This collection of essays takes a fresh and invigorating look at late medieval English society by focusing not on how people lived but on how they saw the world and their place in it. Alongside contributions on how different social groups saw themselves and were seen by others are more general discussions of key aspects of fifteenth-century life: attitudes to the rule of law, to the power of the ruler, to education, to honour and service and finally to death. These essays, which include a selection of attractive and often unusual illustrations, create a unique introduction to a troubled and controversial century, which in the past has been seen variously as 'the waning of the middle ages' and the forcing ground of modern society.

FIFTEENTH-CENTURY ATTITUDES

*F*ifteenth-century attitudes

PERCEPTIONS OF SOCIETY
IN LATE MEDIEVAL
ENGLAND

Edited by

Rosemary Horrox

CAMBRIDGE
UNIVERSITY PRESS

Published by the Press Syndicate of the University of Cambridge
The Pitt Building, Trumpington Street, Cambridge CB2 1RP
40 West 20th Street, New York, NY 10011-4211, USA
10 Stamford Road, Oakleigh, Melbourne 3166, Australia

First published 1994

Printed in Great Britain at the University Press, Cambridge

A catalogue record for this book is available from the British Library

Library of Congress cataloguing in publication data

Fifteenth-century attitudes: perceptions of society in late medieval
England / edited by Rosemary Horrox.
p.   cm.
Includes bibliographical references and index.
ISBN 0 521 40483 5
1. Great Britain – History – Lancaster and York, 1399–1485.
2. England – Social conditions – 1066–1485. 3. Fifteenth century.
I. Horrox, Rosemary.
DA245.F52 1992 *1994*
942.04–dc20   94–5622 CIP

ISBN 0 521 40483 5 hardback

Contents

CONTENTS

Illustrations

Illustrations appear by the kind permission of the following: the Controller of Her Majesty's Stationery Office (6): Margaret Aston (30); Bibliothèque de l'Arsenal and Photographie Bibliothèque Nationale, Paris (18); the British Library, London (11, 13, 27); the Bodleian Library, Oxford (8, 9, 19, 20, 23, 26); the Syndics of Cambridge University Library (25); the Courtauld Institute of Art, University of London (29); Glasgow Museums, the Burrell Collection (21); the Provost and Scholars of King's College, Cambridge (4, 15); Musée Condé, Chantilly, and Photographie Giraudon (2); the Earl of Verulam and the Trustees of the National Gallery, London (10); the Trustees of the National Library of Scotland (17); the Royal Commission on the Historical Monuments of England (5, 16, 24); the Science and Engineering Research Council and the Royal Observatory, Scotland (14); the Trustees of the Wallace Collection, London (1, 7); Brian Waters (22); the Dean and Chapter of Westminster Abbey (3). Picture research by Peter Hammond and the editor, with thanks to Margaret Condon.

INTRODUCTION

Rosemary Horrox

Seventy years ago the place of the fifteenth century in the historical cycle was clear, it was the 'waning' of the middle ages: the downturn before the wheel swung upwards again towards the glories of the Reformation and Renaissance. Since Huizinga wrote, late medievalists, predictably enough, have become restive under this disparagement. No one, after all, wishes to see 'their' period as an unfortunate hiatus. Outside the academic community, however, the negative image has kept its potency. This surely owes something to Huizinga himself, who contrived to make the decadence of the late middle ages enormously seductive, with its scent of blood and roses.[1] In England it probably owes more to the power of the Tudor myth: the Shakespearian picture of the century as four generations of bloodshed and anarchy between the deposition of Richard II in 1399 and the arrival of Henry VII as restorer and redeemer in 1485.

Myths cast long shadows. No historian now accepts the Shakespearian model, but it has left behind a certain uneasiness in handling the century. Most late medievalists, whether consciously or not, have set themselves to 'rescue' the century from its earlier negative image; to play down the lawlessness and violence, and present it as a buoyant, upbeat period of increased personal wealth and self-determination: an 'age of ambition', when the fall in population brought about by recurrent outbreaks of bubonic plague from the mid-fourteenth century raised wages and opened up the job market. There have been dissident voices. The much reduced population inevitably had a depressive effect on national levels of trade and industrial output, and it is possible to see the fifteenth century in recessionary terms. Towns, in particular, found their traditional sources of income (property rent and levies on internal trade) falling in the fifteenth century. But none of this is incompatible with an increase in individual productivity and spending power. Late medieval towns, unlike their early modern successors, had not yet found a way of taxing the private wealth of their inhabitants on a regular basis, and their genuine (and strident) howls of financial distress co-exist with extremely wealthy townsmen, who were cheerfully pouring private money into building projects

---

[1] J. Huizinga, *The Waning of the Middle Ages* (Harmondsworth, 1968), p. 25: 'So violent and motley was life, that it bore the mixed smell of blood and of roses. The men of that time always oscillate between the fear of hell and the most naive joy, between cruelty and tenderness, between harsh asceticism and insane attachments to the delights of this world, between hatred and goodness, always running to extremes.'

like the enlargement of urban churches, while civic building projects, including the upkeep of walls or pavements, languished. A private benefactor, Robert Holme, met most of the cost of lead water pipes to replace the open dykes which brought fresh water into Hull; twelve years later, in the middle of a cash crisis, the city ripped up the piping and sold the lead.[2]

Living standards for most people rose, and the availability of well-paid work must, although it is hard to quantify, have given individuals a greater sense of control over their own affairs. In the countryside, unfreedom was becoming an irrelevance as the economic tide set against landowners and in favour of tenants. The sense of opportunity, that more was possible, manifested itself in a surge of interest in self-improvement. The fifteenth-century best sellers were school books and handbooks of practical *self*-instruction, and numerous contemporary wills testify to the importance attached to education. John Hedlam, who made his will in 1461, is unusual only in the explicitness with which he spells out his motives. His land was left to his eldest son; his goods, after his debts had been met, were to go to the schooling of his younger children: 'for they have no other goods to help them with, but if God will of his mercy prefer them in cunning [learning], to the which I beseech God increase them'.[3] Against this background the founding of God's House (later Christ's College) in Cambridge explicitly to make good the national shortage of grammar masters should be taken not as evidence of the parlous state of schooling, but of the insatiable demand building up from below. That demand was still largely utilitarian and vocational, but there are hints of a belief, which was to become stronger in the following century, that education was a good in itself as well as a means to an end.

The widening of opportunity had a darker side. Historians inevitably see the successes. Contemporaries saw the failures as well, and were more ambivalent about the successful as a result. Ambition had always been unpopular with moralists, who regarded it as a potent amalgam of pride, covetousness and ingratitude. But other men, too, were uncomfortable with it – not because they thought the desire to better oneself was wrong (as the moralists tended to do), but because of the tactics which might be adopted in pursuit of self-advancement. A popular fifteenth-century compendium of wise advice has a telling comparison between a man who willingly abstains from self-indulgence, who deserves to be called temperate, and a man who abstains and hates his abstinence, who should be called ambitious.[4] It is assumed that ambition entails selfish and cynical calculation – whereas men should act out of an open and generous spirit, in which case reward would be well deserved.

The tension between success and failure can sometimes be glimpsed in the acquisition of land. It was axiomatic that anyone who achieved wealth or influence should invest their gains in land as soon as possible. Land was power, in a way that

---

[2] *The Victoria County History* (hereafter *VCH*): *York, East Riding*, I (1969), p. 371.
[3] Borthwick Institute of Historical Research, York, Probate Register 2, fol. 451.
[4] C. F. Bühler (ed.), *The Dicts and Sayings of the Philosophers*, Early English Text Society (hereafter EETS), orig. series 211 (1941 for 1939), p. 170.

wealth by itself was not; and, unlike personal influence, could be handed down to subsequent generations. The value attached to land, however, meant that the land market was extremely sluggish. There was plenty of land to rent, but no one would sell land unless they had no choice, and acquiring it, at least on a significant scale, was rarely a straightforward matter of purchase between two equals. The most effective way to come by land was through marriage, which gave a safe title and a ready-made niche in local society. Otherwise it was often a case of profiting by an owner's misfortune, whether economic (in the case of families which had to sell up or mortgage their estates) or political (in the case of forfeiture for treason). Some of the contemporary odium attached to lawyers may have derived from awareness that they were well placed to acquire land from families in difficulties, as Judge William Paston's career demonstrated.

The acquisition of land did not concern the whole population. But contemporaries may have been conscious of a more general way in which opportunities for some were being bought by the misfortunes of others. Many of the social trends of the period derived from the fact that the population was being held artificially low by epidemic disease. There is a sense, therefore, in which the comfortable living standards and increased opportunities of the survivors were paid for by high mortality levels among family and friends. Certainly men and women were haunted by a sense of the fragility of success. 'For the mercy of God', wrote one Paston correspondent, 'remember the unstableness of this world.'[5] Perhaps this helps to explain why, although there are some signs that attitudes to the poor were hardening, levels of charitable giving held up. Apart from the religious requirement of performing good works, the successful may have felt a superstitious urge to register a sense of gratitude.

What men feared was a sudden catastrophe beyond their control. Contemporary guild ordinances, defining which categories of members could be given charitable help, waxed eloquent on the mishaps which could bring respectable folk to poverty. The Palmers' guild of Ludlow made provision for members brought to want through theft, fire, shipwreck, the collapse of their house, imprisonment, unjust seizure of their property or grievous sickness. Guilds were adamant, however, that help was not to be extended to the feckless and improvident; those whose loss had come through their 'own lust, or gluttony, or dice-play or other folly'.[6] In the same way licences to beg were careful to spell out that no personal culpability was involved. In 1484 Edmund Philpot of Twickenham was given a royal licence to solicit alms after his dwelling house and twelve adjoining tenements were 'suddenly burnt to his utter undoing'. He had an extra claim upon men's charity for he had previously 'kept after his degree a good household, by the which many poor creatures were refreshed'.[7]

---

[5] N. Davis (ed.), *Paston Letters and Papers of the Fifteenth Century* (2 vols., Oxford, 1971–6), II, no. 688 (lines 57–8).

[6] Lucy Toulmin Smith (ed.), *English Gilds*, EETS, orig. series 40 (1870), pp. 166, 193–4.

[7] R. E. Horrox and P. W. Hammond (eds.), *British Library Harleian Manuscript 433* (4 vols., 1979–83), II, p. 88.

Philpot's dramatic descent from giver to recipient of charity was guaranteed to play on contemporary anxieties about the mutability of fortune. Those who had been born poor could not always be assured of an equally warm response. Given the contemporary perception that there was plenty of well-paid work about if only people could be bothered to take it, the able-bodied poor were likely to be viewed with some mistrust. There was a widespread sense that employees were getting above themselves. The increased leisure which they could buy with their higher wages annoyed their employers, who would have preferred them to work longer hours, and offended the contemporary sense of what was proper behaviour for each social group. The Black Death had been quickly followed by the first sumptuary legislation, which attempted to curb extravagance and enforce social distinctions by defining what types of cloth and fur each social group could wear. Not surprisingly the attempt was a total failure, but the legislation was repeated, with modifications, throughout the fifteenth century. In 1482 the Commons were still complaining that the legislation was not being observed and that as a result the 'said realm is brought into over great misery and poverty, and like to run to greater'.[8]

Sumptuary legislation was designed to ensure that each social group behaved appropriately, and to that extent it is evidence of some contemporary discomfort with the fact that increased spending power was breaking down the *visible* distinctions between social categories. But the legislation cannot be interpreted as a criticism of social mobility as such, let alone as an attempt to limit it. Its message was simply that people should dress in conformity with their status. A peasant should dress (and behave) like a peasant, but a peasant who had become an estate official should dress (and behave) like an estate official. A few theorists attempted to argue – in the teeth of practical experience – that behaviour was innate and that leaving one's allotted niche in society was therefore not only morally wrong but likely to be an embarrassing failure as well. But most observers were more pragmatic. Upward social mobility was a fact of life. Pushy and aggressive individuals might be deprecated, the general trend was not.

Contemporary grumbling that people did not know their place is not, therefore, evidence of a social hierarchy which felt itself under serious attack. There is very little evidence of social groups closing ranks against new recruits. Surviving criticism of the upwardly mobile tends to be from below: from the people left behind who resented being lorded over by people no better than themselves. There is, it is true, a scatter of attempts to limit periods of 'misrule' when the social order was turned upside down – attempts which were to become far more insistent in the sixteenth century. But most of these early attacks were made by clerics, like Archbishop Arundel of York, who in 1391 forbade the clergy of Beverley minster their 'ancient and corrupt custom' of choosing a King of Fools.[9] Secular lords still

---

[8] *Rotuli Parliamentorum* (6 vols., 1767–77), VI, p. 220.
[9] *VCH: York, East Riding*, VI (1989), p. 62.

seem to have found misrule amusing and acceptable, and hence, presumably, 'safe' – in other words they knew that the real hierarchy was firm and would be restored.

Any sense of insecurity among the fifteenth-century aristocracy and gentry had more to do with political than social pressures. The middle of the century brought a major civil war, and although the periods of military activity were relatively brief, the resulting tensions were enormous. The war arose from the most stressful dilemma medieval political society could face: what was to be done with a king (in this case Henry VI) who had signally failed. This dilemma was not, of course, new – two kings had been deposed in the previous century – but that did not make it any easier to resolve. Opposing the king was treason, and therefore dangerous – for the standard penalty for treason was now death, and the total disinheriting of the traitor's heirs. But opposition was also ideologically frightening. The king was the embodiment of order; the one man who could stand above conflict and resolve it. His removal – or even his control – therefore represented a fundamental assault on order. The problem for contemporaries was whether two wrongs ever made a right. Whether, in other words, the king's own failure to maintain order could justify his removal – and lift the stigma of treason from the men who did it.

In 1460 Henry VI's main critic, his cousin Richard duke of York, sidestepped the whole issue by claiming that he, not Henry, was the rightful king of England. This was the obvious solution to York's own problem, which was that his attack on Henry's associates had led to his being branded a traitor, but it introduced a new and frightening complication. There were now two claimants to the throne of England; for a time indeed, from 1461 to 1471, there were two crowned kings. This profoundly destabilized political life, since any opposition to the reigning king could now be validated as support for the 'rightful' claimant.

But if disaffection thereby became easier, everything else about high politics became more difficult, and more frightening. It behoved men to be careful, and a sense of wariness pervades contemporary letters. John Paston warned his brother in 1471, after the Yorkists had returned to power: 'I pray you be wary of your guiding, and in chief of your language, so that from henceforth by your language no man may perceive that you favour any person contrary to the king's pleasure.'[10] In 1483, after the unexpected death of Edward IV called into question the stability of the past decade, Ralph Hastings, the brother of the dead king's closest friend William lord Hastings, concluded a letter: 'my lord saith that I write always so plainly to him that it feareth him, and therefore I dare not, but shall forbear to write any more so'.[11] Ralph survived the coup of 1483, but his brother did not. Perhaps the fate of lord Hastings was in the mind of the brothers' colleague at Calais, John lord Mountjoy, when he came to make his will in 1485. Mountjoy died in his bed, but he still thought it

---

[10] Davis (ed.), *Paston Letters*, I, no. 263.
[11] *Ibid.*, II, no. 796.

worth warning his sons: 'nor desire to be great about princes, for it is dangerous'.[12]

In spite of Mountjoy's advice, there was never any shortage of men who 'desired to be great about princes', and civil war could bring opportunities as well as catastrophes; but the dangers he had in mind were real enough. One man's misjudgement could bring disaster not only to himself but to his family. The attainder of traitors disinherited their heirs, and although such forfeiture was not, in fact, usually permanent it could cripple a family for a generation, forcing them on to the charity of servants and friends. Even more damagingly, the war raised the odds against a family perpetuating itself in the male line. It is well known that the Wars of the Roses did not, as used to be thought, extinguish the 'old' nobility. There was indeed no such thing. The weakness of male children in the early years of life meant that even under normal conditions families found it difficult to produce surviving male heirs, and the aristocracy was constantly being replenished from outside. But given the natural failure rate, the loss of even one male member by execution or death in battle increased a family's risk of extinction.

When the risks involved in political activity were so high, it is easy to understand why the men of this period found themselves attracted to the idea of Fortune: the goddess whose turning wheel represented the role of chance in human affairs. The message of Fortune was fatalistic: that not even the best laid human plans are proof against unexpected disaster, and that although an individual must take *moral* responsibility for his decisions, he cannot be held to blame for the events which overtake him in the world of action. Awaiting execution in 1483, Anthony earl Rivers fell to meditating on the situation in which he found himself and presumably derived some comfort from the reflection that it was not, after all, his own fault:

> Methinks truly
> Bounden am I,
> And that greatly,
> To be content;
> Seeing plainly
> Fortune doth wry
> All contrary
> From mine intent.
>
> My life was lent
> Me to one intent.
> It is now spent.
> Welcome Fortune!
> But I ne went [never thought]
> Thus to be shent [punished]

---

[12] D. A. L. Morgan, 'The king's affinity in the polity of Yorkist England', *Transactions of the Royal Historical Society*, 5th ser. 23 (1973), 23.

1   Fortune's wheel

But she it meant:
Such is her wont.[13]

The image of Fortune's wheel carried another message, which must have seemed even more apposite to men living through the upheavals of the mid-fifteenth century: that as the wheel continues its revolution anyone who has risen must inevitably fall. The only safety, as Mountjoy argued, was not to seek to be great in the first place; for, as John Lydgate put it:

Who that hath with that queen to do
Contrariously she will his chance dispose.[14]

Similarly any major change was likely to be cancelled out in due course by another. Nothing could be relied upon:

But Fortune with her smiling countenance strange
Of all our purpose may make a sudden change.[15]

For those out of favour this was, of course, a cheering thought. When John Paston, writing to his mother shortly after the battle of Barnet, in which he had backed the wrong side, told her: 'the world, I assure you, is right queasy', he was offering the reflection optimistically, hoping for a future turn of events which would be more favourable to them.[16] But those with something to lose, who were probably always the majority, regarded the prospect of repeated political change with shrinking dismay rather than enthusiasm.

Perhaps the most terrifying realization to come out of the Wars of the Roses was just how fragile political stability could be. In spite of a genuine commitment to its preservation, once things had begun to slide, or the wheel to turn, instability was likely to be self-perpetuating. The only person with authority to halt the cycle was the king, and, far from weakening and discrediting the monarchy, the conflicts of the mid-century ultimately strengthened it, since support for the *de facto* king came to seem the only hope of stability. Edward IV benefited from this perception during his second reign, when the political community was prepared to acquiesce in actions like the manipulation of property descents and the cynical removal of the king's brother Clarence, which would normally have generated considerable uneasiness. But the ultimate beneficiary was Henry VII. He came to the throne after Richard III's usurpation had destroyed – some thought wilfully – the stability achieved by Edward IV. Henry's success in establishing his dynasty owed less to his own efforts than to the wish of the political community to break the cycle of change and violence.

Once instability had turned into civil war, it could only be resolved by violence.

---

[13] P. M. Kendall, *Richard the Third* (1955), p. 212.
[14] R. T. Davies (ed.), *Medieval English Lyrics* (1963), p. 192.
[15] Davis (ed.), *Paston Letters*, I, no. 350.
[16] *Ibid.*, I, no. 261 (line 30).

2　The fortunes of war: blind Fortune turns her wheel and heaven and hell
contend for the souls of the dead

Medieval commanders generally avoided pitched battles, preferring to wage war by attrition. Conventional wisdom viewed battles as chancy affairs, where the right side did not necessarily win. But in a civil war, waged by definition on home ground, it was not possible to adopt a scorched earth policy or settle in for a lengthy campaign of sieges. The only possible tactic was to confront the opposition on the battlefield, and the outcome could dramatically alter the course of events. Neither of the fourteenth-century depositions had involved a trial of armed strength; in the fifteenth century both Edward IV (twice) and Henry VII secured the throne by military victory. The victors welcomed the result as evidence of God's will; the battle being seen as a large-scale trial by combat. But such trials no longer had much place in judicial practice, and the analogy tacitly confirms that the resolution offered by battles was arbitrary.

Pitched battles were also, of course, dangerous. Men died. Victorious commanders would sometimes acknowledge a moral responsibility for the dead of both armies by founding a battlefield chantry, as Henry IV did near Shrewsbury or the Yorkist kings near Towton; or they might make a more personal provision for their own followers. Edward IV associated himself with a chantry for the Kentishmen who had died in his campaign for the throne, and Richard duke of Gloucester endowed masses for his servants who died at Barnet. Ordinary soldiers were always vulnerable, but in civil war or rebellion that vulnerability was extended to their commanders. The convention of sparing the eminent for the sake of ransom did not apply, and commanders on the losing side could expect to die, either in battle or on the scaffold. Not surprisingly armies tended to get smaller as the Wars of the Roses continued, with all but the committed opting to sit at home and see what happened. The victors proved willing to welcome defaulters back into the fold; and although non-combatants presumably forfeited a degree of favour, masterly inactivity became an increasingly tempting option.

This should not be taken as evidence that the aristocracy and gentry of England were ceasing to be a military elite in the fifteenth century, or that chivalry was losing its hold on their imaginations. The problem was rather that civil war was the wrong sort of war. When the combatants knew the 'enemy' and might even consider some of them friends, victory offered little triumph. It also offered little reward, since looting (although it sometimes occurred) was usually frowned on. By contrast, enthusiasm for foreign war held up surprisingly well under difficult circumstances. The Treaty of Troyes radically changed the nature of English involvement in France. In the early stages of the Hundred Years War the characteristic campaign had been the *chevauchée*, a raid across country which occupied one campaigning season, and therefore allowed nobility and gentry to combine military activity with the pursuit of their interests in England. After Troyes the English army in France became an army of occupation, forcing men to choose, in effect, between a military career and their interests as English landowners. Even before Henry V's death some men were jibbing at this degree of commitment, and this response intensified under Henry VI when there was no royal involvement to act as a focus for chivalric aspirations. What is striking is not that some men lost enthusiasm for campaigning under these conditions, but that there remained others, like the duke of Bedford and John Holland, duke of Exeter, who were prepared to make an almost full-time commitment to France, and were much admired by their contemporaries for doing so.

Foreign war was one escape route from the tensions of domestic politics. In the past crusading had been another, and it still held its appeal at the beginning of the century when Richard Beauchamp, earl of Warwick, combined a pilgrimage to the Holy Land with fighting the pagans of eastern Europe. In 1471 Anthony Woodville was planning to go and fight the Moslems in Spain, although the plan apparently fell through. Crusading was not, of course, only an escape route, it was primarily an act of penance and regeneration. Perhaps Woodville saw it as expiation of his involvement in civil war over the previous decade, but it is impossible to be sure how contemporaries regarded such involvement. If they did feel penitence was called for it seems to have been undemonstrative – there is no evidence that the civil war, for all its discomforts, triggered a spiritual crisis.

The civil war of the twelfth century had produced a great surge of support for the Cistercians, then the most austere of the religious orders. Renunciation, whether vicarious or actual, continued to exert a powerful attraction on medieval aristocrats. In the fourteenth century the courtiers of Richard II, who faced their own political dilemmas in the late 1390s, patronized the Carthusians, a connection which lasted into the next generation with Henry V's foundation of the Charterhouse at Sheen. Henry also established the Bridgettines at Syon, who attracted aristocratic support up to the Reformation. But the drive towards renunciation seems to have slackened in the course of the fifteenth century, and although the Observant Franciscans arrived at Windsor in the reign of Edward IV they did not generate much local enthusiasm.

Most people in the fifteenth century seem to have paid their moral debts in the currency of masses and prayers. Lavish testamentary endowments of masses and charitable works may thus be evidence of some anxiety about a lifetime's sins, but they also suggest that the situation was thought to be safely in hand. Purgatory had become a broad thoroughfare to ultimate redemption rather than a strait gate. It was popularly assumed that virtually everyone could avail themselves of the second chance it offered – and those who could not afford post-mortem masses and works of charity could comfort themselves with the thought that the poor suffered their purgatory in this life; although the financial limits of this means-tested redemption were never spelt out.

But if the soul could be salvaged, the body could not. For the church that was exactly as it should be, and moralists throughout the middle ages and beyond used the decay of the human body as a brutal object lesson in the vanity of human pride. It is difficult to resist the conclusion, however, that the horrified fascination with physical corruption which surfaces in the fifteenth century derived from something more urgent than a conventional desire to express the transience of worldly ambition. There is surely a sense that the pleasures of worldly success are guilty pleasures, purchased by the failure and death of others – and that sooner or later a price will be exacted. Success, in other words, is not only fragile but dangerous. As Fortune's wheel turns, those it has raised up are inevitably toppled to destruction: to worldly failure or premature death.

Individuals may have been finding the century uncomfortable, but this is a very long way from arguing that society as a whole was in crisis. The fifteenth century cannot be seen as a world turned upside down. At times the world seemed to be 'going on wheels',[17] but it was still demonstrably the right way up. The increased possibilities for social advancement might generate jealousy, but they did not shake the social hierarchy because men accepted the requirement to behave in conformity with their new status. Significantly, criticism was aimed at members of the lower orders who seemed not to be working hard enough, in other words were not filling their allotted role, rather than at those who had advanced themselves. A very similar point can be made about the political community. Henry VI's failure raised real and frightening problems, but what emerged from the upheavals of the mid-century was essentially a commitment to the existing system. Individual members of the political classes might come in for fierce condemnation, but the balance of power between king, nobles and gentry was not significantly modified.

In the religious arena, too, there was no sense of crisis. The Lollard threat had been minimized, and although the state of the established church has been a matter of fierce controversy there seems very little reason to doubt that it was giving its members what they wanted to receive. There is little evidence of spiritual doubt, but much of undemonstrative acceptance and a confidence that all would be well.

In the mid-fourteenth century the first attack of plague had triggered apocalyptic fears throughout Europe. The fifteenth century was still living with the consequences of plague in all sorts of ways, emotional as well as demographic, but the plague itself had become a fact of life, its recurrence hardly noticed in contemporary chronicles. No one any longer, it seems, expected the world to end. And no one, either, expected the world to change in any very surprising ways. Change could still be contained, just as the geographical discoveries at the end of the century were absorbed with very little difficulty into the prevailing model of the world. Individuals might have been feeling queasy at times, but they were not expecting imminent shipwreck.

---

[17] A. Hanham (ed.), *The Cely Letters, 1472–1488*, EETS, no. 272 (1975), p. 239.

$$\boxed{I}$$

THE KING AND HIS SUBJECTS

G. L. Harriss

The last half of the fifteenth century saw six changes of ruler, all save one by violence. Yet though kings came and went, the necessity of monarchy was not questioned and its theoretical basis remained unchanged. It was universally held that monarchy was instituted by God for the benefit of His people. The king ruled by the grace of God, his person and authority were inviolable, and he received the obedience of his subjects by divine command. His rule should be God-like in quality: rewarding the good and protecting the weak, punishing sinners but showing mercy to the repentant. Justice, in its broadest sense, was the purpose of his government, but it was also the measure by which it was judged. For a king had a duty not only to God, from whom he derived his authority, but to his subjects whose bodies and, indeed, souls, were in his care. God gave the king his realm – whether by inheritance or conquest – not for the ruler's own enjoyment or profit but to make it a Christian commonwealth, a preparation for heaven. To this end he was responsible for defending the realm against its enemies, for enforcing law and order, for inculcating virtue and for ensuring stability and social harmony.

Writing when the English monarchy was at its point of deepest crisis, Sir John Fortescue confronted the problem of how the crown could be strengthened while preserving the liberty of its subjects. Repudiating the French model of a monarchy that could tax and legislate at will, he argued that in England subjects should more readily render obedience and aid to their king because they gave assent to his rule. A king who ruled his realm for his own profit was a tyrant, whereas true kingship was 'an office, in wich he mynestrith to his reaume defence and justice'.[1] The same point was made by the English ambassadors sent to negotiate peace with France in 1439. They were told to remind the French king that 'God made not his people . . . for the princes, but he made the princes for his service and for the wele . . . of his people, that is to say to reule theim in tranquillite namely by the mene of deue ministracion of justice.'[2] Seventy years later Henry VII's disgraced minister, Edmund Dudley, wrote in prison that:

---

[1] Sir John Fortescue, *The Governance of England*, ed. C. Plummer (Oxford, 1885), p. 127.
[2] N. H. Nicolas (ed.), *Proceedings and Ordinances of the Privy Council of England* (hereafter *Proc. PC*) (7 vols., 1834–7), v, p. 357.

as subjects are bounden to ther Prince, so be all kinges bounden to ther subiectes by the comaundyment of god them to maynteigne and supporte . . . for though the people be subiectes to the king yet are thei the people of god, and god hath ordeyned ther prince to protecte them and thei to obey ther prince.[3]

We would be wrong to read into this any suggestion of a contract between king and people, from which the ruler derived his authority or by virtue of which he could be removed if he broke it. Nevertheless this theory of kingship did incorporate a tension between the obedience which subjects owed to a divinely ordained ruler and the moral judgement which subjects made on a king who ruled contrary to the common weal. For if subjects were 'the people of God', could the *Vox Populi*, denouncing an unjust king, be deemed the *Vox Dei*? Could the need to restore good government and preserve the realm justify resistance to, and even the removal of, an evil ruler? Even if that were answered in the affirmative, no constitutional procedure existed to effect it. True, a failure to abide by his coronation oath – to keep the peace, do justice and maintain the laws – laid the king open to a charge of perjury, but he was subject only to God's judgement, not to that of men. The attempt in the early fourteenth century to distinguish between allegiance to the king's person and his office, and justify rebellion as defending kingship against any one king's misrule, failed to take root. Indeed there was no legal process of deposition and kings like Edward II and Richard II, whose unfitness to rule had been formally pronounced by their subjects, were induced to resign. Others, like Henry VI and Edward V, had their rule invalidated on dynastic grounds. Even so, usurpers took pains to present themselves as liberators from past tyranny and reformers of the common weal. Henry IV asserted that the 'rewme was in poynt to be undone for defaut of governance and undoyng of the gode lawes', and Yorkist propaganda in 1461 represented Lancastrian England as 'a gardayne . . . overgrowen many yere with wedys'.[4] Richard III was asked to take the throne to prevent the realm falling 'into extreme miserie and desolation'.[5] Subjects, therefore, might be called on to render a verdict on the government of their kings as part of the process of deposition. But even then the person of the deposed monarch remained sacrosanct, and Henry IV, Edward IV and Richard III each stained their reputation by the regicide of the monarch whom they had deposed. Of the saintly Henry VI's death in the Tower in 1471 the Crowland chronicler wrote: 'may God have mercy and give time for repentance to him, whoever it might be, who dared to lay sacrilegious hands on the Lord's Anointed! And so let the doer merit the title of tyrant and the victim that of glorious martyr.'[6]

Even kings whose authority was fully acknowledged depended on the tacit consent of their subjects to rule effectively. For the crown lacked the coercive power to

---

[3] Edmund Dudley, *The Tree of Commonwealth*, ed. D. M. Brodie (Cambridge, 1948), p. 31.

[4] *Rotuli Parliamentorum* (hereafter *Rot. Parl.*) (6 vols., 1767–77), III, p. 423; T. Wright (ed.), *Political Songs and Poems* (Rolls Series, 2 vols., 1859–61), II, p. 267.

[5] *Rot. Parl.*, VI, p. 240.

[6] N. Pronay and J. Cox (eds.), *The Crowland Chronicle Continuations, 1459–1486* (1986), pp. 129–31.

compel the obedience of the majority of its greater subjects. Without either a standing army or a salaried local bureaucracy, it depended on the support of the propertied classes both to defend and to govern the realm. That support was given partly out of traditional obedience and respect, partly out of self-interest and partly out of a critical perception of the quality of the king's rule. If disobedience was exceptional and punishable, willing obedience had to be elicited and could not be assumed. To that degree the political nation, or propertied classes, rendered continuous judgement on the king.

In the period under review that judgement was passed more explicitly and more frequently than usual, as crisis succeeded crisis and kings bid for support to save, or gain, the throne. In what ways and in what circumstances did kings confront their subjects, and what determined the attitude of subjects to royal authority? In answering this we must distinguish between three categories of subjects, with each of whom the king's relationship was bound to be different. First were those with whom he had regular contact, whose names and something of whose background he could be presumed to know: the lay and spiritual peers and the more prominent members of his court and household. Second there was the political society in town and countryside – the knights, esquires, gentlemen and burgesses – on whom the crown depended as a magistracy to maintain royal government at a local level and carry out royal commands. The king might have personal knowledge of some amongst these and would confront their representatives at parliaments. Thirdly, and merging with the second group at parish level, were the yeomen, husbandmen, small freeholders, copyholders, waged labourers, poorer clergy and, in the towns, the shopkeepers and artisans: all those who comprised 'the people'. Except on rare and particular occasions the distance between monarch and people was unbridged, and all communication was indirect. How, then, did the king impress his personality and policy on each group and what considerations would determine the level of support he received?

Monarchy was, of course, personal not institutionalized, and it was on the person of the monarch that government centred. Bishop Russell who, like other chancellors, took the body politic as the theme of his parliamentary sermon, asked: 'What ys the bely or where ys the wombe of thys grete publick body of Englonde but that and there where the kyng ys hym self, hys court and hys counselle?'[7] The nobility – lay, spiritual and official – were the king's natural counsellors and their attendance at court had symbolic importance. The king's authority was most visibly displayed, and the fidelity of his nobility demonstrated, when he wore his crown in solemn religious processions and sat in state in one of his palaces, with bishops on his right hand and earls on his left. It was thus that Edward IV celebrated the great feasts of the year, at Westminster at Christmastide and at Windsor on St George's day. In special circumstances this served to reaffirm the inviolability of the crown when it had been challenged, as after the first battle of St Albans in 1455, or in 1471 on Edward IV's restoration. On such occasions

---

[7] Printed in S. B. Chrimes, *English Constitutional Ideas in the Fifteenth Century* (Cambridge, 1936), p. 174.

display and largesse were calculated to impress, and the presence of the greater nobility was undoubtedly required.[8] So too was their attendance at parliaments and great councils, to which all were summoned by individual writs, and where major political decisions were discussed. Similarly when the king himself led an army in a foreign war, particularly on the first occasion in his reign, all his nobility were expected to accompany him, to demonstrate their own loyalty and the unity of the nation in arms. Henry V in 1415, Henry VI in 1430, Edward IV in 1475 and Henry VII in 1492 were all attended by most of their magnates. Indeed it was on the nobility's recruitment of retinues that the crown relied for the formation of a royal army. For most of the time, however, nobles resided on their estates, making occasional and personal visits to the court and attending council intermittently. No more than a handful of them were perpetually around the king, either as household officials or paid councillors. Yet even within their own 'countries' the personal allegiance they owed to the crown imposed a special loyalty and duty, for they were answerable to the king for the good order and stability of their area and were expected to set an example to other subjects. Reproaching lord Egremont for creating disturbances in the north in 1453, Henry VI reminded him that he had been elevated to the peerage 'in especial for the keping of the rest and pees of oure lande', and in his sermon of 1483 Bishop Russell told his audience that 'the polityk rule of every region wele ordeigned stondithe in the nobles'.[9]

However, the nobility were a far from uniform body and the king's relations with its different members varied widely. Three groups may be distinguished: those of the blood royal, that is the king's or queen's immediate family; those who had risen or were rising through royal favour such as (in this period) the families of Bourchier, Hastings, Herbert and Howard; and those whose families were of ancient lineage like the houses of Courtenay, de Vere, Mowbray, Neville, Percy and Stafford. The king's family and the king's friends stood close to, and more in need of, his favour than did the ancient nobility. The wealth and influence of the older nobility rested on land; those of the newer families on royal favour and office. Normally power and influence accrued to junior branches of the royal family from the personal service they rendered to the king at court or in war. One thinks of the Hollands under Richard II, the Beauforts under the Lancastrian kings and the Woodvilles under Edward IV. The crown could not from its own resources endow a newly created earl with sufficient land to sustain his dignity, though it could, in the right circumstances, arrange a marriage which would furnish this. It was the availability of land from Lancastrian forfeitures that enabled and encouraged Edward IV to establish his brothers, George and Richard, his wife's family and such parvenus as Hastings and Herbert as important lords in their regions. 'New' nobility of this kind, even if they were of the royal family, remained heavily dependent

---

[8] See 'The Record of Bluemantle Pursuivant, 1471–2', printed in C. L. Kingsford, *English Historical Literature in the Fifteenth Century* (Oxford, 1913), pp. 379–81.

[9] *Proc. PC*, VI, p. 159; Chrimes, *Constitutional Ideas*, p. 172.

3   The coronation of Henry V

on royal favour, both to ensure the fidelity of their own retainers and in the hope of converting their grants of offices, lands and revenues into hereditary titles. For his part Edward IV found himself embroiled in the quarrel between his brothers Clarence and Gloucester over the Warwick lands and in the jealousy aroused by the acquisitive Woodvilles, while later he had to connive in the expansion of Gloucester's power in the north.

In this respect the lineage nobility were more independent of royal favour. Their loyalty was determined less by the hope of further gain than by the fear that the king might seek to disinherit them of their family estates in order to reward others. Awareness of royal displeasure, coupled with jealousy of royal favour to a political rival, lay behind virtually every noble rebellion of the middle ages. Royal patronage could thus be a destabilizing force among a nobility conscious of honour and precedence; indeed it was the extraordinary volume of patronage at the disposal of Edward IV after the Lancastrian defeats that contributed to the political instability of the Yorkist era. All kings, of course, had both the need and the opportunity to replenish the peerage as older families died out, for the power to ennoble rested exclusively in the king's hands. Moreover the monarch could count on the gratitude and dependence of those he promoted and this made them important political allies. Yet a king had to be aware of the personal and territorial consequences of his favour and he needed to maintain a political balance between the court and country nobility, those of his blood and those of ancient lineage.

Beyond these considerations, which we can to some degree analyse, lay the intangible and essentially unknowable quality of the personal relationship between monarch and magnate. What private distrust of Edward IV's clemency persuaded Henry, duke of Somerset, to renege on his oath of loyalty in 1463, and how far did Richard III's attitude to the duke of Buckingham prompt the latter's decision to revolt? What qualities made lord Hastings the boon companion of Edward IV, and what were the feelings of each towards the Woodvilles? In seeking for such vital clues we scarcely know whether we are helped or hindered by the chroniclers and Shakespeare. Yet the style of kingship which a monarch adopted towards his nobility can be identified. Broadly he had two options, either to join them or to beat them: that is, to bind them by friendship or overawe them by fear. Kings who led their nobility in war, like Edward III or Henry V, perforce treated their nobles as comrades in arms, a relationship institutionalized in the establishment of the Order of the Garter. In the different conditions after 1485 Henry VII distanced himself from his magnates, using the threat of punitive fiscal sanctions to engender apprehension and ensure docility. His declared purpose 'was to have many persons in danger at his pleasure'. Edward IV trusted too readily and indiscriminately; Richard III played on others' trust of himself. Either way the king needed to act consistently, for to favour some and distrust others could only implicate the crown in the rivalries and feuds which it was expected to stand above and control. That indeed was the king's supreme function and the test of his authority and ability. The hapless Henry VI's efforts at the loveday of 1458 to repair the feuds unleashed by the slaughter at St Albans contrast with the stern mediations of Henry V or the adroit settlement imposed by Edward IV on his brothers in 1472. Concord among the nobility rested on the king, and upon it, as the sage Bishop Russell observed, 'restith the wele of all the commen'.[10]

Below the peerage were those of lesser rank whose personal attendance on the king was more continuous and more intimate. These courtiers – the knights and esquires of the body and later the gentlemen of the privy chamber – had specific duties in the royal household but might also perform a range of broadly political functions. From some the king would take advice – one thinks of the alleged warning given to Richard III by Catesby and Ratcliffe about his plan to marry Elizabeth of York – while others would be sent on major diplomatic missions or entrusted with strategically vital commands, as was John lord Dinham at Calais in 1484. Even as the court perambulated with the king individual esquires might be detailed to undertake *ad hoc* tasks: to enquire into forfeited lands, convey the king's wishes to a nearby town or summon parties in a dispute into the royal presence. The chamber knight on the king's business, wearing the king's livery, carried the full weight of royal authority. It was, equally, their enjoyment of the king's confidence and familiarity that made them unique channels of petitions for his grace. An incessant stream of petitions for favour, patronage and pardon was directed to the monarch and constituted his normal mode of contact with the world beyond the court. The first two Lancastrian kings set aside an hour or two after dinner when they received and answered their subjects' requests. In fact access to the king's ear was largely governed by those who surrounded him. Knowing someone at court who was willing and able to promote your request was half way to success. In 1479 John Paston lobbied lord Hastings, Bishop Morton and, above all, the courtiers 'which wait most upon the king and lie nightly in his chamber' in order to secure royal favour and intervention on his behalf.[11]

Courtiers, then, were channels of communication, and the Yorkist court was open and accessible. But they could also form a barrier, cocooning the king from criticism and complaint, and lining their pockets at his expense. These were the charges brought against the corrupt clique on whom the popular uprising of 1450 vented its wrath. The Yorkist court attracted far less calumny, but under Henry VII the inner group who served the king personally were formally constituted as the 'privy chamber'. Access to the personal apartment of the king was closely controlled and jealously sought, and the process of distancing the king from even his greater subjects was given a physical dimension. Well might those admitted to the king's counsels be likened to Moses, speaking to God on the mountain and relaying His commands to the people.[12] Yet government in this fashion necessarily bred suspicion and resentment, and it was not surprising that on his accession Henry VIII swept away his father's minions, Empson, Dudley and others. Dudley repeated in his own *Tree of Commonwealth* the stereotyped

---

[10] Chrimes, *Constitutional Ideas*, p. 171.

[11] N. Davis (ed.), *Paston Letters and Papers of the Fifteenth Century* (2 vols., Oxford, 1971–6), I, p. 617.

[12] Bishop Russell's sermon printed in Chrimes, *Constitutional Ideas*, p. 173.

warning, derived from the story of Rehoboam which all medieval kings learnt, to avoid young, covetous and cruel counsellors.[13]

In the later fifteenth century the royal household had an increasingly important role in the government of the localities. More local gentry were put on the household roll, to serve as a link between the centre and the localities. As the number soared to upward of 400, so the nature of household service changed. Many of these attended court on an occasional and part-time basis, their service to the king being primarily rendered within their own locality. There they were the eyes and ears of the crown 'through whom may be known the disposition of the counties', providing a channel for royal influence within the shire in which they were leading members. Serving as sheriffs, justices of the peace and representatives of the shire in parliament, or as commissioners for raising loans and investigating the crown's rights, such men could expect not only royal patronage and favour but the envy and respect of their peers. Then, beyond this circle, defined by their household connection, were all those who held local offices and fees by the king's gift, from the receivers of the reorganized crown estates who accounted to the king's chamber, to the foresters, parkers, bailiffs, castellans and their subordinates. In 1495 an act of parliament reiterated that all such persons holding offices and annuities from the crown were obliged to attend the king's summons to arms.[14] Beyond these, again, were those with no formal or financial attachment to the crown whom the king might nevertheless on occasion command to render a particular service on the promise of future favour. For the king sought service when and where he needed it and those who rendered it did so from a mixture of obligation, honour and reward. In this sense the whole political community was responsive to the royal will and influence, though this co-existed and competed with local and personal interests in all their diversity and complexity.

This brings us to the second category of subjects, the wider political community. The knowledge of the names and circumstances of the leading families in each county with which Edward IV was credited was indeed essential information which the government, it seems, took some pains to acquire. The English crown had never ruled through a permanent local bureaucracy and long tradition dictated that local government should be entrusted to the propertied classes, who should be responsive to the royal commands. Kings wrote letters under the privy seal and signet to individual knights and gentlemen signifying their wishes: ordering them to compose their quarrels, to lend money, to serve in the royal army or to appear at court. Similar letters went to borough corporations – rather than to individual burgesses – and Edward IV was on such friendly terms with the leading citizens of London that in 1482 he entertained the aldermen to a hunt and feast at Waltham. Richard showed comparable favour to the citizens of York. Both kings strove to impress the image of their kingship on the minds of the magistracy in shire and city through personal progresses undertaken at

---

[13] I Kings 12; Dudley, *Tree of Commonwealth*, p. 27; Fortescue, *Governance*, pp. 133, 269.
[14] *Statutes of the Realm*, II (1816), p. 582.

the beginning of the reign. Richard III sought assiduously to inculcate the image of a good prince, demonstrating his sapience at Oxford, doing justice with rigour and compassion, rewarding loyalty with favour, preferring his subjects' love to their riches and displaying his piety. For the personal virtue of the ruler ensured the safety and prosperity of his people, the harmony of virtues in his person betokening the social harmony under his rule. Obedient himself to God, he could justly claim the obedience of his subjects.

Important as were such personal interventions, they made their impress on only a small fraction of the political class. The widespread administering of oaths was not employed in England, as it could be on occasion in France, but in times of political uncertainty the king could seek to ensure support by distributing fees or, more cheaply, badges and livery. For his progress to the north in 1483 Richard III ordered 13,000 livery badges bearing his device of the white boar.[15] The building up of a royal affinity among the gentry of the shires by widespread retaining seems to have been a phenomenon of the reigns of Richard II and Henry IV, and by the end of the fifteenth century most royal retaining took place, as we have seen, within the context of extended household service. By this time so extensive were the crown's landed estates that it disposed of a vast pool of local offices, each of which ensured the holder's loyalty. These estates, notably those in Wales, Cheshire, Lancashire, the north midlands and Yorkshire, provided a reservoir of lords and tenants who could be mobilized for military support if the crown were challenged. Yet even on its own estates the crown depended on the local magistracy whose loyalty in moments of crisis was determined by their assessment of their own interests. From the official account of Edward IV's recovery of his throne in 1471 we know that many at first declined to answer his summons and held themselves aloof. Following the duke of Buckingham's revolt in 1483 the London chronicler described the uncertainty of 'the more party of the gentilmen of England . . . so dysmayed that they knewe nat which party to take but all aventure'.[16] In fact some of Edward IV's affinity joined in the revolt while others stood to Richard. McFarlane was surely right to say that 'the loyalty of the propertied classes was engaged more by the hope of effective rule than by any attachment to a particular ruler or dynasty'.[17]

The opportunity to assess the quality of both the ruler and his rule came in parliament. There the king met the political nation, and together with it enacted measures with the authority of the whole realm. Parliament met on the king's order and his business had priority. Each new monarch in this period began his reign with an act settling his title and the succession to the throne. All were careful to emphasize that they derived their title from God and by rightful succession; but as the act of 1484 declared, 'the manifestation and declaration of this right by the three estates of the

---

[15] C. D. Ross, *Richard III* (1981), p. 150.

[16] J. Bruce (ed.), *Historie of the Arrivall of Edward IV in England*, Camden Soc., old series 1 (1838), pp. 3–4; C. L. Kingsford (ed.), *Chronicles of London* (Oxford, 1908), p. 192.

[17] K. B. McFarlane, 'The Wars of the Roses', in *England in the Fifteenth Century* (1981), p. 256.

realm assembled in parliament and by authority of the same maketh, before all other things, most faith and certainty'.[18] Parliament's right to express the political will of the whole realm was more normally exercised in rendering assent to taxes and laws and in presenting grievances which touched the whole community. For the most part this intercourse between the king and the parliamentary Commons took place through intermediaries. The chancellor was the crown's chief spokesman, opening parliament with a sermon such as that of Bishop Russell, which might dwell on political ideals, like harmony and justice, and conclude with indications of the business of the session.

Similarly it was through their Speaker, appearing with some of the Commons before the king and Lords assembled in full parliament in the Painted Chamber, that the Commons voiced their grievances and made their grants of taxation. The man chosen as Speaker, though elected by the Commons and given freedom to voice their opinions without fear of reprisal, was always high in royal favour and well able to remind the Commons of the crown's needs and view. He evidently exercised some control over the Commons' proceedings, for Bishop Russell remarked that 'yn the lower house . . . alle is directed by the Speker'. Since some of the trusted knights and esquires of the king's household would usually secure election to parliament, royal influence could readily make itself felt in debates. Nor was it unknown for members of the Commons to curry favour with the king by assiduously meeting his wishes or even reporting to him the names of those who had ventured to oppose them. At one point Henry IV publicly promised not to listen to such tale bearers.[19] There was thus no need for the king to attend in person each day – and when he did he of course sat with the Lords – and most members of parliament would be lucky to catch a glimpse of him at the closing or opening session. Earlier, kings like Edward III and Henry IV had on occasion invited both houses to dinner when parliament was dissolved. But in one or two parliaments kings made short speeches to the Commons, occasions rare enough to call for special mention on the parliament roll. In 1453 Henry VI thanked them in person for a notably generous grant of taxes; that was shortly before his mental collapse, and no further royal intervention is recorded in his remaining parliaments. At the close of his first parliament Edward IV thanked the Commons through their Speaker for their 'faithful and loving hearts and their great labours in recovering of my said right and title', a precedent followed by Henry VII. Edward again addressed them in person in 1467, this time at the beginning of parliament, announcing his intention to live of his own and ask taxes only for great and urgent causes touching the common weal.[20]

Taxation was normally the most important function of parliament in the eyes of the king, and often the most contentious. When it was proposed a whole series of reflexes came into play. By constitutional tradition stretching back over two centuries, taxes

---

[18] *Rot. Parl.*, VI, pp. 240–2.
[19] 'Record of Bluemantle Pursuivant'; *Rot. Parl.*, V, p. 461, VI, p. 6; Chrimes, *Constitutional Ideas*, p. 174. On the Speaker, see in general, J. S. Roskell, *The Commons and their Speakers in Medieval Parliaments* (Manchester, 1965), chapter 2.
[20] *Rot. Parl.*, V, pp. 231, 487, 572.

4   Henry VI petitioned by the Lords and Commons

could only be asked for the exceptional needs of the king and the realm, most obviously and usually in time of war. Subjects were obliged to contribute their own goods when the safety of the realm was threatened, though they could only be taxed with their own consent. These two elements – of common obligation and free consent – underlay the debates on taxation that took place in parliament. The crown justified the demand for a tax in terms of the needs of the realm; the Commons discussed, dissected and even – though very rarely – rejected the crown's case. The formal record of the parliament roll almost wholly conceals the debates that undoubtedly took place. Some speeches may have been lengthy and rhetorical, as that of a crown spokesman in the 1472 parliament, preserved in the Canterbury archives.[21] This presented Edward IV's arguments for re-opening the war with France in terms likely to persuade the Commons. Foreign war, they were told, was the most effective way of pacifying the country after the disturbances of recent years, by employing its lawless and warlike members in a pre-emptive strike against a traditional foe whose aggressive intentions were in any case well known. The proffered alliance of the dukes of Brittany and Burgundy offered the unique chance of a swift and easy victory, while the conquest of Normandy and Gascony would provide lands for younger sons and others, and ensure the safety of the sea for merchant shipping. The speaker was trying to persuade the Commons that

---

[21] J. B. Sheppard (ed.), *Literae Cantuarienses* (Rolls Series, 3 vols., 1887–9), III, pp. 274–85.

the war was in their interest, and he made little of the king's traditional claim to the French throne. Nevertheless the Commons remained sceptical and granted taxation reluctantly and with reservations. It took three further sessions and repeated demands before the king eventually secured a total of £118,625 from parliament together with £48,000 from the clergy. The Commons imposed conditions on their grant which showed their distrust of Edward's intentions. They stipulated that money from the first grant was to be returned if the army had not mustered by Michaelmas 1474, and until it was needed it was to be placed in deposits outside the king's control. Further grants likewise set a two-year period in which the money was to be used. In all this the Commons were well within their rights; a century earlier they had similarly placed their grants in the custody of special treasurers and demanded to see the accounts of how the money had been spent. For the crown was required to spend taxes on the purpose for which they had been sought, and it faced fierce criticism if the Commons suspected that the money had been fed into the royal household or spent on the crown's ordinary costs. Edward's decision to abandon his campaign when it had scarcely begun, accepting a treaty with a pension from Louis IX, provoked bitter criticism from his subjects who felt that they had been duped and their taxes wasted. Indeed the Crowland chronicler declared that thereafter Edward no longer dared to seek taxes from his subjects in time of need, and gave this as the reason for his sustained effort to build up a treasure from his own resources.[22]

In fact Edward IV's much publicized intention to live of his own implied no cessation of demands for taxation. For the king's obligation to spend his own wealth on his normal expenses was the counterpart of his right to call upon his subjects to contribute theirs for great and urgent causes which touched the common weal. A king was expected to use his revenues wisely, to plan his budget and stay solvent. Least of all should he allow his household to run into debt, for not only was that dishonourable to the monarch, but it burdened and indeed robbed his subjects. That was the charge brought against Henry VI in 1450, whose accumulated debt of £372,000 so appalled the Commons. Not all of that, by any means, was Henry's own fault, but the heedless prodigality with which he had dispensed lands, money and offices as favours had undoubtedly contributed to the crown's insolvency, and it provoked an irresistible demand that such grants should be taken back into the crown's hands. That proved contentious, for while some thought it was unseemly for a king to take back what he had given, others like Sir John Fortescue argued forcibly that to reconstitute the endowment of the crown would enhance its strength and dignity.[23] Yet there was nothing theoretical or academic about this debate on whether it was the king's duty to reward his servants or to recover his grants in order to restore royal finances. We know that at the height of Jack Cade's revolt in 1450–1 it raged at the court, in the royal

---

[22] Pronay and Cox (eds.), *Crowland Chron.*, pp. 135–9; for popular hostility to the tax of 1469 see J. O. Halliwell (ed.), *A Chronicle . . . by John Warkworth*, Camden Soc., old series 10 (1839), pp. 8–9, 23.
[23] Fortescue, *Governance*, p. 155.

council and in parliament, and a resumption was one of the chief demands of the rebels themselves. This amounted to the most forceful expression in the middle ages of the right of the commons to criticize the king's use of his 'own'. Yet because this criticism was firmly anchored in a convention of good kingship, it could be taken over as royal policy by Henry VI's successors. Both Yorkists and Tudors regularly passed acts of resumption to win public approval and as a means of reviewing royal patronage, insisting that all grants were held at the king's pleasure and were conditional on continuing service. They also adopted the practice of allocating revenues from the crown estates to support their household expenses.

Public finance was the matter where the interests of the crown and its subjects most habitually met, at times in collaboration, at others in conflict. However, a wide range of other concerns, some common and some individual, came before the king by petitions in parliament. The former were presented by the Commons at the prompting of groups or individuals. They could reflect the interests of merchant bodies like the Company of the Staple, seeking to enforce their monopoly over wool exports to Calais, or imposing restrictions on trading by foreign merchants. A variety of crafts, like the silkwomen of London, the bowyers, pewterers, shoemakers, and the different trades engaged in clothmaking, all sought regulation or protection of different kinds. Urban oligarchies quite frequently presented petitions seeking, like those of Bristol and Gloucester, permission to compel houseowners to contribute to the pavage of streets, or in London to remove slaughterhouses beyond the city walls. Dover sought to enforce its monopoly of all passage between Kent and Calais. From the countryside came complaints about the malpractices of sheriffs, or the corruption of the courts, or the activities of lawbreakers. The answer to these was usually to reinforce existing legislation. Though often prompted by particular incidents, such complaints touched matters of common concern; but powerful and, at times, not so powerful individuals could also submit petitions seeking the king's grace and favour.

The political turmoil of these years produced a constant stream of requests from members of the nobility and gentry caught up in factional quarrels for the reversal of attainders and the restoration of their lands. Many with material interests to further, whether lay or ecclesiastical, sought pardons and privileges. Despite the trend, in the last quarter of the century, towards more occasional meetings and the increasing monopoly of its business by the crown, parliament remained the most important and habitual point of contact between the king and the political class as a whole. Its meetings served to disseminate royal intentions and the character of royal government among the population at large. On their return from Westminster members might well be asked to relate the events of the session, as were the Colchester burgesses in 1485.[24] Indeed for over a century before this the news of parliamentary proceedings was eagerly

---

[24] Printed in N. Pronay and J. Taylor (eds.), *Parliamentary Texts of the Later Middle Ages* (Oxford, 1980), pp. 177–96.

sought in the remotest parts of the kingdom. It was a vital channel of communication between the king and his subjects – in either direction.

When we pass beyond the king's contacts with and through the political classes, numbering at most some 10 per cent of the population, to those with the mass of the people, the direct channels of communication were very few. Proclamations were sometimes ordered in shire and city courts, as in 1474 concerning the repayment of royal debts, or in 1495 regulating coinage, weights and measures. At times proclamations were used also to rally political support: to justify the Yorkist successes in 1461 as the work of God, or to blacken the character of Edward IV's regime in 1483. Where official accounts like the *Arrival* and the *History of the Rebellion in Lincolnshire* were directed towards a literate and sophisticated audience, proclamations and sermons caught the ears of artisans, yeomen and peasants. Not that such classes were necessarily either illiterate or uninformed. Jack Cade's professed demand was 'to have the desires of the Commons in the parliament fulfilled' and, as we have seen, there were marked similarities between the reforms sought by the rebels and members of parliament.[25] Awareness of Henry VI's misgovernment – his bankruptcy, the loss of Normandy and the inability to curb local disorder – was widespread, and the names of the courtiers held responsible were circulated in bills and verses nailed to church doors and market crosses. The violence of the mob, in lynching Henry's principal ministers – a duke, two bishops and a lord – could be seen as an act of justice, repairing the deficiencies of the king's own rule. The *Vox Populi*, raised against the king's misgovernment, was indeed the warning of God to an unjust ruler.

But in the eyes of their rulers the people were essentially volatile. In his 1483 sermon Bishop Russell likened them 'unto the unstabille and waverynge rennynge water', for their support could easily be channelled and manipulated by leaders who played on their grievances.[26] Clearly their support was thought worth mobilizing, and the articles of the Yorkist lords in 1460, like those of Warwick and Clarence in 1469, invoked the whole gamut of popular grievances: the crown's indebtedness, the impoverishment of subjects, the burden of taxes, the preservation of justice – and promised to reform the state of the crown and realm.[27] Such pretensions were roundly condemned by the author of the *Somnium Vigilantis*, who denounced the Yorkist rebels against Henry VI, dismissing such popular protest as being 'varyable and . . . groweth of oppynable conceits and not trowth'. He derided the argument that popular support justified the reformers in their revolt: 'the peple favoureth hem, ergo thay be good'.[28]

Bishop Russell's view was uncompromising: the only way to rule the people was by 'drede'. 'Drede is the begynnyng of wyse demenynge', and it was the job of the king's

---

[25] R. Flenley (ed.), *Six Town Chronicles* (Oxford, 1911), p. 130.

[26] Chrimes, *Constitutional Ideas*, p. 169.

[27] Printed in, respectively, J. S. Davies (ed.), *An English Chronicle*, Camden Soc., old series 64 (1856), pp. 86–9, and Halliwell (ed.), *Warkworth's Chron.*, pp. 46–9.

[28] J. P. Gilson, 'A defence of the proscription of the Yorkists in 1459', *English Historical Review* 26 (1911), 521.

lords and officers to exercise it. Where the king ruled his nobility by 'loving treaty', he ruled his people by 'true justice'. By this Russell meant the exemplary justice rendered by a king on judicial progress to curb misdoers: 'the ministracion of justice is wont to be so terrible and precise in processe that alle the pertees and persones adioignaunt quake and tremble for fere'.[29] This was the kind of justice that Edward IV visited upon Kent in the aftermath of Faucomberg's rising, just as Henry VI did following that of Cade. A royal progress was often undertaken with punishment in view, but it could on occasion provide justice of another kind, designed to win hearts by love rather than terror. Richard III, again traversing Kent, proclaimed that all should bring their complaints to the king, and he was to lay the foundations of the Court of Requests for poor men's causes.

The mass of the people, the ruled, were thus seen in widely differing ways. In their own eyes they might appear as avenging angels, the people of God, exacting retribution for the sins of their governors. Noblemen who, at times of political disturbance, fell victim to popular fury included the duke of Suffolk and lord Say in 1450, Richard Neville earl of Salisbury in 1460, Humphrey Stafford earl of Devon in 1469 and Henry Percy earl of Northumberland in 1489. The nobility might also woo the common people, posing as reformers, and using popular discontents to indict their rivals. The crown feared the potential of the mob for revolt and sought stability through intimidation or paternalism. How, in turn, the people viewed the king is less easy to discern. Direct comment on the king's person could be treasonable, and not surprisingly little survives. Chroniclers who report popular reactions often had an axe to grind, and even ballads and political doggerels were written for and not by the people, though they may well reflect the prevailing mood. Nonetheless it seems clear that each king produced a fairly definite impression and was the subject of popular, if summary, judgement. Henry VI was seen as simple and easily led, like a sheep, and though not held blameless for the disasters of his reign, he was pitied rather than hated. Edward IV's self-indulgence was common knowledge before it was denounced by Richard III, but his affability and largesse won him popular applause. Richard's usurpation produced widespread revulsion, though contemporary opinion on his reign remained confused and ambivalent, and the subsequent blackening of his reputation has obscured the verdict of his contemporaries. In 1498 a Spanish envoy reported that Henry VII was disliked, but direct evidence of the popular verdict on his rule is significantly absent.

I began by outlining the dual nature of kingship, which drew its authority from divine right but was held accountable for the welfare of subjects. These were not just academic concepts, or conventions to which lip service was paid; they were facts in the minds of both ruler and ruled, guiding men's political actions and influencing their disputes. Of course belief in such concepts did not displace the struggles for power and

---

[29] Chrimes, *Constitutional Ideas*, pp. 171, 173.

the calculations of self-interest which formed the substance of politics, and they could readily be used as propaganda to win support and legitimize success. But the government of England, even in the turbulent fifteenth century, was not for the most part a perpetual and naked struggle for power. It was mainly about keeping a tolerable level of order, solvency and justice, security for property and person, respect for due authority and defence against external threats. In other words it was about the kind of concerns we have today. In these terms the concept of a society regulated by a divinely ordained hierarchy of authority, and directed towards the common good, provided an essential framework for political life and development. It is tempting to ask whether the political vicissitudes of successive kings in these years did not discredit the notion of divine right and strengthen that of accountability to subjects. If so it marked no permanent shift of emphasis, for the pendulum swung back towards the obedience due to God's anointed in the royal propaganda of Tudor times. If there was a broad development in these years it was surely towards a greater integration of the realm and the identification of the common good with that of the rapidly broadening political class. The spread of literacy, the growing reach of royal authority and the involvement of an increasing sector of society in the processes of government, all helped to narrow the distance between rulers and ruled and stress their mutual interest in stable government. Fortescue's view of England under Edward IV as a college in which 'we shul now mowe enjoye oure owne goode and live undir justice' was not a mere conceit. He was defining a relationship between kingship and the liberty of subjects which differed fundamentally from what he saw in France.[30]

---

[30] Fortescue, *Governance*, pp. 155–6.

LAW AND JUSTICE

Edward Powell

The history of the law in medieval England is often regarded as a dull and difficult subject. Even professional historians tend to shy away from it, deterred by the voluminous records of the courts (some of the plea rolls of the court of common pleas are so large they can only be lifted with difficulty!) and the obscure technicalities of land law. Legal historians are treated as a strange breed, using terms that no one else can understand and cackling with delight over the finer points of the assize of novel disseisin. They probably have only themselves to blame for this state of affairs, since all too often they do not attempt to explain their subject to a wider audience. Nevertheless it is important that they should do so, because the concepts and workings of law and justice are central to any understanding of society and politics in fifteenth-century England. As Dr Eric Ives has pointed out in his study of the career of the lawyer Thomas Kebell (which spanned the Yorkist and Tudor period),[1] English society was extremely 'law-minded'. Legal ways of thinking permeated social relationships and activities, and law formed part of the fabric of everyday life much more than at the present day. For a law-abiding citizen going to court is now a comparatively rare event, but in the fifteenth century it was the badge of citizenship, of the full membership of society. Men (and attendance was overwhelmingly male) went to court not just to litigate or prosecute, but to serve on juries, make indictments and record land transactions. Also, in an age when bureaucratic specialization was not so great as it is today, much of what we would consider administrative or local government business was handled in the courts. For example manorial courts were concerned with the management and regulation of agrarian activity, and justices of the peace were involved with the upkeep of roads and bridges and later, under the Tudors, with administering the Poor Laws, the precursors of social security.

At the highest level the fundamental importance of legal concepts is perfectly illustrated by the famous petition of the three estates calling upon Richard III to assume the throne in 1483. The legal context was vital, because of course Richard was seeking to legitimize his seizure of the throne. After Edward IV's marriage to Elizabeth Woodville, it was alleged,

---

[1] E. W. Ives, *The Common Lawyers of Pre-Reformation England* (Cambridge, 1983), p. 7.

the order of all politic rule was perverted, the laws of God and God's church, and also the laws of nature and of England, and also the laudable customs and liberties of the same, wherein every Englishman is inherite, broken, subverted, and contempned against all reason and justice; so that this land was ruled by self-will and pleasure, fear and dread, all manner of equity and laws laid apart and despised; whereof ensued many inconvenients and mischiefs, as murders, extortions and oppressions, namely of poor and impotent people.[2]

That remarkable passage provides us, in a nutshell, with the essential meaning of law and justice as it was understood in the fifteenth century, and also underlines the close connection made between them and the stability of the body politic. The first point to note is the association of law with order, both in the sense of social hierarchy ('the order of all politic rule') and also in the sense of public order ('murders, extortions and oppressions'), the breakdown of which most seriously affects the poor and defenceless. This analysis is exactly what one would expect of a highly stratified aristocratic society like that of medieval England. The hierarchical structure of society is ingeniously justified as existing for the benefit and protection of its lowest members. Although this may seem to the modern eye to be a transparent piece of class propaganda, it formed a central strand in medieval social theory, and was implicit in the model of society as made up of the three complementary and mutually supportive estates – knights, clergy and peasants.

Secondly we may note the hierarchy that existed within the law itself: the law of God, the law of nature, the law of England and the customs of the realm. It was a medieval commonplace that all law derived ultimately from God. Mankind could not apprehend the eternal law of God directly, but by applying reason (the divine spark which set man apart from and above the animals) he might deduce a body of principles based upon it, that is, the law of nature. It was from the law of nature that the positive laws of human societies were derived, including the laws of England.

It was the *rule of law* which was the distinguishing feature of medieval kingship. Tyranny was characterized by the ruler's wilfulness and his failure to observe the law. In the petition quoted above, Edward IV's rule was in effect denounced as tyrannical ('. . . this land was ruled by self-will and pleasure . . . all manner of equity and laws laid apart and despised . . . '). Richard III was therefore presented as offering a return to kingship under the rule of law in place of the tyranny of his brother's Woodville in-laws. It is interesting and instructive to compare this part of the petition with the articles brought against Richard II at his deposition in 1399. There it was alleged that 'the king refused to keep and defend the just laws and customs of the realm, but according to the whim of his desire he wanted to do whatever appealed to his wishes'.[3]

It is clear also from the petition of 1483 that *reason* was integral to the medieval

[2] *Rotuli Parliamentorum* (6 vols., 1767–77), VI, p. 240.
[3] *Ibid.*, III, p. 419.

concept of law: note that the petition claimed that the laws were ' . . . broken, subverted, and contempned against all reason and justice . . . '. Eternal law was the application of divine reason to the universe, and natural law was the means by which mankind, as rational creatures, participated in the eternal law. In the late middle ages natural law and reason were regarded as virtually synonymous, and were routinely invoked in the law courts as much as in the legal treatises of writers like Sir John Fortescue in the fifteenth century and Christopher St German in the sixteenth. Petitioners seeking the equitable jurisdiction of the king's council or chancery requested, as a matter of form, the remedy dictated by law and reason.

Justice gets only a passing mention in this Ricardian text, but there were two standard definitions of justice in the middle ages, one from Roman law, the other Biblical. The first was the maxim *suum cuique tribuere* attributed to the Roman jurist Ulpian: 'justice is the constant and unfailing will to give each his right'. This was adopted by the thirteenth-century English law writer Bracton. The second comes from St Matthew's gospel (7: 12): 'all things whatsoever ye would that men should do to you, do ye even so to them, for this is the law and the prophets'. This was adopted by Sir John Fortescue, lord chief justice under Henry VI and tutor to his son Prince Edward, as the 'golden rule' embodying the law of nature. The emphasis here is on the notions of fair dealing and reciprocity. An intriguing third definition of justice was provided by Bishop Robert Stillington, chancellor to Edward IV, in his speech to the parliament of 1467:

> Wherefore first be asked, what is justice? Justice is every person to do his office that he is put in according to his estate and degree, and as for this land it is understood that it standeth by three estates and above that one principal: that is to wit Lords Spiritual, Lords Temporal and Commons, and over that Estate Royal above, as our sovereign Lord the King.[4]

Such a definition is striking both for its particularity to the English context and for its stress on order and degree. It takes us full circle to the association of law and justice with hierarchy and public order.

To summarize, we can identify three basic points fundamental to fifteenth-century attitudes to law and justice: law was of divine origin, it had to be in accordance with reason, and justice entailed giving each man his due. Two obvious objections may be raised to such an analysis. First, the concepts described are very abstract, sounding impressive in theological and legal treatises but having little relevance to everyday life in England at the end of the middle ages; and secondly that they represent the dominant ideology of the ruling class and were promoted to maintain the status quo.

There is undoubtedly an element of truth in both objections. They are not serious enough, however, to allow us to dismiss such ideas as so much hot air, to be set aside and ignored when we examine the workings of the legal system. The concepts of law

---

[4] *Ibid.*, v, pp. 622–3.

and justice discussed above did indeed help to uphold a very stratified social structure. On the other hand they provided the basis for a powerful critique of the ruling classes in their administration of the law. They offered a yardstick, a set of standards against which the day-to-day practice of the law could be measured and its shortcomings exposed. The constant litany of complaint against corruption and the abuse of the law was firmly grounded in those concepts, as is apparent from sources like petitions to parliament, contemporary poems and songs of complaint, and popular manifestoes at times of rebellion such as the Peasants' Revolt of 1381 and Jack Cade's rising in Kent in 1450. It is therefore important to bear them in mind as we turn to examine the practical workings of the law in fifteenth-century England.

By comparison with the other kingdoms of Europe there can be little doubt that England possessed an advanced and highly centralized legal system, epitomized in the institutions of the common law. This was a legacy of the early political unification of the realm, achieved before the end of the Anglo-Saxon era, and of the administrative and legal innovations carried out by the Norman and Angevin kings in the centuries after 1066. By the fourteenth century Westminster was already emerging as the administrative capital of the kingdom. It was there, in Westminster Hall within the royal palace, that the four central royal courts – king's bench, common pleas, chancery and exchequer – administered the common law. In the shires the king's government had long been carried out by the sheriff and lesser officials such as the coroner. The sheriff was responsible for serving writs and arresting offenders to appear in court, and also for empanelling juries to try civil and criminal cases (a duty which made the sheriff's office the target of much bribery and intimidation during our period). The coroner held inquests on the dead and recorded outlawries in the county court. From the fourteenth century onwards, however, judicial responsibilities for local government fell increasingly upon the justices of the peace. By the Yorkist period, indeed, the JPs were well on the way to becoming the all-purpose workhorses of royal government in the shires. In 1461, for example, in the first parliament of Edward IV, the jurisdiction of the old sheriff's tourn was transferred to the JPs. Their main sessions were held four times a year (hence the term quarter sessions), and they enjoyed an extensive criminal jurisdiction, covering all types of offence from murder and robbery to minor assaults and petty theft. They also had considerable responsibility for the regulation of economic activity: they were, for example, entrusted with the enforcement of the labour legislation passed after the Black Death to hold down wages and limit the mobility of workers.

The link between the centre and the localities was provided by the circuit commissions of assize and gaol delivery. The assize judges were appointed mainly from the judges and serjeants of the Westminster courts, and they went out on circuit twice a year, in spring and summer. Their jurisdiction was comprehensive, including a wide range of civil cases and all the most serious criminal offences apart from treason. The gaol delivery commission gave the judges the power to try all prisoners held in the county gaol on suspicion or on indictment for felony. The work of the assize judges overlapped with that of the JPs, over whom they exercised a supervisory role. On his appointment, an assize judge was nominated to the bench of every county within

5 Robbery with violence: the devil, disguised as a pilgrim, strangles a young man
who has offered him alms

his circuit. The assizes continued to function even in the thick of the Wars of the Roses.
Records survive, for instance, from the south-western circuit for the summer assizes of
1460 in the uncertain period following the battle of Northampton (although admittedly
there were numerous fines for non-attendance!). The system of royal justice at a
local level, based on the twin pillars of quarter sessions and assizes, was thus firmly
established by the late fourteenth century. It provided the bedrock of judicial
administration until the abolition of the assize circuits in the 1970s.

Despite possessing such comparatively advanced legal institutions, however, late
medieval England does not have much of a reputation for justice and public order. On
the contrary, both in the popular mind and among professional historians the period is
usually written off as a time of unparalleled violence, lawlessness and corruption, an
inglorious prelude to the establishment of strong, orderly government under the
Tudors. It is true that there is strong evidence to support such a view. As far back as
the early fourteenth century the notorious Folville gang, a band of gentry outlaws,
terrorized the midlands unchecked for the best part of a decade and were never

punished for their crimes. Indeed they flouted the king's justice in the most outrageous manner, murdering one royal judge, Roger Bellers, and kidnapping another, Richard Willoughby, until he paid a ransom of 1,300 marks. The wider implications of the failure of justice in the fifteenth century have been demonstrated by Professor Robin Storey in his classic study *The End of the House of Lancaster*, which documents the escalation of disorder through a series of spectacular breaches of the peace which led ultimately to the Wars of the Roses. One of the most shocking and brutal crimes of that period in the eyes of contemporaries was the murder of Nicholas Radford by Sir Thomas Courtenay and his followers in 1455. Radford, a Devon lawyer, was a counsellor of Lord Bonville, the bitter rival of Courtenay's father the earl of Devon. Courtenay's men stormed and looted Radford's house, tipped his invalid wife out of bed to steal her sheets, dragged Radford outside and stabbed him to death.

Besides such instances of wanton violence there is also abundant evidence of corruption and abuse of justice – bribery, maintenance and intimidation – at every level of society. The Paston letters reveal the extent to which such practices were part of the routine pursuit of legal disputes. Reviewing the legal history of the late middle ages Professor John Bellamy concluded gloomily that 'not one investigator has been able to indicate even a few years of effective policing in the period 1290–1485'.[5]

Were things really as bad as Professor Bellamy's prognosis suggests? In part the traditional view of the late medieval period as unusually violent and lawless is simply due to the fact that we have better and more numerous records. In the words of K. B. McFarlane, 'it is the very richness of the sources which has given the later middle ages a bad name'.[6] This does not, however, take us very far. On the face of it royal justice in the fifteenth century still left much to be desired. Indeed it appears to have been failing in its primary functions of enforcing the law and doing justice.

We should not, however, make the mistake of assessing the performance of the medieval legal system by modern standards. There is a very real danger here of making anachronistic judgements. Because the system we are examining is the ancestor of our own and looks familiar in many respects, historians have all too often made the unspoken assumption that it functioned in the same way as ours does. However this overlooks the obvious fact that the medieval state was quite different in structure and resources from the modern state. In particular, medieval kings had no standing army or police force at their disposal. The maintenance of public order must therefore be considered in a completely different social and political context from that with which we are familiar. This point is easily forgotten as we shake our heads at the lawlessness and corruption of fifteenth-century England.

The point is neatly illustrated by the account of a nineteenth-century dispute given by Professor Alan Harding.[7] Early in the reign of Queen Victoria the possession of

---

[5] J. G. Bellamy, *Crime and Public Order in England in the Later Middle Ages* (1973), p. 4.
[6] K. B. McFarlane, *The Nobility of Later Medieval England* (Oxford, 1973), p. 114.
[7] A. Harding, *The Law Courts of Medieval England* (1973), p. 94.

Stansfield Hall in Norfolk was disputed using means which the Pastons themselves might have adopted four centuries earlier. While the owner, Isaac Jermy, was away, the claimant, Mr Larner, appeared with some eighty men, all cheering and waving their hats. They evicted Jermy's servants and barricaded themselves in the house. Later Jermy returned, and being a justice of the peace read the Riot Act outside his own front door. The incident was brought to a close by the appearance of a troop of Dragoon Guards from Norwich. They surrounded the house and loaded their weapons, and Larner's men were given five minutes to surrender. The relevance of this story lies in the crucial question: what is to be done when there are no Dragoon Guards to be called out? For it is on that question that much of late medieval legal history turns.

The answer lies in the local communities. In the circumstances I have described the crown was bound to rely heavily on the support of local society in its efforts to enforce the law and maintain public order. Principally this meant the landowning classes, who ran the shires and filled the magistrates' bench and other local administrative offices. But it also included the lower ranks of yeomen and substantial villagers who served on juries which indicted offenders before the coroners and JPs and tried accused felons at gaol delivery.

Inevitably this degree of local influence meant that the courts were vulnerable to pressure from the powerful members of local society – the classic symptom of the evils of bastard feudalism. A great noble might overawe court proceedings within his 'country' in order to obtain an unjust verdict. An extreme example was the famous case of Ankarette Twynho, who in 1477 was abducted in Somerset on the instructions of George, duke of Clarence, brought to Warwick, the seat of the duke's power, and indicted, convicted and executed in a single day on a charge of poisoning Isabella Neville, duchess of Clarence. More rarely, an entire community might close ranks and refuse to co-operate with royal justices if it felt its interests threatened. This happened, for example, in Devon during Henry V's reign, when the king attempted to prosecute the breach of maritime truces as piracy.[8]

Nevertheless the effect of local influence was not always negative, because there were strong forces at work which militated towards the containment of disorder and conflict. One was that it reflected badly upon a great lord if he allowed disputes between members of his retinue to fester unresolved and degenerate into violence. As John Paston put it, it was 'disworship to my lord [of Norfolk] that two of his men should debate so near him'.[9] Another factor was that the legal system offered ample opportunity for out-of-court negotiation and conciliation during proceedings, and magnates and leading gentry were expected to use their influence to promote the peaceful conciliation and settlement of disputes, which they might do by informal negotiations or by formal arbitration procedures. Such attempts at peace-making might

---

[8] E. Powell, *Kingship, Law and Society: Criminal Justice in the Reign of Henry V* (Oxford, 1989), pp. 201–5.

[9] Sir John Fortescue, *The Governance of England*, ed. C. Plummer (Oxford, 1885), p. 30 n. 1.

not always be successful, but they stood more chance of achieving the lasting resolution of disputes than the final judgement in a lawsuit, which left a clear winner – and a clear loser.

In the last assessment the maintenance of public order in late medieval England rested as much upon social and political relationships as upon judicial institutions. The king had the ultimate responsibility for law and order, as he acknowledged in his coronation oath. There was little he could do, however, without the support, or at least acquiescence, of his greater subjects. He therefore had to exercise effective political management over his nobility and gentry and to satisfy their aspirations for advancement in royal service, military and governmental. It was the king's duty to create the conditions in which peace and order could flourish; but their day-to-day implementation at local level rested with the greater landowners in the shires. Where the king's role was critical was of course in curbing feuding and violence within the nobility itself. This was less a matter of the strength and integrity of judicial institutions than of the political abilities and the sheer force of personality of the king himself.

If we bear in mind the distinctive social and political context in which the fifteenth-century legal system functioned, therefore, we can begin to see in better perspective some of the familiar issues relating to public order – in particular the questions of judicial corruption, bastard feudalism and gentry violence. This in turn will enable us to assess how wide was the gap between the contemporary ideals of justice in fifteenth-century England (which have been outlined above) and the reality. Such a gulf probably exists in all societies – not least our own – but the assumption has been that it was particularly wide in the fifteenth century. Was this really so?

As far as bribery and corruption are concerned the gap between the ideals and the reality of justice seems to have been less wide in the fifteenth century than it was in the fourteenth. The fourteenth century was truly the heroic age of judicial corruption, as a result of the rapid expansion of the common law in the previous two centuries and the laicization of the judiciary. It was a century in which there were enormous fortunes to be made as a royal judge – the Scrope brothers made so much money under Edward II and Edward III that they both established baronial families. However the personal risks involved were also much greater than in the following century: judges often went in fear of their lives and several were killed, including Chief Justice John Cavendish at the hands of the rebels in 1381. In the fifteenth century judicial office was less remunerative but also less dangerous, and it is harder to find evidence of outright bribery and retaining. The corrupt 'high justice of England' immortalized in the earliest Robin Hood ballad reflects the freewheeling times of the early fourteenth century rather than the more cautious spirit of the age of Thomas Littleton and Sir John Fortescue. Judges did continue to receive sweeteners, as we see from the correspondence of Mayor John Shillingford of Exeter, but not on the munificent scale of the Scropes and their contemporaries. Mayor Shillingford was engaged in a long-running dispute with the bishop of Exeter in the middle years of the fifteenth century. The case came into chancery, and on one occasion Shillingford sent the lord chancellor 'two stately pickerels and two stately tenches, for which my lord Chancellor

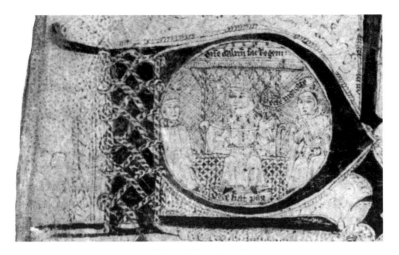

6   Henry VI as lawgiver

gave right great thanks and made right much thereof'.[10] We should probably see this kind of gift less as an example of flagrant bribery and more as the medieval equivalent of the business lunch; it is hard to envisage a case being decided on the strength of a good fish course, even in the fifteenth century. On the other hand the extensive records of the litigation of Sir John Fastolf of Norfolk, a contemporary of the Pastons and a veteran of the Hundred Years War, reveal some cases of more direct and cruder methods. There are several instances where Fastolf paid cash to secure the 'friendship' of useful people, such as the clerk of the judge Sir William Yelverton, and to speed up the hearing of his cases in court. Litigants regularly solicited ministers and men in the king's confidence for their support, reflecting the persistently personal character of government in the fifteenth century and the lack of a tradition of public service in the face of the traditional concepts of good lordship inherent in bastard feudalism. Clients in lawsuits saw no reason why what was normal elsewhere in society should be omitted because the law was involved, nor did patrons feel great inhibitions about getting involved, not least the king – the good lord of all good lords.

It is important to put such evidence into perspective, however. In the second half of the fifteenth century (by contrast with 100 years earlier) evidence for the most direct sort of bribery of the judiciary and the upper ranks of the legal profession is not common. In the records which survive, such as the letters of the Paston family and Mayor Shillingford, as well as the Fastolf archives, only a small proportion of references to gifts and payments for legal services smack of outright corruption.

---

[10] Ives, *Common Lawyers*, p. 309.

Less progress was made at the local level, where justices of the peace continued to receive fees and retainers, often taking several small fees from local landowners, towns and religious houses. But again this may not have been a matter of simple corruption. Since the workings of the peace commission depended upon a small number of diligent justices in each county, who served with great regularity, such fees were no doubt the means whereby such semi-professionals supplemented their salary of 4s per day and made their devotion to duty worthwhile. Because of the comparatively limited scale of their operations and the diversity of their caseload, it would not have been worth the while of any one patron to grant them a large retainer. But a system of general benefit could have been sustained by a number of patrons paying small fees to JPs to ensure that county peace-keeping was done by experienced and able men. Such fees would to an extent have cancelled each other out and have provided a general landowners' consensus behind a partly 'privatized' system of local justice. Far more prominent than the JPs in the corruption of justice was the sheriff and his staff. In fifteenth-century accounts of legal expenses payments to sheriffs and their underlings are commonplace, and in the Paston letters comments on the necessity of gaining the support of the sheriff in legal proceedings comfortably outnumber comparable references to the JPs. This of course reflects the pivotal role played by the sheriff in executing judicial process, most notably his responsibilities for serving writs and empanelling juries.

Whether or not corruption was openly discernible, the influence of lordship was only too evident throughout the workings of the legal system in the fifteenth century, justifying the ubiquitous complaint that 'law goeth as lordship biddeth'. In part this reflects the persistent identification in late medieval England between landownership and the exercise of judicial authority, despite the triumph of royal justice over feudal jurisdictions. In the scheme of the three orders the knightly order shared with the king the responsibility for doing justice as well as defending the realm. Conversely, the king sometimes behaved like a private lord. There was as yet no tradition of altruistic public service among the king's servants, even those whose income derived substantially from the crown. Royal servants continued to see their relationship with the king as one of personal loyalty and service in return for profit. The exploitation of royal office for private profit is characteristic of medieval government – although of course it extends far beyond, into the reigns of the Tudors and Stuarts. Thomas Hoccleve, in his work *The Regement of Princes*, voices the attitudes of all royal servants when in his address to Prince Henry (later Henry V) he harps on the inadequacy of his income as a clerk in the privy scal office, and drops unsubtle hints that Henry should provide him with an annual retainer.

It comes as no surprise therefore to find late medieval kings interceding on behalf of their men with local officials. For example in 1451 Robert Hungerford, lord Moleyns, who was involved in a dispute with John Paston over possession of the manor of Gresham in Norfolk, was indicted with his men for riotous disorder. Paston had high hopes of a conviction, which would of course have impeded Moleyns in his campaign to secure Gresham, but to his dismay the king, Henry VI, intervened:

The sheriff is not so whole as he was [wrote Paston's servants] for now he will show but a part of his friendship . . . also the sheriff informed us that he hath writing from the king that he shall make such a panel to acquit the Lord Moleyns. And he told us, and as far as we can conceive and feel, the sheriff will panel gentlemen to acquit the lord, and jurors to acquit his men; and we suppose that this is by the motion and means of the other party.[11]

This is a classic example of the manipulation of the law through bastard feudalism – the only noteworthy feature being that the lord involved in exerting pressure on the sheriff happened to be the king.

Inevitably the magnates and gentry followed the example thus set by the king. As I have suggested, these classes played a substantial part in the administration of local justice. In the fifteenth century they continued to exercise a similar degree of judicial control, through the peace commissions and other local offices, to that which they had done in earlier centuries through the feudal and hundred courts. The crucial difference was that they did so now more explicitly as royal commissioners, but this did not have the effect automatically of modifying their behaviour or of imbuing them with a precocious sense of disinterested public duty. They continued to equate their own political and territorial interests with those of the local communities which they led. If their behaviour was modified, it was only as a result of overwhelming public clamour and outcry – as with the practice of the retaining of royal judges, which came to an abrupt end at the close of the fourteenth century. A remarkable case from the reign of Henry IV illustrates the extent to which the public interest, even at a very high level, might be subordinated to the private. John, lord Lovell, a member of the king's council, was in dispute with a certain William Doyle over the manor of Hinton in Northamptonshire. In 1403 there was a burglary at the treasury of receipt at Westminster where legal records were kept, including feet of fines – deeds recording agreements and conveyances of land. The culprit was a servant of Lovell's called John Freeman, who had made off with all the bundles of feet of fines for Northamptonshire between 1331 and 1336. The purpose of this theft was to remove all record of an agreement made at that time which was an important piece of evidence in Doyle's case against Lovell. Freeman had committed a very serious – even treasonable – offence, and perhaps he had been rather overzealous in pursuit of his lord's interests. Nevertheless he was still Lovell's man, and it was Lovell's duty to protect him. The case was referred to the king's council at a session which Lovell attended, and remarkably (in view of the fact that he had been indicted in the court of king's bench for treason) Freeman was granted bail, on Lovell's security, to appear in king's bench at Easter 1403. He failed to appear as bailed, and when he finally did come to court over a year later it was merely to present a pardon, no doubt procured through Lovell's good offices.

---

[11] N. Davis (ed.), *Paston Letters and Papers of the Fifteenth Century* (2 vols., Oxford, 1971–6), II, nos. 477, 479.

There can be little doubt then that the realities of wealth and political power in late medieval England invariably influenced, and sometimes distorted, the workings of the law. The law was not a closed system, but reflected the character and needs of the society it served. In particular, political considerations intruded into cases where law regulated the allocation and distribution of the principal sources of wealth and power, which in the fifteenth century chiefly meant land. Nor were the officials who operated the legal machinery immune from these pressures. They shared the values and assumptions of society at large, and were themselves part of an hierarchical structure based on lordship and patronage. There have been a number of in-depth studies recently which have confirmed how vital were the power and political connections of disputants to their success in winning lawsuits. Even such a substantial figure as Sir John Fastolf experienced endless trouble with his lawsuits in East Anglia in the 1440s because his opponents were backed by the all-powerful duke of Suffolk.

We might therefore seek an explanation for what we consider to be the endemic judicial malpractices of fifteenth-century England in the nature of the social and political structure of the age. While such a point of view has much to commend it, perhaps it is also a touch anachronistic. For it would be wrong to assume that the exercise of lordly influence was entirely at odds with contemporary expectations of justice. It is important to bear in mind the emphasis upon order and hierarchy in medieval concepts of law. If justice meant giving each man his due, that did not mean each man's due was the same: justice did not automatically entail equality, as we assume it should today. Furthermore, as we have seen, great lords retained considerable responsibilities for upholding the interests of their followers and resolving their disputes. Even a noble as erratic as George, duke of Clarence, played the role of good lord by arbitrating in his retainers' disputes and making peace between them. This remained an essential aspect of lordship. Throughout the late middle ages the councils of great magnates exercised a form of equitable jurisdiction supplementary to that of the royal court of chancery. Arguably, therefore, there were still situations where it was considered right and proper that 'law goeth where lordship biddeth'.

The final element we must touch upon in considering the gulf between the ideal and reality of late medieval justice is violence. The era of the Wars of the Roses was of course notoriously one of political violence, stemming from the collapse of the Lancastrian regime under Henry VI. The spectacular nature of these disorders has been fully chronicled by Professor Storey. However, if we look behind the headlines as it were, the striking fact about English society is that force and violence were far less prevalent than they were in the rest of Europe. The effectiveness of the king's peace, established gradually over several centuries, was such that England was less militarized than the continent. Royal castles in many parts of the country were falling into disrepair, and only in the north and the Welsh marches did the strongholds of private lords pose a potential threat to royal power. Perhaps the most remarkable feature of the Wars of the Roses was not the level of violence involved but that it took so long to break out. It is interesting to note that in the conduct of lawsuits in the fifteenth century, the threat of violence is much more common than its actual occurrence. The use of force was a matter much more of last than of first resort for disputants, and battle was joined more readily in complex and protracted litigation in the courts. Allegations of violence, on the other hand, were part of the everyday cut and thrust of the disputing process. Crimes like the murder of Nicholas Radford by the Courtenays attracted such attention because they were genuinely shocking by contemporary standards, in a society which was becoming used to the restraint of baronial violence.

No rehabilitation of the late medieval legal system can ever be entirely convincing. There is a case to be made, however, that the reputation of the fifteenth century for lawlessness, corruption and injustice is not wholly deserved. There was indeed a gap between contemporary ideals and reality, but those ideals were very high, and it remains a matter for debate whether the gap was any wider then than it is in modern society.

The most important point, which cannot be overemphasized, is that the workings of the law were inextricably bound up with those of society. Law was a mirror of the social order. There is overwhelming evidence in the fifteenth century of attempts to influence and manipulate the course of justice, but the methods principally employed sprang out of the traditional bonds of family, lordship and service which still formed the basis of the social structure. Maintenance, for example, which is usually seen by historians as the bane of the late medieval legal system, only became an offence during the reign of Edward I in the late thirteenth century; historically it was one of the main obligations of lordship. Likewise bribery, the epitome of corruption from a twentieth-century viewpoint, is less easy to condemn in a society where legal officials were inadequately paid and gift-giving was an essential courtesy. In short, the more closely we place the law in its contemporary context, the more accurately we shall see it in perspective.

$$\boxed{3}$$

ARISTOCRACY

Kate Mertes

The past seems fixed for many people because it is over and done with. But history is an enquiry into a dynamic process, a world no less changeable and evolving than our own. A study of the aristocracy of England in the 1400s does not exhibit crisis or complacency, but a culture responding to the tensions of its times. The political turmoil of fifteenth-century England wrought many changes for established noble and gentle families, for better or for worse. The aristocracy was forced to respond to economic changes such as the decline in rents, as well as more gradual historical processes begun much earlier, such as the demise of purely feudal institutions and the development of urban power and wealth. Certainly there were even some challenges to the very existence of hierarchical social order, as indeed there had always been. But by and large the idea of aristocracy itself survived the fifteenth century without any real erosion of its force as a political, economic and social control. That is not to say, however, that it was an idea without tension, or that it was not subject to more subtle changes of emphasis. The nobility of the fifteenth century were a distinctive breed, and understanding them is central to developing a feel for the entire period in whose history they loom so largely. Also, the evolution of fifteenth-century noble society is an important stage in the history of the nobility, linking their established past with the much greater challenges to aristocratic life that arose in the early modern period.

Traditionally the subject of the aristocracy has been approached as a question of political manoeuvring, economic control or 'class' ascendancy. But one of the things that makes aristocracies so tenacious in clinging to power, and so hard to enter or indeed leave, is their existence as a culture as well as a political institution – a complex web of habits, traditions, relationships, behaviours, assumptions and beliefs which gave them a common world and enables us to talk about them as a unit. The American historian David Hackett Fischer calls these 'folkways', originally a sociological term describing the dynamic systems and structures which allow a culture to function.[1] These 'folkways' are not always subject to intense or disinterested scrutiny by the group that espouses them, but they are often consciously and deliberately perpetuated.

The advantage of looking at social groups as cultures rather than as strictly political

---

[1] D. H. Fischer, *Albion's Seed* (Oxford, 1989), pp. 7–13.

42

or economic entities is that it makes it possible to enter their mental world more fully, and to recognize the dynamic nature of the group in question. Rather than finding crisis or decay in every change that overtakes them we are more easily able to see the continuities and the evolutionary changes that enable aristocracy, or indeed any culture, to survive the events it lives through. In considering the idea of aristocracy in fifteenth-century England, the whole cultural milieu can give us valuable clues about nobles' conception of themselves and their lives, who they were and what purposes they served.

Of necessity this will generally be a view of the aristocracy as they saw themselves. Very few others have passed their opinions down to us; many of the clerics who composed some of the texts from which we draw evidence were themselves part of the aristocratic culture. The members of the noble classes were often themselves the most interested in codifying and passing on the idea of aristocracy. While the vast majority of English people were not aristocrats, and probably had rather different ideas about this dominant culture than did its members, if we want to get at the culture of the nobility, its lived nature rather than its intellectual presentation as an abstract idea, this internal approach makes sense. Indeed, sometimes the most telling elements in a discourse on nobility lie in the author's unconscious assumptions rather than in carefully worked out theories.

In approaching these topics most of the traditional sources on the idea of nobility may prove useful, but in this essay a major touchstone will be courtesy books. These were enormously popular, extremely common little tracts, ranging in length from a few doggerel verses to carefully arranged book-length texts, detailing the behaviour and attitudes necessary to proper socialization as a gentleperson. Some are clearly aimed at children; others have a wider intended audience. Some are aimed at and seem to speak of ordinary people, but even these seem to have been used mainly by nobles. While ostensibly aimed at the children of yeoman farmers and artisans, poems like 'The Godemans Son' and 'The Godewyfe's Doghtere' mostly survive in noble common-place books.[2] Courtesy books were a kind of popular culture of the nobility, and exist in their thousands, scribbled down and commented upon in commonplace books, the backs of bibles, accounting records and letters, alongside recipes for cold medicines and records of gambling debts. One of the most popular, 'Stans Puer Ad Mensam', survives in no less than eighty renditions. A good printed source for these books is still F. J. Furnivall's *Babees' Book*, first published by the Early English Text Society in 1868, but many more examples can be drawn from surviving manuscripts.

Historians' concepts of nobility have traditionally been taken from contemporary treatises such as the Knight of La Tour-Landry and the works of Olivier de la Marche and Castiglione, William Harrison and Sir John Fortescue. These directly address the issue of nobility as a concept, but via an intellectual culture far removed from the

---

[2] Unless otherwise noted, the courtesy books referred to can be found in F. J. Furnivall (ed.), *Early English Meals and Manners*, Early English Text Society (hereafter EETS), 32 (1868).

lives of many nobles, who after all were mostly very ordinary people. Contemporary chronicles and histories, such as Hardyng's chronicle and the Anonimalle chronicle of Richard II's reign, also provide less direct but revealing statements from diverse sources which are useful for unveiling unconscious assumptions and attitudes about nobility, but they can be ambiguous at best. Courtesy books have the advantage of being a direct, simple, sometimes almost naive commentary on nobles' ways and duties, which were endorsed through their use by gentlepeople of all stations. Using courtesy books as well as more traditional sources, we can begin to approach the culture of aristocracy in fifteenth-century England.

In the space of an article it is not possible to convey every aspect of that culture, but by looking at several core aspects of late medieval noble life we can hope to capture some of the essence of being a gentleperson at that time. Each of these aspects is a kind of nexus of interrelated concerns closely tied to ideas of nobility and central to the practice of noble culture. First of all it will be worthwhile to look at just who inhabited this culture we wish to study. Joel Rosenthal, in his very useful book *Nobles and the Noble Life, 1295–1500*, restricted his discussion of the aristocracy to those people called to sit in parliament as the king's peers, and their families – for his purposes a useful distinct group, but, as he himself admitted, in many ways an artificial one. Other authors have focused on those who held their land at the top of the feudal heap, but by the fifteenth century that sort of distinction had come to mean little.

In a general consideration of the idea of nobility it is most useful to take the widest view, considering those at the fringes as well as at the core of the aristocratic condition. This group of people can best be defined as those who obtained most of their wealth and authority from their command of a rural landholding, and who were not such smallholders that they were compelled to farm their own fields. They form a group of diverse estate but common interests. Despite the range of incomes, social backgrounds and power this definition covers, these people shared a culture. They married amongst each other, fostered children with each other, sat on the same commissions of the peace, formed political alliances and fought beside each other, and led lives based on the land and the power it could convey, and they tended to have similar ideas about aristocracy. Moreover, they were all happy to use terms such as 'noble' and 'gentle' in talking about themselves and their condition, and although they recognized the vast differences in estate between dynasties like the earls of Oxford and families like the Heighams, a minor gentle family under the earls' clientage, the continuum of hierarchies between them was itself part of the whole idea of nobility.

As a result, in this essay the words gentle, aristocratic and noble, and their various derivations, are used mostly as synonyms, as they generally were in the late middle ages. The distinction between the country gentry on the one hand and the nobility or peerage on the other is a product of the seventeenth and eighteenth centuries and did not exist in the 1400s. The word aristocrat comes ultimately from the Greek *aristos*, meaning good, and *kratos*, ruler, and has a long history in the ancient world as meaning both noble as in nobly born and good as in morally good. It was not much used in English before the sixteenth century, but does appear in some fifteenth-century French and Latin texts.

Gentle, on the other hand, was probably the most common term fifteenth-century aristocrats were likely to apply to themselves. Originally from the Latin *gentilis* meaning from the same tribe or clan, it gained its special sense of meaning from the best families, being well bred, in Old French and was used as such in English as early as 1225. In the fifteenth century it was not used in the truly modern sense of kindly, patient or soft but did carry a blend of connotations such as refinement, good manners and honourable behaviour, a kind of code of honour learned and lived by the ideal gentleperson.

Noble is from the Latin *nobilis* and originally meant well known or famous, quickly coming to be used to mean of good birth or family connections, belonging to an important family. It was a common word in English, Anglo-French and the Latin used in England all through the middle ages.[3] These three terms' origins and usage parallel some important facts about aristocracy as a group in fifteenth-century England. It was not a group of phrases with negative connotations. Sayings like 'drunk as a lord' date from the seventeenth and eighteenth centuries, when feelings about the aristocracy were decidedly more mixed. On the contrary, Jesus is often described as noble, and especially as gentle, in the middle ages. The nobility were, or were expected to be, good people. While this idea of natural moral superiority was not unchallenged and indeed was held in tension by the learned behavioural code carried in the use of the term gentility, the *aristos* in aristocrat still had real force.

But the *kratos* is equally important. The political authority and economic clout of the group as a whole was central to their existence and purpose. The modern idea of genteel poverty and obscurity was foreign to the late middle ages. Good birth also played a crucial role in the idea of nobility. The clannishness implied by the etymologies of noble and gentle suggest the importance of family background and marital alliance to the concept of nobility, and marriage and the family must be one of the first folkways examined in any study of medieval English aristocracy. It was very much an aristocracy of inheritance, and family and marital alliances weighed heavily in the continuation of its culture. At the same time, family and marriage were a source of tension, for the main challenges to a noble's position lay through the relatives of blood and marriage vying for the same sources of wealth and power, whilst a noble's main allies lay in that same network of relationships. Marriage and family were sources of emotional satisfaction, but they were also calculated battlegrounds for the winning of influence and the victorious accumulation of estates.

Marriage among the gentle classes primarily served the purpose of cementing family alliances and consolidating estates and fortunes. Every document discovered, every text reinterpreted confirms the view that all nobles and gentles, male and female, expected their marriages to serve their families economically and politically. This is not to say that love bore no relationship at all to the marriage bed, but it did so in a

---

[3] All etymological information is derived from the *Oxford English Dictionary*.

curiously conventional way. The Stonor letters and papers bear witness to the courtship of William Stonor and Elizabeth Ryche, a wealthy London widow. William and his brother Thomas traded frequent and presumably heartfelt remarks about her beauty and good nature, but their wording is remarkably standard and unvarying, whilst intricate and novel considerations concerning the disposal of her fortune and her connections with the London wool trade take up most of their time. Likewise, Elizabeth and William in their early letters express many kindly and loving feelings towards each other, but the substance and thrust of their communications was towards economic and political concerns.[4] Love matches between socially compatible couples were considered charming and appropriate, but romantic affairs with inappropriate people, such as Margery Paston's involvement with her parents' steward, were looked upon with horror. Love was usually a matter, not of natural passion, but of nurtured emotions of respect and shared familial goals which created an alliance between the partners. Tales of star-crossed lovers may have been popular then as now, but they awoke decidedly different, often negative emotions in the breasts of contemporaries, who viewed them as dark morality tales rather than the triumphs of true love we tend to see. Courtesy books like the 9th earl of Northumberland's instructions to his son Algernon, stressing politeness and respect between couples, convey a very good sense of the temperature of most marital relationships.[5]

Marriages were ideally happy, but this was subordinate to the propagation of family. It might be tempting to speculate that emotional ties were strongest between related family members, but this is not necessarily true, because these same relations could be rivals for wealth and power. The notion of family itself was less a matter of loyalty to the members of that family than a more abstract devotion to the perpetuation of the name. Courtesy books like 'The Noble Babees Noble Boke', for instance, often talk of family honour and the importance of obtaining good lordship for the purpose of maintaining it, but while they urge respect towards parents they almost never mention brothers or sisters, let alone more distant cousins, uncles or aunts. The English system of primogeniture, which preserved a single line of a family at the expense of 'extra' children, discouraged a clannish view of family solidarity and encouraged the perpetuation of family as lineage. Indeed, primogeniture and the familial values it espoused could actually create hostility between family members. Brothers, especially, vied for a limited share of wealth, and fathers were often looking over their shoulders at sons eager for their inheritance. Mothers and sons frequently ended up in court after the death of the father and husband, arguing over the distribution of land between the rights of the heir and the widow's jointure or dower. It is telling that some of the closest emotional family relationships of which evidence has survived should be between fathers and daughters, and between brothers and sisters such as Thomas

---

[4] C. L. Kingsford (ed.), *The Stonor Letters and Papers, 1290–1483*, Camden Soc., 3rd series 29–30 (1919); *idem*, 'Supplementary Stonor letters and papers', *Camden Miscellany XXIII*, Camden Soc., 3rd series 34 (1924). See especially letters 172–80.

[5] Printed in *Archaeologia* 27 (1838), 306–58.

Arundel, bishop of Ely, and his widowed sister Joan,[6] who were seldom in direct competition with each other for wealth and authority.

In practice and in theory perpetuating the family honour came down to a matter of keeping its wealth and estates concentrated in a single lineage, and in helping relatives to a position wherein they might contribute to the sustenance of that lineage by either a sound marriage or a useful position with another aristocrat whose alliance would be of use. Thus William Paston was put into the service of the 13th earl of Oxford by his parents, and his parents' and siblings' letters to him are full of reminders to advance the cause of the family. Courtesy books tend to repeat these abjurations: 'Caxton's Book of Curtesye', among others, stresses the advantages a young boy can bring to his family through good service to a noble lord.[7] Family advancement was considered to be part of the natural tendency of the nobly born, and courtesy books use it as a motivation not needing any comment or explanation in the same way that modern parents expect children to understand the basic fairness of doing unto others as one would be done by.

Family and marital relations amongst fifteenth-century English nobles may seem emotionally bleak to us, but we must remember that aristocrats did not expect the intensity of familial closeness that we do, and perhaps they were capable of bringing the same passion to their notion of family as we do to ours. Family – concern with its advancement and regard for the honour and duty it conveyed – was the core of what it was to be noble in the fifteenth century. This did not always lead to an excessive concern with genealogy, in part because people then did not have the same historical sense of the past as was to evolve in the sixteenth and seventeenth centuries. Collateral descent and claims of cousinship were of less matter to a nobility based on primogeniture than they were to European aristocrats who perceived nobility flowing down alike through all descendants. Though keeping track of distant relatives remained important in a world where the direct line was often extinguished by death, disease and lack of issue, one's father's name was sufficient to place one in the social order. But if one's precise relationship to distant ancestors was not always a major concern of English gentlepeople, one's precise place in the contemporary social hierarchy always was.

Every courtesy book that survives is intensely focused on the importance of knowing and understanding social rank in all its potential ramifications – who has precedence in seating arrangements, when entering and leaving a room, in receiving the first cut of meat or the first cup of wine. Being able to distinguish the minute variations of rank and to act appropriately concerning them is treated both as a matter of nature – nobility is immediately recognizable by the nobly born – and nurture, a result of careful tutoring and instruction laid out by the courtesy books and urged by them to be committed to memory. The author of 'The Book of Precedence' considers every

---

6 M. Aston, *Thomas Arundel: A Study of Church Life in the Reign of Richard II* (Oxford, 1967), pp. 171–4.

7 F. J. Furnivall (ed.), *Caxton's Book of Curtesye*, EETS extra series 3 (1868).

potential complication of rank and relationship for his listeners to learn by heart.[8] This concern with social order reflects some of the basic nature of an aristocratic society centred on family lineage. Recognition of social hierarchies allowed participants to feel secure in the niche they inherited while at the same time establishing guidelines for recognized, unthreatening relationships between nobles of different states which might lead to family advancement. The social order of feudalism having collapsed and taken its relative assurances with it, fifteenth-century precedence rules regulated the complex dance of good lordship and clientage which allowed noble culture to adapt and evolve.

Nobles were quite sincere in their belief that the purpose of the ruler is to serve and protect the ruled, a concept adapted from Christian theology and applied to the social contract. As early as the eighth or ninth centuries the need of a vassal for a good lord who would reward faithful service and look after followers was dealt with as a major theme in literature. By the fifteenth century the term was still very common, though it perhaps implied a less direct relationship between lord and servant. Except in the poetic sense, it was not a dialogue between rich and poor, but between nobles of greater and lesser degree. Thus the dukes of Buckingham could appeal to the king for good lordship while a whole host of noble families like the Knivets and the de la Mares could appeal for the same to him, and in turn be appealed to by more minor gentry.

The mechanisms of good lordship and faithful service were exercised through a number of avenues: fostering, household service, military alliances, political support on county commissions, intercession with other nobles or at court, introductions to other influential people, marriage arrangements, the payment of annuities. Client families almost badgered their patrons with requests for tangible and intangible favours, but this complex network of support meant that great lords could almost always rely on their client families to act in their interests, and one can see why the provision of badges and livery to people outside the lord's household caused so much consternation and the enactment of so many laws against the practice; it could easily lead to an establishment of a kind of private army. In many cases this happened anyway. Lord Moleyns, for instance, was able to engage his client families in a private war against the Pastons over the rightful ownership of the manor of Gresham.

Families which pushed too hard for too many favours, or jumped the ranks of good lordship by appealing too high on the ladder, were often disliked or actively attacked for their presumption. The Woodvilles were hardly the upstart clan contemporaries accused them of being; they had a perfectly acceptable gentle lineage. But when Elizabeth Woodville married King Edward IV the family obtained a good lordship supposedly reserved for the highest nobles, and this threatened the whole process which kept noble social structure functioning. They had, in a sense, shown their lack of natural nobility by ignoring and therefore disturbing the lines of precedence by which noble culture continued to flourish. Social order for fifteenth-century English aristocrats was by no means a static thing; on the contrary, it created means for

8 F. J. Furnivall (ed.), *Queene Elizabethes Achademy etc*, EETS extra series 8 (1869).

advancement. But without a clearly defined ranking system there was nothing up which to advance. If family was the root of nobility, precedence was its trunk and branches, and the custom of clientage was the sap that nourished it.

Land, its acquisition, maintenance and consolidation, was in that case the sustaining ground, both literally and figuratively, of the noble tree. While nobles had other means of access to wealth and power, land was by far the most important resource for noble families. It produced the material gains and occasions for the exercise of authority which kept the nobility in the ascendancy. We can readily understand the value of land in terms of potential material benefits, but the political power land also conveyed is something that we may find less familiar. We must remember that while most people in the fifteenth century lived and worked on rural holdings, only a very small number could actually be said to possess land. Most farmers and rural labourers were tenants of many sorts who held land through a complex system of rents, fines and fees, remnants of feudal tenure or substitutions of payment for its original purpose of armed support in return for the right to farm land. The nobility and gentry held their land, for the most part, outright, although again some elements of feudal tenure still clung in the death fines and marriage fines some nobles were liable to pay. In the monetary value of rents and the crops, wool and minerals the land produced, nobles gained much material wealth. But more importantly, they gained authority from their landholding. Landholders, once the gods of the little land they ruled, still retained political authority over their manors. They had a limited but important judicial role in manorial courts, deciding many cases of petty personal and property crime; and it was their status as landholders that got them appointed to the commissions of the peace that played such a large role in county affairs, and sometimes brought them to parliament.

Perhaps most importantly, landholders retained their very old authority over the lives of their tenants. A crucial assumption in the fifteenth century was that if one paid rent it established a relationship in which the landholder had to be a good lord, and one had to render service to that good lord in a more general sense than paying one's rent on time. Lords were expected to listen to complaints and rectify them when possible, to extend favours and advance the causes of dependants. Tenants, on the other hand, were expected to support their lord, from providing personal service to supporting private quarrels. Although the death of feudalism had effectively ended military service in return for land tenure, in practice the good lordship/clientage relationship had its basis in that landholding system, and some of its tenets of loyalty and service were continued quite strongly in the fifteenth-century tenant/landlord relationship. John Mowbray drew many of his military followers in the French wars of 1416–17 from among his tenants.[9] On a higher level, the landlord/tenant relationship fuelled the good lordship/clientage relationship within the nobility. In most cases the client families of a noble were the same families that had held land from that family feudally. The Stafford family's affinity is a case in point; many of their client families were or had

---

[9] Berkeley Castle muniments, box no. 9, roll of war payments.

been tenants as well.[10] Because of the common assumption of authoritarian and supportive roles on the part of the landholder, the possession of estates conveyed far more in the way of potential power than their simple monetary value might suggest.

Although many urban merchants were by the fifteenth century as wealthy or wealthier than members of the noble classes, their lack of land continued to restrict their actual power as a potential political force. The power and prestige landholding could bring was in part mind over matter. Tenants followed their lord not merely because the noble family they adhered to could in many cases solve their problems and advance them, but because a very deep-rooted assumption of English culture was that they could and should do so, an assumption held most strongly and forcefully by the nobility itself. The network of support and service upholding aristocratic culture was primarily based on landholding, which provided a power base and a source of wealth on which nobles survived and from which they drew meaning and purpose.

As well as land, wealth was the prerogative of the gently-born, if not always in fact, at least in theory. As has been pointed out, many of medieval England's urban-based merchants had as much or more money than many gentry, and this was one reason why this group was so hard for contemporaries to place in the social system. For wealth was in some ways almost a definition of aristocracy. We are quite used to the concept of the vulgar *nouveau riche* and the impoverished gentry, but these concepts were really alien to fifteenth-century society.

We can see why wealth was so closely allied to gentility if we remember that aristocratic authority rested upon the ability to extend good lordship to client families, and this frequently required some outlay. A lord who broadcast his wealth in his day-to-day existence was not 'showing off' in our sense of the phrase so much as advertising that he or she was liberal with wealth. A quiet elegance hardly showed the expansive nature that best evinced good lordship. Nobles who rode through the countryside in gaudy cavalcade or entered towns with enormous pageantry, dispensing alms with careless abandon, were sending quite explicit messages about both their ability and their propensity to provide rich pickings for adherents. Such conspicuous consumption is not unlike the power lunches and designer mania which we think of as characterizing the 1980s, but fifteenth-century people were not at all morally ambiguous about it, as we are. The church not only did not weigh against it; bishops, nobles in their own right, used the same conspicuous display of wealth to gain their own followers and impress and delight their flocks. Contemporaries expressed an enormous, sincere and unqualified delight in this sort of display: George Cavendish, gentleman-usher to Cardinal Wolsey, devotes large portions of his biography of the churchman to fulsome descriptions of his retinue as examples of what a good master Wolsey was.[11]

---

[10] C. Rawcliffe, *The Staffords, Earls of Stafford and Dukes of Buckingham, 1394–1521* (Cambridge, 1978), appendices B–D.

[11] George Cavendish, *The Life and Death of Cardinal Wolsey*, ed. R. Sylvester, EETS 243 (1957), especially pp. 23–5.

There was one occasion, however, in which noble displays of wealth were considered with unease or trepidation. When things were unsettled politically such displays could rouse adherents to open war between rival nobles' factions, often with calamitous results. A number of English kings, most notably Edward IV, tried to suppress ostentatious parades through the capital in an effort to quell unrest in difficult times, but it was more from a desire to suppress rivals and keep the peace temporarily than through any idea that this display was inherently improper. On the contrary, it was well recognized that the display of wealth and the showering of largesse upon the population was a thoroughly proper duty of the aristocracy.

By the fifteenth century conspicuous consumption was not simply a matter of what nobles did, but of what they were. Courtesy books like 'The ABC of Aristotle' and 'The Noble Babees Noble Boke' are quite clear that presenting a good appearance and dispensing largesse at all appropriate occasions were a matter not just of noble duty but of noble nature. Indeed, by the fifteenth century descriptions of aristocracy were more likely to stress the spontaneously extravagant and liberal character of nobility than its warlike character, previously the chief personal characteristic of the gentleperson. While client families were still most likely to cleave to the greater families in their home district who would once have been their feudal overlords, the demise of some families and the rise of others meant that shifting loyalties were always a possibility. A liberal nature was likely to win the advantage.

The liberal nature was, however, also a carefully nurtured one. Largesse may appear to have been thrown with gay abandon, but in most cases it was carefully planned rather than a spontaneous expression. Nobles kept careful records of their distributions of alms and often went out provided with a prearranged sum for distributing in the places in which they showed themselves. Liberal lords had to keep an eye on their concern for precedence and rank in dispensing largesse, and also on the unfortunate need to mind the coffers.

Falling rents and rising prices put many fifteenth-century nobles in an economic bind they were not used to dealing with. Faced with the problem of maintaining and even increasing their liberality, many aristocrats became surprisingly shrewd at cutting costs. Liberality was not by any means the same thing as profligacy. Great lords with enormous establishments and concomitant enormous potential for waste imitated the royal household by commissioning books detailing the expense procedures and cost-cutting measures to be implemented, and the ways to avoid waste and overspending while still engaging a large staff and providing frequent hospitality and alms. All levels of the aristocracy kept a close eye on expenditure; many lords signed every page of every account, carefully scrutinizing and correcting entries. Because apparently natural and spontaneous liberality was carefully nurtured and meticulously planned, nobles were able to maintain their estate with a reputation for good lordship without losing their wealth in the process.

Good lordship depended upon political influence as well as the distribution of wealth, and late medieval nobility maintained political clout by acting both as warriors and statesmen. The earliest English medieval idea of social structure was a simple three-tiered arrangement: 'men of work', 'men of prayer' and 'men of war'. Though

7   Men of war: fifteenth-century armour

significantly lacking in some respects – women and merchants, for instance, have no place in the social structure – it served well enough in medieval minds to become a truism throughout several centuries. The aristocracy were classed as 'men of war', and indeed the origins of most ancient nobility lie in their role as soldiers; families able to pull together and lead a fighting unit, in return for which they received the grants of land and royal favours which created the groundbase for their power and wealth and also gave them a recruiting ground for more fighting men.

Despite the unrest of the fifteenth century and the not infrequent battles the nobility and gentry participated in during it, by the late middle ages the aristocracy

8   Stag-hunting

were certainly not dependent upon the field of battle as a means for advancement. The 'men of war' label continued to stick, however, in contemporary conceptions about nobility, and perhaps nowhere more so than amongst the aristocracy themselves. Courtesy books stress the need for military training and practice. Education was becoming more closely identified with gentility, and courtesy books like John Russell's 'Boke of Nurture' hold up as a bad example the uncouth noble who is proud of his inability to read, but they also stress that a true gentleman does not neglect military prowess. Interestingly the stress is not so much upon learning to use a sword but on keeping in training, even in books aimed solely at children. A natural skill in arms was the mark of a noble person, but that skill had to be cultivated.

If the nobility continued to view themselves as a warrior class this view was sublimated in life, largely into two main activities: hunting and politics. It may seem odd to combine these but in many ways they represent the evolution of the leisure time on the one hand, and the work on the other, of a warrior culture. In many aboriginal cultures the warrior and the hunter are still one; the same skill with weapons is involved, the same sort of fortitude is required and both hunting and war protect the community at some times and provide for its needs at others. Even by the early middle ages few nobles actually needed to rely upon their hunting skills to feed themselves; hunting had become a sport for them. But skill at the hunt, and interestingly the ability to cut up and divide the kill properly between participants, remained a sign of nobility; witness, in the romance 'Tristan and Isolde', Tristan's inborn knowledge of how to hunt and slaughter a deer, clearly indicating to King Mark's court that this wild man was of noble birth. Sumptuary laws regulating who could hunt what animals and who could use what falcons to hunt with indicate the noble status still tied to the art of the hunt. In the fifteenth century practically all courtesy books contain precise details about how to carve and serve meat, who to serve first and to whom to serve which parts;

a vestige of the elaborate rituals connected with the slaughter of hunted deer, and the sign of a truly noble nature, it was treated by courtesy books with immense seriousness, beyond the practical demands of good manners. Several surviving courtesy books, most notably 'The Boke of Carving', are devoted entirely to this skill. It was part of the way noble culture recognized and maintained precedence boundaries, and one of the rituals which kept that culture opaque to outsiders.

Politicking has something of the same vestigial qualities for the work of a warrior culture that hunting has for its leisure. Even in the most tumultuous years of the later middle ages, few nobles spent large amounts of their lives on the battlefield. They had traded arms for a no less difficult and occasionally deadly pastime with the same ends of obtaining control, authority and wealth.

Sitting on county peace commissions was for many minor gentry the place where they met important local nobles and established clientage alliances that led to the rise of family fortunes. An ability to help establish and carry through policies at these commissions, and the ability to arbitrate differences between one's tenants, was crucial to one's reputation for good lordship and faithful service with those above and below. At a higher level, the same jockeying for the ear of the influential and the formation of alliances, and the need to establish a reputation for shrewdness in negotiating political differences, led to success at court. The greater nobility depended upon membership of the king's affinity to obtain annuities, favourable judgements and involvement in national policy-making; the royal chamber knights frequently worked as special commissioners, constables and justices on the king's business.

The chivalric ideal was a knight who fought to protect dependants, served the over-lord faithfully and thereby advanced self, good name and family. Fifteenth-century nobles had the same aim; they had a real sense of duty to their clients and tenants and a real sense of respect for their overlords, necessary qualities to maintain the social structure that gave their lives purpose, as well as a fierce desire to embellish the family. In a more settled time they were able successfully to translate warrior values into the maintenance of peace without relinquishing their status.

It is not surprising, therefore, that gentility in the fifteenth century had taken on the sense of a behavioural code of mannerliness closer to our use of the term. Courtesy books lay an enormous stress on the need for good behaviour and proper manners, in the three senses of knowing the right way to do something; knowing one's place in society; and knowing how to behave decently towards others. Those courtesy books which are aimed chiefly at children are the most insistent about the importance of good manners, for perhaps obvious reasons, but all courtesy books, including those aimed at adults, equate good manners with gentility and nobility of mind.

This is not, of course, a new idea. As far back as the thirteenth century, the romances of Chrestien de Troyes were stressing politeness, respect for others and an accommo-dating personality as some of the marks of gentleness. But in the fifteenth century this concept of manners making (gentle)man seems to have taken over as a dominant strain in the definition of nobility. Shakespeare's literary models of fifteenth-century noblemen in his history plays often shape our perception of the late medieval aristocrat as a choleric soul, quick to anger and sensitive to any potential slight to his or her honour; but this vision fits more closely the roaring boys of sixteenth-century London rather than fifteenth-century nobles themselves. The bloody street brawls described by Hardyng and other chroniclers were often instigated to make a political point, rather than a spontaneous quarrel between nobles and their factions. The majority of gentlepeople were a great deal more suave than we might expect. Courtesy books sometimes take the trouble to paint a disgusted picture of the hard-drinking, swearing, hunt-mad, illiterate up-country noble proud of his rough ways as a significant picture of how nobles are not supposed to behave; John Russell's 'Boke of Nurture' and 'The Boke of Carvyng' both set up such a colourful figure in order to knock him down.

Some courtesy books stress the equivalency of noble birth and a noble nature, while others are quite clear that gentility lies not in birth but in manners, and that a gentle-person is as much made as born; the poem 'The Godemans Son' is a classic example of this. This tension between nature and nurture was never really resolved throughout the fifteenth century, nor were the consequences it might have for noble constructs of society. If behaviour makes one a gentleperson and behaviour can be taught, as the very existence of courtesy books suggests, what ramifications does this have for the social hierarchy whose very rigidity sustained noble culture? One might want to consider the sixteenth- and seventeenth-century successors of the courtesy books so frequently parodied in Jacobean and Restoration dramas, which quite openly aimed to teach the children of prosperous merchants how to become gentry. Ideas about gentility as they stood in the fifteenth century might well have conspired with changing social conditions in the sixteenth to encourage this particular phenomenon. But the nature of those parodies is significant – such bourgeois imitators are depicted as succeeding largely in being vulgar. Whether one attributes this to nature or nurture, what can be told from fifteenth-century courtesy books is that gentility was not a matter simply of learning manners but of acculturation, of learning the whole complex ways of a social class with its own traditions and habits.

Most courtesy books assume the reader is set in a great noble household. Many noble children and young adults, the majority perhaps, spent at least part of their teenage years in the service of a noble, usually one to whom his or her family was a client, or even at the royal court if highly born. These young people served meals, helped their masters and mistresses to dress, undertook minor duties and were generally supposed to act as ornaments to the household. In many cases they finished their formal education here, in the company of other sprigs of gentility with whom they would likely associate in later life. Courtesy books were frequently purchased for their instruction to back up the practical lessons they learnt in their daily duties. In 1503/4, the 3rd duke of Buckingham's accounts record the purchase of courtesy books along with penknives, pencases, primers and grammars for the duke's children, wards and pages.[12]

This sort of upbringing was tailored to the production of courtiers. Though boys

---

[12] Staffordshire Record Office, D 641/1/3/7.

were usually instructed in the arts of war – the same account mentioned above also lists bows, arrows and armour for the children – the main lessons all these children learnt lay in their acculturation into a society where good service brought the ear and the favour of the one served. They learned that giving service meant advantage and position rather than subservience; and even quite young children were encouraged to press family advancement by their parents. The Paston, Stonor and Plumpton letters all contain examples of fostered children reporting progress of the family's standing with their fosterers. There is very little sense either of sycophancy or hypocrisy in these relationships which we might be tempted to see. Though late in the next century courtier-like behaviour became much condemned, in the fifteenth century good service was considered naturally and rightly to lead to good lordship. Great nobles did not feel preyed upon by their followers; the clientage relationship was the cement of their whole social structure. Nobles did not expect that their client families served them with any sort of altruistic aim; it was a practical relationship no less sacred for its expectation of an evenhanded give and take.

Late medieval nobility's ideas about God and religion had something of the same flavour. As in most cultures, there was no universal level of religious fervour amongst the late medieval English nobility. Some were intensely pious, some conventionally so and a few were outright disbelievers. That old historical term for the middle ages, 'The Age of Faith', should not be taken to mean that all people were equally godfearing. But whatever the intensity of their religious feelings, the aristocracy did almost universally believe in the power of the church, and did what they felt was their duty to obey it and promote it.

There has sometimes been a tendency in the past to set the secular aristocracy against the princes of the church and the clergy in general, as if they were opposing camps with different agendas in the middle ages. The old medieval division of society between 'men of war' and 'men of prayer' has tended to encourage this supposition, but it is fundamentally mistaken. Certainly there could be tension between the church and the aristocracy, and particularly in the early middle ages some nobles were adamantly anti-clerical – Henry II's quarrel with Thomas Becket had the support of many of his nobles, who felt the church was overprivileged particularly in its judicial freedoms and over-inclined to interfere in governmental matters. But even then most nobles regarded the church's position as a matter of degree rather than kind. It was not so much a question of whether or not the church had a right to meddle in secular affairs as of how much authority they should rightly have, and how much authority secular powers should have over them.

It is important to remember that, rather than having different cultures, the nobility and the clergy in fact shared a culture in most cases. Many clerics, and almost all the bishops, priors, abbots and other high officials of the church, came from noble and gentle families themselves. The church could and did promote the bright children of the poor, but they were always the exception. The noble whispering into one ear of the king might very well be the brother or the cousin of the bishop whispering into his other ear, and they might very well be whispering the same thing. Like the aristocracy, the church was a major landholder, and its shepherds tended to utilize their estates to

9   Merry-making at court

establish power bases and clientage networks in the same way to establish their own authority and that of the church hierarchy in their region. As a result the political policies they were likely to support tended to follow the same patterns as those of their aristocratic brethren. Church princes brought up in an aristocratic culture were very aware of possibilities for family advancement, and even more than nobles were inclined to support collateral family members, being heirless. Rather than being rivals with very different backgrounds and agendas, the secular and the religious hierarchies were inclined to be allies.

Not infrequently they shared the same attitude to religion. Twentieth-century theories about established churches as forms of political control and 'opiates of the people' would be quite alien to medieval nobles' way of thinking, and such thinking also takes no account of the very real faith many nobles secular and sacred held. But medieval aristocrats did believe that obedience to the church's teachings and disciplines went hand in hand with acceptance of the social structure and of aristocratic authority, and assumed that one reinforced the other. Breakaway religious movements were viewed as dangerous challenges to political authority as well as challenges to the authority of God, and sometimes rightly so – movements like Lollardy, the Hussites and the Waldensians combined social critique with religious challenge. While in the sixteenth and seventeenth centuries more nobles were to come to embrace non-traditional creeds, in the fifteenth century the vast majority of gentlepeople sincerely viewed the established church as the dispenser of God's wisdom and authority in the same way that they viewed themselves as natural political authorities.

As a result, most nobles felt they had a duty to conform to the pieties laid down by the church, as good examples, as a subtle and often unconscious reinforcement of their own social position, and as believers. Lords may have varied in their level of fervour, but their religious culture followed familiar lines. Courtesy books such as 'The Lytylle Childrens Lytil Boke' are uniform in their adjurations to hear a mass and say one's prayers daily as a habit as personal and ordinary as washing the face and combing the hair: 'Aryse by time out of thi bedde / And blysse thi brest and thi forehede / Than wasche thi hondes and thi face / Keme thi hede and Aske God grace . . . '. Careful examination of the candle consumption in aristocratic chapels indicates that masses most probably were said daily in the majority of households, and some ordinances regulating household customs fine servants who fail to show up at the daily service without a good reason. In many establishments it was common for the entire divine office or matins and compline to be said daily as well.

These comments show already, though, the personal aspect of religious worship in aristocratic culture. While it is difficult to be sure, nobles did not appear to attend public masses except on special occasions; the noble household was its own parish. The obligation so often felt by noble families in the eighteenth and nineteenth centuries and even today, that they have a duty to be seen at the parish service, does not seem to have been at all true in the later middle ages. Most nobles had at least one and often several chapels, including many privy chapels where mass was heard by the nobility without their larger household.

Aristocrats were not averse to using religious occasions for their own ends. Edward, 3rd duke of Buckingham, organized a major pilgrimage to the burial place of Henry VI's son Edward in 1508, with the clear intention of reminding Henry VII of his family's historic attachment to the Lancastrian cause; his party included important clients and political supporters.[13] On a more normal level, noble families were inclined to turn family saints' days and religious holidays into massive extensions of good lordship, feeding the poor of the neighbourhood and re-establishing ties with client families invited to the feast. But once again it would be wrong to see this as a cynical manipulation of other people's faith. The gentry had just as much, perhaps more, belief than the poor, and that belief was very closely tied to their perception that God had ordered the social structure of the world and put them in the place they held. As such it is hardly surprising that they established connections between their own aggrandizement and the greater glory of God. Their religious behaviour was a natural extension of their beliefs but also a nurturing of its force as a social control and political weapon.

---

[13] Public Record Office, Exchequer (Treasury of Receipt) Miscellaneous, E 36/220.

The tension between nature and nurture in concepts of nobility in fifteenth-century England is perhaps most obvious in the consideration of manners and behaviour, but it runs as a curious thread all through the many aspects of noble culture. It is one of the most distinctive things about fifteenth-century discourse on the nature of aristocracy, although contemporary commentators never used that phraseology, nor did they engage in that kind of direct comparative contrast which we do in discussing, say, nature and nurture in child-rearing. Rather, one comes across constant juxtapositions of these two approaches to what makes a person noble in sometimes seemingly contradictory ways. The assertion of the inborn right to gentility seems to have existed side by side with an equally strong notion of the need to teach nobility, and of the relationship between individual behaviour and being noble, with the concomitant implication that nobility could be increased, decreased or even lost altogether. This tension is central to an understanding of the culture of the aristocracy in fifteenth-century England.

The whole idea of a heritable aristocratic ascendancy depends upon the belief that noble qualities are natural, inborn. Without it the entire idea of amassing and passing on power and wealth through the generations, of labouring to maintain a familial line, loses much of its point. At the same time, such a view of noble character as inborn can and in some cases has led to abuses which are destructive of the very aristocratic position which prompted the abuse, and medieval nobles were well aware of this – pride was, after all, one of the seven deadliest of sins. A too rigid view of the inherent nature of a group can also lead to stagnation and an inability to change; for how and why does one alter the natural state? The tension between nature and nurture in noble culture maintained its flexibility of response and its ability to adapt behaviour and outlook to changing circumstances.

Massive changes in the politics and economics of early modern England would eventually force the aristocracy into a crisis nonetheless real for being partly a crisis of perception, which eroded wide public acceptance of and regard for the social placement of the nobility, and led to a split in its very members by the growing perception of differences between gentry and nobility as separate groups with different interests. Noble society's experience of the events that rocked its foundations in the seventeenth century changed but did not destroy it. One is tempted to suggest that this is not just a matter of raw power and simple economics, although these are clearly crucial factors. The ability of even modern upper classes to resist infiltration and regain hegemony within a very tiny minority must in part be due to its establishment as a culture of shared values imbibed from early childhood which encourages behaviour promoting group ascendancy; a culture which those not born to it find immensely difficult, like any culture, to understand and share in all its complexities.

The aristocracy of fifteenth-century England are part of a continuum of noble culture that has evolved and survived up to the present day. If their folkways contributed in part to the difficulties their early modern heirs faced, they also contributed to the strengths that enabled them to change and survive. Whatever one's feelings about the idea of an aristocracy one has to recognize that they formed a far more cohesive unit than the self-interested powermongers they are sometimes portrayed as; they had their own pieties, passions and value systems which supported and regulated their actions. Understanding the fifteenth century requires that we try to understand fully the complex systems and motivations of its most dominant social group.

$$\boxed{4}$$

SERVICE

Rosemary Horrox

Service has some claim to be considered the dominant ethic of the middle ages. This essay is mainly concerned with the social and political manifestations of service, but it is important to recognize that these rested upon attitudes which were very deeply rooted in medieval society. That society, to a degree which modern readers sometimes find disconcerting, was based on hierarchy. Human society, mirroring the whole created universe, was arranged in order of importance. There is no doubt that this orderliness was found satisfying in itself. Medieval writing bears witness to a passion for arranging things in order and for resolving all the possible ambiguities and contradictions which might arise. The minutely detailed lists of precedence to be found in late medieval courtesy books reflect not only a sense that it was socially important to seat people in the right order at the dinner table, but a sheer pleasure in working out the minutiae of relative status.

Hierarchy was seen as a reflection of the divine order which created and sustained the universe. Even the nine orders of angels constituted a hierarchy, from the three superior orders (seraphim, cherubim and thrones) around the throne of God, to the three lesser orders (principalities, archangels and angels) who concerned themselves with the affairs of mankind. Given this divine endorsement, deference to those above you was not only a desirable social courtesy, but the very essence of order. As the fourteenth-century preacher John Bromyard put it (using an image more famously employed by Shakespeare): 'The order of these various ranks in the community ought to be like the position of strings upon the harp . . . if the strings are disarranged the melody jars.'[1] This is not to say that social mobility was considered improper, let alone impossible, in the middle ages. It is true that some writers tried to argue precisely this, on the grounds that behaviour is dictated by the social class into which the individual was born: once a peasant always a peasant; or, more potently perhaps, once a knight always a knight. In Malory's *Morte d'Arthur* we meet Torre, the putative son of Aries the cowherd, whose precocious passion for tournaments and war reveals that he is in fact the son of King Pellinore. The border ballads enshrine similar assumptions, most crudely in *Glasgerion* where it gradually dawns on the princess in the darkness of her

---

[1] G. R. Owst, *Literature and Pulpit in Medieval England* (Oxford, 2nd edn, 1961), p. 558; Shakespeare, *Troilus and Cressida* 1.3: 'Take but degree away, untune that string / And hark! what discord follows.'

bedroom that the man making love to her is not the king's son Glasgerion but his servant. The clinching evidence, after the servant has been able to explain away his tousled hair and homespun stockings, comes when he makes love on the floor.[2]

Such literary tropes did not, however, reflect reality. Indeed the very urgency with which some theorists argued for behaviour as a function of birth rather than upbringing is surely evidence of awareness that they were living in a world where social barriers were not immutable. In a society where standing was intimately bound up with 'face' – what contemporaries called *worship* – a man's origins might be something about which he felt social anxiety. In 1433 the controller of the English garrison in Bayeux, William Packington esquire, killed a soldier for jeering in a pub that Packington had been a retail haberdasher and thus was 'no sort of gentleman'.[3] Given the value set on tradition, and the perception that the past validated the present, there must also have been a fairly widespread sense that inherited status was the best sort to have. But in the end worship was a matter of behaviour and life style, and the emphasis on due order translated into a sense that people should behave in conformity with the level at which they happened to find themselves.

This essentially pragmatic perception of hierarchy was commonplace in the later middle ages. 'Manners maketh man' is a proverb recorded from at least the mid-fourteenth century. It now tends to be taken as a pithy expression of the importance of courtesy – good manners – but this was not what it meant to a medieval hearer. In the mid-fifteenth century it was recorded as 'Ever manner and clothing maketh man'; in other words an individual is defined by what he wears and how he behaves.[4] Of course there remains a potential ambiguity here. The proverb could carry the elitist assumption that if someone pretends to be what he is not, his behaviour will betray him. But it is unlikely that this was seen as its primary meaning, otherwise William Wykeham, founder of Winchester and New College, would hardly have taken it as his personal motto. For him it was surely a statement of the validity of acquired behaviour in defining individual value – and specifically, no doubt, the importance of virtue and learning rather than birth. Bromyard agreed. His comments on misplaced harp strings are not directed against lowly social climbers as such: 'If the strings are disarranged the melody jars, as when he who is unworthy in respect of manners, knowledge and wisdom is set in a high position through bribery, favour or inordinate love. Behold the string out of its place which destroys the whole melody!'

None of this is to deny the importance of hierarchy or its acceptance by contemporaries; on the contrary. Packington would not have reacted as he did had he not believed that such things mattered. Nor was hierarchy merely a matter of constructing theoretical models. It demanded deference to one's superiors, and that deference perpetually (and, no doubt, often almost unconsciously) coloured all social and

---

[2] F. J. Child, *The English and Scottish Popular Ballads* (5 vols., 1882–98), II, no. 67.
[3] D. A. L. Morgan, 'The individual style of the English gentleman', in M. Jones (ed.), *Gentry and Lesser Nobility in Late Medieval Europe* (Gloucester, 1986), p. 23.
[4] *The Oxford Dictionary of English Proverbs* (1975), p. 508.

political intercourse – not only in speaking, but in body language too: doffing a hat, giving place, rising to one's feet.

Such deference, and the obedience which it implied, were general requirements. But they are also the essential underpinning of the more specific manifestations of service which form the subject of this essay. All forms of medieval activity rested on service. All households but the very poorest had domestic servants. Employees in agriculture and industry were generally described as servants, and this is not a mere semantic quibble. Service was defined not by the nature of the tasks being performed, but by the relationship involved: that of master and man. Not all medieval employees, of course, conformed to this model. Some hired out their labour as required, and often appear in records with *communis* prefixed to their craft (a common shepherd or common tiler, for example) to distinguish them from workers who stood in a service relationship. The implication, at least in the late middle ages when the shortage of workers was causing anxiety, was that the servant was more respectable than the worker hired by the job, because he had a master to answer for him. As this suggests, the servant's subordination was not only economic. In many respects servants, especially those living in their master's household, were seen rather in the same way as children – and the words used for the two categories could often blur, as in the English page or French *garçon*.

The service relationship could thus be found at all levels of society. A scullion washing dishes was performing service, but so was a nobleman carrying part of the regalia in the king's coronation. Some distinctions have to be made, and the crucial one is between honourable and menial service. This is not a distinction based on function (although it may sometimes look as though it is), but on the status of the servant. The menial servant has no independent standing aside from the performance of his task; the honourable servant has. It is the difference between the tapster in a tavern and the esquire pouring the king's wine at dinner – or, more revealingly, between the servant pouring wine on the lower tables in the king's hall and the servant pouring wine on the top table. The job is the same, but the servant on the top table will be a landowner; his harassed counterpart further down the hall will be of humble status, reliant on his job in the royal household to earn a living.

This still leaves a very wide range of men whose service could be regarded as honourable – from the heads of major gentry families to younger sons who were almost entirely dependent on their lord for authority and status. They would all have felt, however, that they inhabited the same world; a cohesion strengthened by the fact that one man's servant might well be another man's lord (a term which will be used in what follows to denote any superior, not only members of the peerage). All of them regarded service as open-ended, rather than a matter of performing certain pre-defined functions. It was essentially a personal relationship between two men, in which the servant could legitimately be asked to do whatever the lord needed done at that moment – always provided, of course, that the task was not incompatible with the servant's own status.

An esquire in the service of a nobleman might thus find himself acting as steward or receiver of a group of his lord's manors, sitting on his council, coming into the household to attend upon him for part of the year and raising troops for him in war.

Lesser figures might act as administrators or domestic servants. All of them would also be called upon to perform a plethora of *ad hoc* tasks, which tend to leave fewer traces in the extant records but probably represented a more substantial burden. The sheer slog of service can be glimpsed in this letter to John Prince, a much put-upon servant of Cecily duchess of York:

> My brother Sandes and I were never so sorry for man as we have been for you since your departing, considering that so many men be slain daily, and also your great cost and charge for to ride with 2 men and 3 horses for so long a time, and the time of business and harvest, being at so great cost outward, at home and here in the law. It is a great heaviness to us that love you as often as we think upon it.[5]

The writer goes on to make an explicit (and unfavourable) comparison of the fee Prince was receiving with the burdens being placed on him. Clearly there was some contemporary sense of what constituted fair treatment; but it is equally clear that although servants might allow themselves the luxury of a grumble to a sympathetic listener, they accepted the rough with the smooth. John Paston II, miserably out of his depth at his first entry into the king's service, was advised by his uncle to stick it out, since departure would look like shirking 'which should cause him not to be had in favour'.[6]

The servant's readiness to shoulder such burdens becomes more understandable when one looks at the other assumptions involved in the relationship. The honourable servant was generally a man of some independent standing. This indeed was what made his service attractive. His influence would allow him to carry out his lord's commands more efficiently, and at the same time his status enhanced his lord's worship by demonstrating that the lord was able to attract people who mattered into his service. Similar considerations prevailed at all levels of honourable service. John Russe, a servant of the Pastons, put his finger on precisely this point when he asked for his master's help in securing the office of controller of customs at Yarmouth. The job would give him influence among the merchant community: 'with whom and with all men I call myself a servant of yours'.[7]

The fact that the servant was offering a degree of independent power or status needs to be stressed. Service today tends to be seen as a relationship enshrining the servant's inferiority, and in social terms this was of course true in the fifteenth century. The honourable servant, however elevated, owed his master deference – and it is a reflection of that inequality that even quasi-menial service could become honourable when performed for someone of sufficiently superior status. It was on this basis that dressing the king, or waiting on him at table, were seen as valued, high-status jobs. But this is not the whole picture. When a lord asked his servant to act for him he was

[5] Essex Record Office (hereafter ERO), D/DCe/L/57.
[6] N. Davis (ed.), *Paston Letters and Papers of the Fifteenth Century* (2 vols., Oxford, 1971–6), I, no. 116. The spelling in all extracts has been modernized.
[7] *Ibid.*, II, no. 666.

tacitly acknowledging that in some respects the servant was more influential, or more skilled, or simply better placed, than the lord himself. In the mid-1450s Richard Neville, earl of Warwick, wrote to John Paston I to enlist his help in a local matter; to ask for his service, in short:

> Worshipful and my right trusty and welbeloved friend, I greet you well. And forasmuch as I have purchased of the worshipful and my welbeloved friend prior of Walsingham two manors in Little Snoring . . . I desire and heartily pray you that you will show to me and my feoffees in my name your good will and favour so that I may by your friendship the more peaceably enjoy my forsaid purchase. And moreover I pray you to give credence in this matter to my welbeloved chaplain Sir John Southwell, bearer of this my letter, and in the same matter to be my faithful friend as my great trust is in you; wherein you shall do to me a singular pleasure and cause me to be to you right good lord.[8]

Paston was not formally Warwick's servant, and the earl's careful tone betrays that he knows himself to be asking a favour. But the tone is not so very different in a letter of the same period from Paston's 'especial good lord' the earl of Oxford. All that is missing is the offer of good lordship, which was presumably taken for granted:

> Right trusty and welbeloved friend we greet you right heartily well. And forsomuch as we be informed that one Thomas Kecham, a servant of our right welbeloved brother Sir Richard Vere, knight, hath to do with Sir Harry Inglose, knight, in a certain matter in which your good mastership may cause his singular ease . . . we pray you heartily that at the reverence of us and this our writing you will take the labour upon you to speak unto the said Sir Harry . . . In which faithfully doing we shall offer you hearty thanks.[9]

The relationship of lord and man is thus more evenly balanced than an emphasis on deference and hierarchy would suggest. Indeed, it is, in an important sense, mutual; something that menial service could never be. This mutuality becomes even clearer when one explores the rewards of service. Service self-evidently benefited the lord and it is accordingly very easy to see it as something which needed to be 'bought' by him with patronage and favour. Many servants did receive rewards from their lords, and all surely hoped to do so. The easiest to trace are tangible grants of land, office or money, made by letters under the lord's seal. But equally important were the less formal manifestations of favour, such as help in a law case or towards a good marriage. The earl of Oxford, negotiating a marriage on behalf of his servant Thomas Denys, offered to visit the lady himself if that would help. Edward IV contented himself with writing to the lady on whom one of his servants had fixed his affections:

> Our welbeloved servant N, bailiff of our town of C, hath so grounded, established and set his heart and inward affection upon you over all other women by way of good, true and faithful love according to the pleasure of God and not otherwise. Which to be brought unto an amiable and goodly conclusion would be to our great pleasure . . . [We pray] that at our

---

8 *Ibid.*, II, no. 505.
9 *Ibid.*, II, no. 476.

instance you would be the more heartily disposed towards a final end and matrimonial conclusion . . . You shall not only purvey you of such a fellow as shall be to your worship, heart's ease and profit in time coming, but also shall cause us for his sake to be unto you right good and gracious lord at all times hereafter.[10]

A lord who looked after his servants' interests was, in contemporary parlance, a 'good lord'. Significantly, as the letters quoted above reveal, this concept never needed to be defined, but was simply invoked. Its potency is also demonstrated by the way in which it spills into other social contexts. 'Good master' came to be used in exactly the same way. John Russe began his letter to John Paston: 'Right worshipful sir and my honourable and worshipful master, I recommend me to you in my most humble wise.' Even 'good brother' came to carry something of the same weight of meaning.

The possibility of material gain provided a powerful incentive to service, and a lord who was unable to offer it (through poverty or political ineffectiveness) or unwilling to offer it (through miserliness or narrow favouritism) would inevitably seem a less attractive master as a result. But the concept of buying service nevertheless remains too crude. For one thing, everyone knew that material gain was only a possibility, never a certainty, and that it had to be earned. Patronage was not the down payment which secured service. If anything the reverse was true: service was the weekly gamble in a sweepstake which might one day pay out.

Even this, however, is probably the wrong emphasis. The assumption that service was a chore which needed to be sweetened by favour is itself fundamentally flawed. Service was its own reward, and most people wanted to serve at least as much as lords wanted service. For the servant, his links with a lord constituted a public statement of the value attached to his abilities or standing. More important, carrying out the lord's commands allowed him to demonstrate his own power. Power, after all, only becomes manifest by being used, and obedience to the commands of a superior gave servants a legitimate arena in which to demonstrate their own influence. At the same time that influence would be subtly increased. A man acting for a nobleman enjoyed more power than he might claim in his own right – and the same effect was even more marked when someone acted for the king.

Service was a symbiotic relationship, and it cannot be argued that one side was dependent on the other without immediately adding that the reverse was also true – a perception which has important consequences for any discussion of the *relative* importance of nobility and gentry in the late middle ages. When an earl asked a knight to become his steward and play a role in the running of his estates, this was at one and the same time an expression of the earl's superiority – since he was in a position to make a knight work for him – and evidence of the earl's need for the support of lesser landowners if his lordship was to be effective at a local level.

Power is notoriously difficult to quantify, but something of the complexity of the

---

[10] *Ibid.*, II, no. 490; British Library, Additional MS 48031A, fol. 53.

relationship under discussion can be glimpsed in the rewards which office could command. When an earl appointed a steward he would almost certainly give him an annual fee, perhaps as much as £20. That in itself was a sign of the donor's social superiority. In the middle ages men often gave gifts to their superiors, but never money. Towns sent food and wine to local dignitaries when they wanted their goodwill, but tipped those dignitaries' servants in cash. In noble households this distinction was ritualized in New Year gifts of gloves from servants to their master, while the lord put coins into his servants' boxes on the same day.[11] A fee, however welcome, was a sign of social subordination. But it would not be the limit of the servant's gains from that office. It would be augmented, and quite probably exceeded, by gifts from people with whom the official had dealing – gifts which acknowledged the power the servant himself was wielding within the office, and which owed nothing directly to the lord's influence.

The fact that service both recognized and enhanced the importance of the servant helps to explain why service was considered honourable and why men of very considerable standing were prepared to serve. Even the great nobility, traditionally seen by historians as virtually autonomous forces, submitted to the pull of royal service and thereby showed that they valued the endorsement which it gave to their own power. When a medieval king likened himself to the sun conferring light on the other heavenly bodies (his nobility), the image can strike the modern reader as offensively autocratic, but contemporaries are unlikely to have found its implications out of the ordinary, let alone shocking.[12]

Giving, as well as receiving, service was thus part of the life style of the great. It was also a recognized career for the less great, and as such was perhaps the most effective method of social advancement in the later middle ages. The upper levels of late medieval society were much more open than is often assumed, and this is surely in part explained by the fact that the elite and those who wished to join their ranks shared the same service-based culture. The late medieval elite clearly felt that *menial* employees were getting above themselves, but any resentment or hostility towards the social pretensions of honourable servants came from below, not above. Many of the elite had themselves risen through service and were not ashamed to publish the fact. The funeral effigy of John Tiptoft, earl of Worcester, shows him wearing his royal livery collar, and Thomas Howard, earl of Surrey wanted to be remembered as a former household servant of Edward IV in his epitaph.

As such epitaphs remind us, men took pride in their service connections and wanted them to be noticed and remembered. When John Mirk, in his *Instructions for Parish Priests*, itemized the questions to be asked in confession he suggested that confessors should ask whether the penitent had been proud of the trust reposed in him by a lord

---

11 Thomas Percy (ed.), *The Regulations and Establishment of the Household of Henry Algernon Percy, the Fifth Earl of Northumberland* (1770), pp. 344–5.

12 R. E. Horrox and P. W. Hammond (eds.), *British Library Harleian Manuscript 433* (4 vols., 1979–83), I, p. 81.

or lady.[13] Most late medieval servants would have had to plead guilty. Edward Grimston, a servant of Henry VI who took the opportunity while in Flanders on royal business to have his portrait painted by Petrus Christus, chose to be shown casually fingering his Lancastrian livery collar. Reynold Bray decorated his chantry at Windsor not only with his own badge, but with the symbols of the Beaufort and Tudor families through whom he had risen to power.[14]

Service to the great was undoubtedly felt to confer honour by association – which explains why men wanted their service to be remembered even after their death. But living servants had other reasons for publicizing their proximity to the great. The knowledge that they had powerful backing could give them an edge in any dispute, even if their lord did not intervene directly. In such situations livery clothing or badges could become a potent form of visual intimidation. No doubt servants also derived a more innocent enjoyment from the vicarious respect which came their way when their service affiliations became known. John Paston III, talent-spotting for his master William lord Hastings, clearly took enormous pleasure in flaunting his association with the most powerful man at Edward IV's court, and the scope which that gave him for bustling around offering favours. One of his finds was Richard Stratton:

> And when I had shown him mine intent he was agreeable and very glad if that it might please your lordship to accept him into your service, whereto I promised him my poor help as far as I durst move your good lordship for him . . . He desired me to move Master Fitzwalter to be good master to him in this behalf, and so I did; and he was very glad and agreeable thereto, saying if his son had been of age, and all the servants he hath might be in any wise acceptable to your lordship, that they all and himself in like wise shall be at your commandment while he liveth.[15]

Service could confer honour, but it was also expected to engage the honour of those involved – lord and servant alike. A lord's honour, in this respect, demanded that he uphold the interests of his servants. When in 1477 a servant of the duke of Clarence, Thomas Burdett, was executed for the treasonable offence of casting the king's horoscope to forecast his death, the duke appeared before the royal council and ordered the reading of Burdett's protestation of innocence. This quixotic action (which landed the duke himself in the Tower) has usually been interpreted as a rather stupid act of defiance; but the duke probably saw himself as doing no more than his honour as Burdett's lord demanded. The countess of Oxford articulated a general principle when she came to the rescue of the family servant James Arblaster: 'he shall not be so bare of friends nor goods but that I will see him helped'.[16] Her husband was not always

---

[13] John Myrc, *Instructions for Parish Priests*, ed. E. Peacock, Early English Text Society, orig. series 31 (1868), p. 34.

[14] Illustration 10; M. Condon, 'From caitiff and villain to pater patriae: Reynold Bray and the profits of office', in M. A. Hicks (ed.), *Profit, Piety and the Professions in Later Medieval England* (Gloucester, 1990), p. 159.

[15] Davis (ed.), *Paston Letters*, I, no. 370.

[16] *Ibid.*, II, no. 501.

10   Edward Grimston, holding his Lancastrian livery collar

so scrupulous. When Oxford's servant Thomas Denys gave cause of offence, the earl
had Thomas's pregnant wife Agnes imprisoned. Agnes had only married Denys in the
first place under pressure from the earl, who had enlisted John Paston's help in
the matter. Paston evidently regarded her harassment as totally unacceptable and wrote
to tell the earl so: 'if she be destroyed by this marriage my conscience thinketh I am
bound to recompense her after my poor and simple power . . . For God's love, my lord,
remember how the gentlewoman is encumbered only for your sake.'[17]

A servant's honour, conversely, demanded that he show obedience to his master; not
just the generalized obedience due to any social superior, but a readiness to carry out
the lord's specific commands. This was so central to perceptions of service that a
fifteenth-century coiner of collective nouns opted for 'an obeissance' of servants –
a word implying both deference and obedience.[18] A servant who failed in this
requirement would incur shame, as well as forfeiting his chance of future benefit. As
John Paston I reminded the duke of Norfolk: 'It is not behoveful for any prince lightly
to give trust or apply to the desires of any persons that have given him cause of
mistrust.'[19] Lords themselves were prepared to make the same point more bluntly,
threatening to be the 'heavy lord' of offenders.

One of the most brutally explicit discussions of service from the servant's viewpoint
comes from John Paston III. The family's ill-judged support of the readeption of
Henry VI had left them in urgent need of a patron at court, and Anthony earl Rivers
offered Paston his lordship (and, specifically, his help in obtaining a royal pardon) if
Paston would accompany him on his planned crusade against the Moslems in Spain.
Paston was not keen, recognizing immediately that Rivers was not a particularly useful
patron given the king's annoyance at his planned expedition: 'The king hath said of him
that when so ever he hath most to do, then the lord Scales will soonest ask leave to
depart.' Some six months later, with Rivers still in England and planning to leave the
following spring, Paston wrote frankly about the situation to his elder brother: 'My
acquaintance with the lord Rivers is none otherwise but as it hath been always, saving
if he go now to Portugal to be at a day upon the Saracens I purpose and have promised
to be there with him; and that journey done, as Wykes says, farewell he.'[20] In spite of
his manifest reservations about Rivers, Paston clearly had every intention of keeping his
side of the bargain.

In this case, Paston's obedience was required in a single matter only. For most
servants, obedience was an open-ended commitment, and it was a commonplace for
servants to offer their 'daily service at all times'.[21] Even here, however, it was largely
obedience to *specific* commands which was envisaged. A servant was not expected to

[17] *Ibid.*, I, no. 49.
[18] Magdalene College, Cambridge, MS Pepys 1047, printed in facsimile by G. A. J. Hodgett, *Stere Hit Well* (Adelaide, n.d.), p. 8.
[19] Davis (ed.), *Paston Letters*, I, no. 65.
[20] *Ibid.*, I, nos. 347, 350.
[21] T. Stapleton (ed.), *Plumpton Correspondence*, Camden Soc., orig. series 4 (1839), p. 25.

devote himself totally to his master's interests. Given that most honourable servants had their own interests and concerns they would hardly have found such a prospect attractive. It was this specificity which made it possible for men to serve more than one master. Just as lawyers could offer their professional service to more than one employer, so the non-professional gentry and lesser nobility could act on behalf of various lords. In the 1460s John lord Howard was not only one of the king's carvers and chamberlain of the duke of Norfolk, but also acted as steward for (among others) the duchess of York, the duke of Suffolk, lord Grey of Powys and lady Scrope.[22] The men who offered Sir William Plumpton their 'daily service at all times' were servants in the royal household, but apparently made the promise with no sense of impropriety.

Many historians have looked askance at these multiple bonds of service. They have assumed that service ought to be exclusive: that a man ought to serve one master and that anything else is at best a diminution of loyalty and at worst positively disloyal. But this is introducing a new – and anachronistic – element into the discussion. Loyalty (*loyaulte*) was indeed something which the middle ages valued very highly. It was one of the primary chivalric virtues; recited like a mantra in the mottoes of aristocratic families. But it never appears in letters offering and requesting service, and nor, more to the point, do its English equivalents faith and fidelity. Even the most effusive petitioners fought shy of them. The Durham gentleman Gerard Salvin who, unusually, did make a point of offering the duke of Gloucester his undivided service in the 1470s, spoke simply of his 'true intent and service that I intend to do towards your good grace'.[23] It is hard to resist the conclusion that by 'loyalty' contemporaries meant something altogether more exalted than the requirements of service: the quasi-religious devotion owed to the king and vowed in the oath of homage performed by tenants in chief.[24]

There is a sense, therefore, in which modern critics are blaming the fifteenth century for not living up to ideals which it had not set itself in the first place. Multiple connections were not frowned on in the middle ages. On the contrary, they were often seen as desirable. The best sort of servant was the one who was well connected and who could get things done, not one who had no existence outside the orbit of his master. However, not all these connections would be given equal weight. In a society so obsessed by hierarchy it is hardly surprising that individuals recognized a hierarchy of obligation – indeed they had to, because some forms of service could only be performed for one lord at once. This is most obviously true of military service, and helps to explain why it is from military contexts that the most minute detailings of responsibilities and rewards survive. But in peace as well a man would acknowledge a 'right especial good lord' or 'especial good master', who had the first call on his services. A few lords tried to formalize this, by insisting that their retainers were not paid a fee by anyone else

---

[22] T. H. Turner (ed.), *Manners and Household Expenses of England in the Thirteenth and Fifteenth Centuries* (Roxburghe Club, 1841), pp. 456–7.

[23] R. Surtees, *The History and Antiquities of the County Palatine of Durham* (4 vols., 1816–40), IV, p. 115.

[24] Horrox and Hammond (eds.), *Harleian Manuscript 433*, III, pp. 180, 182.

(just as by this period kings insisted that royal judges were not paid annual fees by anyone but the king), but this did not preclude the co-existence of other, less formal links.

To say that exclusivity was not an essential element in service relationships is not to suggest that service was no more than the naked pursuit of self-interest, with men shamelessly acquiring and abandoning masters to profit themselves. Service was a matter of honour. The oaths taken by royal officials may not mention loyalty or fidelity, but there is real moral force in them all the same:

> You shall swear that well and truly you shall serve our sovereign lord the king . . . You shall do and purchase the king's profit in all that ye may reasonably do . . . Where you shall know any wrong or prejudice to be done to the king, you shall put and do all your power and diligence that to redress.[25]

Nor was this only wishful thinking on the part of the lords. When Thomas Denys acted contrary to the interests of his lord the earl of Oxford, John Paston's condemnation was forthright: '[he has] right unwisely demeaned him to his shame and greatest rebuke that ever he had in his life; wherefore it is right well done that his person be punished'.[26]

Under normal conditions it was usually possible for a servant to discharge his obligations honourably to more than one master. But there were times when this became impossible, and obedience to one lord would entail disobedience to another. The civil war in the middle of the century must have confronted many men with hard decisions about where their first duty lay. It certainly raised the penalties for miscalculation; but the difficulty of such decisions did not only lie in the complex calculations of survival and self-interest which they involved – honour had to be satisfied as well.

In practice, as far as one can tell, these calculations were viewed sympathetically by contemporary observers. Treachery, of course, was not. The traitor to his lord was the most despised of men. But the servant who had to make up his mind to jump one way rather than another does seem to have been viewed tolerantly. In part, no doubt, this was because men found it useful to have links with both sides, to minimize the dangers of defeat. But it was also the only possible approach in a closely interwoven political society where almost everyone was linked, by family or service, to everyone else. The Wars of the Roses could become an occasion for playing out local and personal grievances on a national scale – a way of legitimating what was essentially a private resort to violence – and yet the overriding impression is that they engendered far less bitterness than the civil wars of the seventeenth century.

This is not to say that such conflicts were easily or comfortably resolved. The fifteenth-century liking for chivalric romances could be seen as evidence of a longing for a lost golden age of uncomplicated loyalties; although Malory reminded his readers

---

[25] *Ibid.*, III, pp. 173–4.
[26] Davis (ed.), *Paston Letters*, I, no. 49.

that the Round Table itself was in the end not immune from internal conflict and tormenting personal decisions. Foreign war, too, might seem to offer an escape. Not, as has sometimes been suggested, because it gave an outlet for brutality which would otherwise be turned against fellow-countrymen; but because foreign conflict raised fewer perplexing questions about just who was the enemy. The English aristocracy became noticeably parochial in the fifteenth century, and few any longer had close kinsmen on the continent.

Civil war might put men under exceptional pressure, but service also generated its own tensions. Service, as stressed above, was a personal relationship, and personal relationships are never a matter of precise or rational calculation. 'Good lordship' owed at least as much to a lord's charisma as to the extent of his land or the size of his moneybags. To earn his lord's favour a servant had to demonstrate his usefulness. But the greatest rewards did not go to the simply useful, however reliable and efficient; they went to the man the lord liked best. This was recognized as inevitable, but it could still trigger resentment and jealousies, particularly in the small worlds of royal and noble courts. It also meant that promotion or advancement was, in the last resort, irrational. This opened the way for men to try equally irrational means, such as charms and spells, to win favour. From the twelfth century courtiers had been considered particularly prone to resort to sorcerers, either to advance themselves or destroy rivals, and the fifteenth century saw accusations of witchcraft or necromancy used as potent political smears.

Favour was not only irrational but transient. 'Lord's love changeth oft' was proverbial in the fifteenth century.[27] It is not surprising that contemporaries turned to astrologers to tell them what would happen in the political arena as readily as they looked to them to help trace stolen goods or for advice on the best time to have sexual intercourse in order to conceive a male child. Knowledge was power; but the resort to astrology was also a tacit admission that power and favour were matters beyond human control. The widespread contemporary fascination with the wheel of Fortune carried the same message: one's own efforts could only carry one so far, success and failure alike were subject to capricious external forces.

The type of service described here sustained all aspects of fifteenth-century life. Government and the maintenance of law would both have been impossible without it, as would military campaigning or estate management. It is the reality behind the 'bastard feudalism' so often taken as characteristic of the late middle ages. This is a term far more often used than defined. Originally it was meant to distinguish the later middle ages from earlier centuries when, it was believed, relationships between king and nobles, or lords and knights, rested securely on the ownership of land: a man's lord was whoever he held land from. As a result, the argument went, relationships were stable and clear cut. In the later middle ages this pattern of tenurial lordship broke

---

[27] R. T. Davies (ed.), *Medieval English Lyrics* (1966), no. 65; *Oxford Dict. of Proverbs*, p. 909.

down, and was replaced by the use of cash fees to mark lordship, or by even more fluid associations reliant on goodwill and self-interest. These relationships, it was argued, were essentially opportunistic and short term, and therefore inherently unstable. They led directly to the political instability and lawlessness which was thought to characterize the fifteenth century.

No historian would now be happy with this dichotomy, both aspects of which have come under increasing attack. It rests on far too simplistic a view of feudalism, which is here presented as a tenurial pyramid in which each man had one lord. In reality this simple pattern prevailed, if at all, for only a short time after the Norman Conquest, when William I's possession of *all* of England allowed him a clean slate on which to draw tenurial relationships. In the feudal period many men held land from more than one lord; and in any case land, it is clear, was never the only factor in relationships between lords and their men – although it is the one which has left by far the best records. But if feudal relationships were not as straightforward as used to be thought; nor, it is now argued, was 'bastard feudalism' as fluid. Fifteenth-century men did not have an absolutely free hand in seeking lordship, unless they were landless younger sons setting out to make their fortune. Landowners would naturally look to a lord with interests in the area where they held land, since it was there, in what contemporaries would have called their 'country', that their main interests lay. Most noble retinues had a strongly localized core – and, were the aristocratic estate to change hands, most of that core would naturally look to the nobleman's successor for lordship.

Once a relationship was in place it was not easily or lightly broken. This was partly because it did not need to be. The acceptance of multiple allegiances meant that a relationship which no longer seemed very valuable could often be left to atrophy rather than being fully broken. But there were also positive pressures which kept a service relationship in being. Honour was undoubtedly one. Self-interest was another. Rewards were generally given for past service and severing a relationship meant abandoning that investment. In addition, men who flitted from lord to lord would get themselves a bad name. Richard duke of Gloucester, scolding one of his servants, said 'that he knew him well enough, and how that he had laboured to have been in household with the earl of Arundel, with the lord Dacre, with the lord Cobham and other'.[28] Multiple connections might be valuable, but itchy feet were clearly to be deprecated.

The debate over 'bastard feudalism' has been bedevilled by two major problems. One has been a confusion of means and ends. It has usually been tacitly assumed that the grant of land or a money fee *created* a relationship. In fact it did not. It recognized an existing relationship, and different forms of recognition do not necessarily entail a difference in the nature of the relationship itself. Relationships formalized by the grant of a cash fee are not inherently less stable than those formalized by the grant of land – although since land was a more desirable reward than money its use does say something

---

[28] ERO, D/DQ 14/124/3/40.

11 Herod orders the Massacre of the Innocents

about the closeness of the relationship involved. It has been too easily forgotten that the availability of land in the generation after the Conquest was quite exceptional – and that the gift of land could never again be the primary method of marking a service relationship.

The other problem is that the argument has acquired a powerful, but largely unstated, moral dimension. As the pejorative force of '*bastard* feudalism' makes clear, early writers on the subject felt that the relationships they identified in the later middle ages were morally suspect. They saw them as designed to be easily broken and hence indicative of a selfishly cynical attitude to service and, indeed, to authority itself. This perception surely owed something to the nineteenth-century tendency to see land as inherently more respectable than filthy lucre. But whatever the explanation, this disapproval forced later writers to attempt the moral rehabilitation of 'bastard feudalism' alongside its historical re-evaluation. Some of the most influential recent writing on the subject has accordingly presented 'bastard feudalism' as a force for social and political stability, providing men with a network of friendly equals and superiors to help them through a dangerous and competitive world.

In reality, as one would expect of a system based on personal relationships, this sort of generalization is as suspect in its way as the old moral absolutes. The system certainly had its positive side. Its most obvious benefit – so obvious indeed that it tends to be overlooked – was that it provided a very effective way of getting things done without creating an elaborate salaried bureaucracy. In this respect the closest modern parallel is probably to be found in the world of high-profile charity fund raising. But the benefits were not purely utilitarian. Because lords, including the king, were relying on other people to take action for them, there were practical limits on their ability to act in ways profoundly unacceptable to contemporary opinion.

It is true that the pressure to obey might lead a servant to carry out his master's wishes regardless of morality or public opinion. Contemporaries saw the Massacre of the Innocents as a chilling example. In the Wakefield cycle Herod assures his knights that if they do the job 'Ye shall find me friendly', and, the slaughter completed, they return eagerly for their reward. The knights in the Coventry cycle are less hard boiled, but still obey:

> We must fulfil Herod's commandment
> Else be we as traitors and cast all in care.[29]

They comfort themselves with the belief that the moral responsibility is Herod's, not their own, but the audience would have known that this was wishful thinking. Moralists throughout the middle ages hammered home the message that obedience to a superior's commands would be no defence at the Last Judgement:

> If thou serve a lord of price [worth]
> Be not too boisterous [violent] in thine service
> Damn not thine soul in no wise,
> For service is no heritage.[30]

As the insistence of the moralists betrays, things were not quite so easy in the real world. The men implicated in the murder of the duke of Gloucester in 1397 later pleaded *force majeure* and received a sympathetic hearing from their peers, who must have appreciated the difficulty of saying 'no' to Richard II. But most men would have had a sticking point, and a lord who persistently flouted accepted norms would in the end cease to command obedience – as Richard II himself was to find.

As this shows, contemporaries were well aware that service had a negative side. Servants themselves were the objects of vociferous criticism. This reached a crescendo in the late fourteenth century. Bureaucrats and other servants were the primary targets of the 1381 rising – in part, no doubt, because they were more vulnerable to physical attack than their well-defended masters, but also surely because of a sense that they were abusing their power. The preacher John Bromyard was unusual in suggesting that servants might themselves be victims of the system, and that the amiable and charming young men who turned into 'cruel, hellish and diabolical lions' had no choice: 'it behoves them to enrich their lord. Otherwise they will not be reputed discreet, nor will they be able to hope for greater things for themselves.'[31]

What evidently worried Bromyard was a sense that servants were likely to be more vicious than their masters – not because they were unfit to exercise power but because they were under pressure to get results. Over two centuries later Sir Walter Raleigh was to return to the attack:

> Tell men of high condition
> That manage the estate
> Their purpose is ambition,
> Their practice only hate.[32]

---

[29] A. C. Cawley (ed.), *Everyman and Medieval Mystery Plays* (1967), pp. 122, 125–7; Peter Happé (ed.), *English Mystery Plays* (Harmondsworth, 1984), pp. 376–7.
[30] Davies (ed.), *Medieval English Lyrics*, no. 65.
[31] Owst, *Literature and Pulpit*, p. 323.
[32] Sir Walter Raleigh, *The Lie*, stanza 4.

Less is heard of this particular complaint in the fifteenth century, but it is unlikely to have gone away altogether. Certainly hostility to arrogant and pretentious servants did not. It surfaces in the first shepherds' play in the Towneley cycle, where the shepherds grumble about the 'boasters and braggers' armed with long knives, which they are quick to turn against their critics. Such men go as proudly as lords, for all their tangled hair, and speak in loud, hectoring tones:

> I wot not who's better
> Nor who is the greater
> The lad or his master
> So stoutly he strides.[33]

In theory it was the lord's responsibility to curb this sort of behaviour, partly because he had a social duty to uphold order, more specifically because it would reflect upon his own honour if he let his servants run wild. Men who approached a lord for redress would thus always tactfully adopt the convention that if a lord had failed to discipline his servants it must be because he was ignorant of the problem. In the mid-fourteenth century the exasperated critics of the Berkeley servant Thomas de Bradeston claimed that although he was a little saint at court, he was a raging lion when at large in his own countryside.[34] The reality, of course, was never so simple. As Bromyard knew, the lord might be the beneficiary of his servants' actions. Even where he was not, the exercise of power was one of the rewards of service. How could a lord undermine his servants when good lordship demanded that he maintain their interests? If his own honour was seriously impugned – perhaps by action taken explicitly in his name but without his knowledge – he might well take a strong line, but there was always a difficult balancing act involved.

The requirement of lord and servant to uphold each other's interests brought another problem in its wake. The complex network of relationships could act as a means of containing conflict, but conflict could never be excluded altogether and once it had arisen those involved were likely to feel that their worship demanded a successful conclusion. Sir John Fastolf, mobilizing his friends and servants in a law case, spelt out what losing would mean to him:

> For in good faith I dread most the shame and the rebuke that we should have if the matter concerning the award went contrary against your intent and mine, as God defend, for then great cost and labour were lost. And the great rebuke and villany should grieve me worst of all, for nowadays you know well that law goeth as it is favoured.[35]

Once lords were engaged on behalf of their servants, such conflicts could be transformed into overt trials of strength. As one of Richard duke of Gloucester's servants

---

[33] Happé (ed.), *English Mystery Plays*, pp. 247–8.
[34] N. Saul, *Knights and Esquires: The Gloucestershire Gentry in the Fourteenth Century* (Oxford, 1981), p. 77.
[35] Davis (ed.), *Paston Letters*, II, no. 520.

jeered to an opponent, 'Now shall thou see whether of my lord's man or of my lady's shall have the better.'[36]

The account of that sneer came, predictably, from the opponent. From the servant's own perspective lordly backing was not aggressive but defensive – perhaps his only hope of achieving justice. Gerard Salvin wrote piteously to the same duke of Gloucester describing his enemies' attempts to murder him and begging the duke to take up his case.[37] One man's good and tender lord was another man's overbearing thug; just as one man's legitimate intervention was another man's riot. Whatever reservations and criticisms men may have harboured about the system they could hardly afford to stand outside it.

Confronted with these ambiguities it is not surprising that several writers, attempting to reach a verdict on 'bastard feudalism', have taken refuge in pragmatism and argued that the system was neither good nor bad in itself but simply held a mirror up to political society. On this argument its quality depended on the quality of the lords who controlled it: 'weak' lordship produced chaos, 'strong' lordship could make the system work to everyone's benefit. At first sight, this seems likely enough. Given that society was hierarchical, the obvious way to resolve conflict or deal with misbehaviour was for someone greater than the protagonists to knock heads together. Ultimately that was the king's role, and if he failed to perform it (as Henry VI did) the tensions could become intolerable.

But 'bastard feudalism' was not (as this interpretation assumes) simply the expression of lordship, but of service; and that, as we have seen, was not a one-way relationship. Men took commands from their masters, but the lord depended on his servants and therefore had to be responsive to them and sometimes, through them, to a wider constituency. John Russe wrote to his master John Paston, then in the thick of the dispute over the Fastolf inheritance:

> Men say you will neither follow the advice of your own kindred or of your council, but only your own wilfulness, which, but grace be, shall be your destruction. It is my part to inform your mastership as the common voice is. God better it . . . for it is half a death to me to hear the general voice of the people.[38]

The complexities of the service relationship are not an index of the variable efficacy of lordship, but of the ambiguities of contemporary attitudes and behaviour. In the end bastard feudalism eludes definition not because it mirrored political society but because it *was* that society.

---

[36] ERO, D/DQ 14/124/3/15.
[37] Surtees, *Durham*, IV, p. 115.
[38] Davis (ed.), *Paston Letters*, II, no. 671.

5

EDUCATION AND ADVANCEMENT

Michael J. Bennett

The word 'education' would have sounded strange in fifteenth-century England. The Latin verb 'educare' was commonly used by men of learning to mean 'to rear' or 'to teach', but 'educatio' as an abstract noun would have seemed new-fangled even to them. Generally speaking, English people used more concrete and specific terminology: 'nurture', 'instruction', 'teaching', 'learning' and 'schooling'. Still, it can be surmised that the more general term would have been comprehensible to English speakers. The verb 'educare' had certainly been anglicized by the 1440s, when in his life of St Elizabeth of Hungary, Osbern Bokenham relates that she promised, if she were blessed with children, to 'educaten' them in God's service.[1] Though less common, the noun 'educatio' must likewise have been known. The *Promptorium Parvulorum* helpfully offered 'educatio' as the Latin for 'nourishing in manners and conditions'.[2] Even if the word did not become common in England until the Age of Elizabeth, when so many Latinisms were definitively domesticated, it is not too anachronistic to talk of 'education' in fifteenth-century England.

A survey of 'education' involves bringing into purview the whole range of activities, informal and formal, by which young people were socialized, taught patterns of behaviour and belief, and equipped with skills and knowledge. In fifteenth-century England, as in modern times, 'education' and 'schooling' cannot be regarded as synonymous. Traditionally, histories of education in medieval England have been somewhat narrowly conceived. In the past decade or so, a number of scholars have sought to broaden the scope of the history of education, moving outside the school-walls to investigate a wider range of social and cultural concerns. In this broadening perspective, attitudes to education in fifteenth-century England seem a natural focus of interest, especially given the well-known expansion of educational provision in Tudor times and the developments in educational thought associated with the Renaissance.

A consideration of educational attitudes naturally leads to a consideration of the relationship between education and social advancement. The later middle ages in

---

[1] M. S. Serjeantson (ed.), *Bokenham's Lives of Holy Women*, Early English Text Society (hereafter EETS) 206 (1936), line 9678.

[2] A. L. Mayhew (ed.), *Promptorium Parvulorum, the 1st English–Latin Dictionary*, EETS extra series 102 (1908), p. 309.

England have been aptly described as 'an age of ambition'. The Black Death of 1348–9 and succeeding epidemics cut deep swathes through all sections of the workforce, giving unprecedented bargaining power to labour. The mobilization of the population for war in the fourteenth and early fifteenth centuries, the increasing scope of government and law, as well as the continuing recruitment into the church, added to the demand for trained personnel. Men (and even women) with talent and skills had particular opportunities to advance themselves materially, occupationally and even socially. In such circumstances it is appropriate to consider the role of education in advancement, and the relationship of careerism to changing attitudes to education.

Education in fifteenth-century England began in the home, and for the majority of people it ended there. High infant mortality rates, perhaps even more than limitation of opportunity, were to blame. There is a grim aptness in the fact that coroners' inquests provide the main evidence for the manner in which children learned by watching, aping and assisting their parents in their daily tasks. Happily, until around the age of seven or eight play was the main activity for village children. Thenceforward household chores became more routine, especially perhaps for girls: baby-minding, watching and stirring food on the boil, drawing water and collecting firewood. 'Education' at this level was, when not wholly instinctual, severely constrained by the exigencies of daily life. The socialization of the girls and boys naturally reflected the division of labour between the parents. Girls learned how to cook and bake, attend to the animals in the yard, wash and mend clothes, spin and weave. Boys, who on the whole enjoyed a more extended childhood, learned how to work in the fields, to fish and hunt, and to work in wood and metal. In this fashion many children in the countryside learned the rudiments of the skills necessary for their life style.

Education at this level represented an education in life. Children were being socialized both into particular sets of roles and into a whole wider culture which gave them meaning. At village level, the culture was necessarily highly localized and largely oral, but it can be assumed that, along with the skills associated with the peasant life, knowledge and expertise of a more general sort, traditions of story-telling, song and dance, medicine and magic, and the like, were passed down from one generation to the next. In the towns greater concentrations of people and wealth made for a richer brew. Guilds served to transmit a way of life as well as trade-skills; forms of conviviality and ceremony as well as standards of craftsmanship. The merchants and members of professional groups, like the gentry and nobility, maintained and sought to pass on life styles of some complexity and refinement.

Above all, children were being socialized into a Christian culture. The rite of baptism itself involved a commitment to education on the part of parents and godparents. Priests likewise had a duty to catechize young children, and to test their knowledge of the faith at particular times. For most children the process of learning their ABC was inextricably bound up with learning their Lord's Prayer and Hail Mary. Even into adult life, the requirements of the Christian life provided many people with the main rationale for learning the alphabet and memorizing words. After all, basic literacy, as opposed to the higher literacy associated with Latin education, had little practical value for most people in the later middle ages. Even in the towns, where proclamations and other notices were posted, the usefulness of reading would have been more apparent than real. For many people, in the towns as well as the country-side, the main stimulus to word recognition would have been an inscription in a stained glass window or a line from scripture included in a wall-painting. Religious devotion, though, provided some men and women with the incentive to go further. Despite ecclesiastical censure and suspicion, the circulation of religious works in the vernacular increased markedly in the fifteenth century, especially after the introduction of printing. If book-ownership was largely the preserve of the social elite, pious layfolk of more humble station met in groups to pore over a rough quire brought by an itinerant preacher. The Lollards, in particular, encouraged literacy, and in various places at various times maintained their own illicit schools.

The church, though wary of lay literacy, had a clear institutional commitment to education. At all levels of its operations, it had a need for trained personnel, and a main requirement on the parochial clergy was not only to expound the faith but to offer wider instruction. Prime responsibility was placed not on the parish priest but on the parish clerk, but all depended on the calibre of the men concerned. The norm must have been small-group teaching on an informal basis, perhaps in the church porch. 'Petty' schools, as they were called, were generally free, though perhaps payments in kind were expected. The pupils themselves reciprocated by running errands and doing odd-jobs, as well as by assisting the priest in church. Even when a clerical schoolmaster was taking fees, chores of this sort might well be demanded; the parents of one pupil complained that their son was required 'to wash pots, pans, dishes and to dice meat in the kitchen'.[3] The need for choristers, if nothing else, inclined larger parish churches as well as monasteries and cathedrals to establish 'song-schools'. By opening the doors to a large number of boys, the clergy could conduct a process of selection, and it seems likely that, even for the poorest boy, a fine voice and proficiency in music were a passport to the best schools in the countryside.

Sentimentality towards children was not lacking in fifteenth-century England. It is comforting to believe that in their earliest years at least most children were able to grow and learn through self-discovery and play, to benefit from the gentle instruction of their elders, and to have some acquaintance, however nodding, with 'schooling', however makeshift and informal. In the later middle ages, however, childhood was all too brief, and for many children between the ages of eight and ten life suddenly became more serious. From this time onwards girls and boys became increasingly useful to their parents in the home and in the fields. The prospects of most youngsters were thus bounded by the occupations of their parents and kinsmen. Of course, many adults had specialized skills to impart, even in the countryside. 'What craftsman', Sir John

---

[3] S. L. Thrupp, *The Merchant Class of Medieval London* (Chicago, 1948), p. 159.

Fortescue asked rhetorically around 1470, 'is so negligent of his child's profit that he does not instruct him in crafts when he is young, by which he may afterwards gain the comforts of life? Thus a carpenter teaches his son to cut with an axe, the smith his son to work with a hammer.'[4] Quite commonly, though, this stage involved a break with the parental home. Children might be placed in the households of kinsmen or friends, where in return for service they were taught whatever skills or knowledge their surrogate parents were able and willing to impart. Clergymen, without children of their own, were doubtless ready enough to assume this role for a nephew with the right aptitude. Training a poor young kinsman in 'clerisy' was the acceptable face of nepotism in the late medieval church.

It is hard to escape the conclusion that for almost all children the die was cast by the age of eight or, at most, ten. The decisions taken then were largely determined by the family's circumstances, but must have been informed by some estimate of the child's aptitudes. Continuing in school from this point onwards must have pre-supposed a basic competence in reading, writing and arithmetic. Though sometimes spiced with business French and accounting skills, Latin grammar was thenceforward the staple diet. Presumably most parents would have tried hard to find ways and means to keep an apt son, though rarely an able daughter, at school for at least a few more years. Even a smattering of Latin might be helpful in life; some priests knew little more. The ability to read a verse from the psalter and thus claim 'benefit of clergy' might even save a young ne'er-do-well from the gallows. As William Langland wrote in *Piers Plowman*:

> Well may the bairn bless whoever set him to books,
> That living after letters saved him, life and soul.
> *Dominus pars hereditatis mee* is a merry verse,
> That hath taken from Tyburn twenty strong thieves.[5]

Needless to say, educational opportunities beyond the elementary level were limited. The capacity of the clergy to teach Latin cannot be assumed. While there were few university graduates resident in the countryside, some villages were fortunate in the quality and dedication of their parish clergy. The regularity with which grammar books appear in the inventories of country clergymen is suggestive. From anecdotal evidence relating to the early schooling of a number of notable churchmen, much depended on the chance availability in the district of a man willing and able to teach. Thomas Rotherham, archbishop of York, counted among his blessings the arrival of such a person in his home town in the early fifteenth century. Thomas Cranmer, later archbishop of Canterbury, was acquiring in the late 1490s a solid grounding in Latin grammar in his native Aslockton, albeit from a 'rude parish clerk . . . in barbarous

---

[4] Sir John Fortescue, *De Laudibus Legum Anglie*, ed. S. B. Chrimes (Cambridge, 1949), pp. 18–19.
[5] Langland, *Piers Plowman: The B Version*, ed. G. Kane and E. T. Donaldson (1975), passus XII, lines 187–90 (spelling modernized).

times'.[6] There must have been many unsung heroes among the country clergy who provided windows on the world to the bright boys of their own and neighbouring parishes. Roger Godeale, rector of Bainton, in the early fifteenth century, can be taken as representative of his breed. On his epitaph his efforts as a teacher to the youth of his corner of Yorkshire are specifically commemorated.[7]

In earlier times monasteries performed a vital role in teaching Latin grammar. In addition to making provision for choir-boys and novices, the 'almonry' schools traditionally offered instruction to a wider clientele. It is generally assumed that in educational terms, as in other matters, the monasteries were in decline in the fifteenth century. From visitation records, for example, it is clear that the existence of a large and wealthy monastery was no guarantee of a functioning school. Nonetheless in some districts, especially perhaps the north of England, monasteries provided vital facilities, and the likelihood is that many poor clerks owed their education, and sometimes their love of learning, to monks and friars. At the same time it might be that some of the smaller houses were supporting themselves financially by taking in fee-paying pupils. Nunneries seem to have been especially active in this sort of education, operating as finishing schools for the daughters of the gentry and the bourgeoisie. Thus Jane Scrope, the tender-hearted maid whose pet bird is elegized in John Skelton's *Philip Sparrow*, was taught and perhaps encouraged in her sensibility by the nuns at Carrow near Norwich.

For most country boys, the pursuit of an education in grammar meant moving to a town. A school in each rural deanery would have been the ideal. The rudiments of such a system have been discerned in Norfolk. In reality this level of provision cannot have been general in late medieval England. Educational facilities could not be guaranteed in all towns; even cathedral schools were occasionally subject to closure. For the most part, though, a grammar school was no further away than the nearest substantial market town, less than ten miles in most parts of the country. The larger urban centres may even have offered a greater range of provision. Many monasteries, after all, especially the old Benedictine houses, the nunneries and the friaries, were sited in towns. In some towns, too, there were private schools functioning alongside the established schools, and freelance schoolmasters seeking to challenge the educational monopolies claimed by local religious bodies.

The emergence of the endowed school was a development of prime significance. The middle decades of the fourteenth century saw the establishment of a number of collegiate churches with well-defined educational functions. The most generous and visionary patron of learning was William Wykeham, bishop of Winchester and chancellor of England. In the 1370s he moved from the informal sponsorship of a schoolmaster at Winchester and a group of scholars at Oxford to the formal endow-

---

[6] J. G. Nichols (ed.), *Narratives of the Days of the Reformation*, Camden Soc., old series 77 (1859), p. 218.
[7] M. Stephenson, 'Monumental brasses in the East Riding', *Yorkshire Archaeological Journal* 12 (1893), 198.

ment of two linked colleges, one for some seventy schoolboys at Winchester and the other what became known as New College, Oxford. Given the grandeur of their conception, Wykeham's foundations could scarcely be emulated, save by royal patronage, but they were nonetheless very influential, not least through the agency of their distinguished alumni. A related but more modest and thus more serviceable model pioneered at this time was the chantry school. Like colleges of priests, chantries were primarily established for purposes other than providing education for children. Still, in the last decades of the fourteenth century a number of chantry foundations involved provision for teaching. The earliest appears to have been at Wotton under Edge, Gloucestershire, founded by Lady Katherine Berkeley in 1384, though apparently after an earlier attempt. According to the statutes, the chaplain was not only to sing masses for her soul but also to offer instruction in grammar freely to all comers. Grandiose or modest, the endowed schools of the late fourteenth century established models of public schooling which were to dominate the educational landscape for half a millennium.

Nonetheless it should not be too readily assumed that the scale of educational provision was increasing in the later middle ages. Even by the end of the fifteenth century the number of endowed schools was small, and their share of the educational market was fairly negligible. New foundations were in any case matched by the decay and disappearance of many old schools, not least in the monasteries. The Black Death and subsequent epidemics not only decimated the educated elite but also undermined the wealth of the traditional sponsors of education. The founders of new endowed schools saw themselves not as launching a new wave of educational expansion for the laity so much as seeking to stem a precipitate decline in the stock of educated clergy. In all likelihood the number of functioning schools in the 1370s was smaller than a hundred years previously. If an informed contemporary commentator is to be believed, there was a further collapse between the 1380s and 1430s. In a petition of 1439 seeking a licence for an endowment for teacher-training at Cambridge, William Bingham alleged that in the counties east of Southampton and Coventry and south of Ripon there were no less than seventy schools, all functioning within the last fifty years, void through the 'great scarcity of masters of grammar'.[8]

Concern about the lack of educational provision found the highest expression in the second quarter of the fifteenth century. The drive for a better educated priesthood had been given a sharp edge by the challenge of Lollardy, and from the 1420s many prominent churchmen sought to endow schools. Anxieties about heresy prompted Bishop Pecock to advocate, somewhat rashly, a wholesale programme of vernacular instruction in theology for the laity. It was the personal commitment of Henry VI, though, which made educational concerns distinctly fashionable. Eton College, on which he lavished attention and money in the 1440s, is the grandest monument to this wave of interest. Among the other patrons of education close to the court, William

---

[8] A. F. Leach (ed.), *Educational Charters and Documents 598–1909* (Cambridge, 1911), pp. 402–3.

Wainfleet, bishop of Winchester, is worthy of special attention. His Lincolnshire background is obscure and nothing is known of his education beyond an association with Oxford. By 1430 he was headmaster of Winchester College whence in 1441 he was 'poached' by Henry VI for the provostship of Eton. He was one of a number of schoolteachers who attained high preferment at this time, and true to his calling used his personal wealth to endow grammar schools in Oxford and in his native village of Wainfleet.

Solicitude regarding educational provision is especially well evidenced in the capital. William Bingham, who sought to promote teacher-training in 1439, was parson of St John Zachary in London. In 1446 the archbishop of Canterbury and the bishop of London, perhaps somewhat defensively, increased to five the number of properly authorized schools in the city. In the following year, the parsons of four London parishes petitioned parliament for a further increase in provision. Pointing to the multitude of young people seeking schooling in London, including many who came into the city for want of schools in their own districts, they asked to be allowed to appoint schoolmasters in their parishes. The educationalist lobby was well able to apply the laws of supply and demand to schooling: 'for where there is great number of learners and few teachers, and all the learners be compelled to go to the same few teachers and to none others, the masters wax rich in money and the learners poor in cunning, as experience only sheweth.'[9]

If England lost more schools than it gained in the hundred years after the Black Death, it is important to appreciate that the country's population declined in this period even more precipitately. In other words, the ratio of schools to people in all likelihood increased. In measuring levels of educational provision, there are problems, too, with the simple enumeration of established 'schools' because it is quite clear that a lot of education was carried out informally. Individual canons, monks and friars sometimes offered private instruction when institutional support lapsed. The households of noblemen and prominent churchmen who maintained tutors likewise took in kinsmen and members of a wider connection. There were many homes, middle class as well as noble households, where teaching was done, either by a chaplain or clerk. In such cases, too, poorer boys, the sons of retainers and dependants, sometimes sat alongside the sons and daughters of the house, if for no other reason than to make up numbers.

Then, too, there is a danger in overlooking the massive contribution made by the smaller and informal 'schools' clustered around Oxford, Cambridge and London. The existence of 'cramming establishments' and 'finishing schools' around the university towns and the capital is well enough known, and the large number of pupils necessarily involved has sometimes been recognized. The church authorities in 1446 were more concerned with controlling a burgeoning industry than with a lack of teaching activity. Their petition bewailed the number of unqualified masters in the city

---

[9] *Ibid.*, pp. 416–20.

who presumed to hold schools 'in great deceit both of their scholars and of the friends that find them'.[10] It might well have been the case, too, that higher-level schooling was becoming increasingly concentrated, at the expense of country towns, in London and other major centres. Such schools seem to have been accessible to young people from districts where provision was less adequate. There is certainly evidence that a couple of years of schooling at Oxford was within the thinking of the gentry and wealthier freeholders from other parts of England.

As regards other forms of education, the emphasis given to the grammar schools is even more misplaced. In the transmission of information and skills household education and apprenticeship were obviously vital. In the later middle ages, as in most other times, young people learned most by spending hours patiently watching their elders, assisting in progressively more complex operations, and in time demonstrating their own mastery of the skills. Such a mode of learning was by no means confined to what nowadays would be regarded as trades. It was in this fashion that most young men sought instruction in administration, accounting or the common law, or, for that matter, prepared for the priesthood. Apprenticeship arrangements, in any case, did not necessarily imply an end to formal education. Masters and mistresses sometimes undertook to release apprentices for schooling, and in the larger cities there were schools catering for their needs. In the early fifteenth century William Kingswill ran a cramming establishment in London for would-be apprentices in accounting and business French. It would seem, too, that the Inns of Court and the royal court provided formal schooling for the young men in their charge.

It would likewise be inappropriate to draw too firm a line between the processes of learning and earning a living. Few youths could have been wholly innocent of the need to support themselves, even if it might be doing menial jobs for their teachers. Apprentices more obviously worked in return for training. Young men pursuing a legal education at Westminster, whether or not formally enrolled in the Inns of Court, probably soon came to involve themselves in discussion of cases, and to act as agents of kinsmen and friends in the country. The universities, of course, did tend to require a larger commitment to learning. There were men at Oxford and Cambridge studying for doctorates in the laws or theology who had spent upwards of thirty years in formal education. Yet even they had served as private tutors and then as 'regent masters', that is as masters of arts fulfilling university requirements to teach for two years after graduation. Most would have acquired church livings or administrative responsibilities in college or university. All shared in the public role of the *studium*, the community of scholars, in counselling kings and defending the faith.

In the later middle ages evidence of learning for the sake of learning is limited. It would be wrong, though, to regard attitudes to education as being crassly utilitarian. For

---

[10] *Ibid.*, p. 417.

12 A schoolmaster and his pupils

many ordinary people, pedagogy was primarily moral education, an education in the Christian life. If a contemporary poem is any guide, lack of schooling implied indiscipline not illiteracy:

> This book is made for childer young
> At the school that bide not long
> Soon it may be conned and had
> And make them good if they be bad.[11]

When seeking to understand the impulses that led people to teach themselves to read, to provide an education for their children or to endow schools, it is necessary to bear in mind the strength of purely religious motivation. In so far as many teachers and learners thought in terms of 'advancement' it was 'advancement' in the eyes of God rather than in the reputation of the world.

Even when viewed solely in secular terms, education was as much the means by which young people were fitted to succeed their parents as a facilitator of social mobility. The assumption was that children were fitted by their very birth to particular roles in life, and that their education should be appropriate to their station. Yet late medieval England was no caste society. The Christian clergy, after all, were not an hereditary estate, but an order depending on recruitment from the wider society. In his observations on education, Fortescue drew an interesting distinction between the ways in which craftsmen and clergy were trained: the former are taught their trades by their parents, while 'he who desires to minister in spiritual matters is trained in letters'.[12] The church's need for literate clerics, and the clergy's celibacy or near-celibacy, provided the conditions for the growth and development of a nation-wide network of schools.

Access to education was neither free nor equal. According to a statute of 1406, 'any man or woman, of whatever estate or condition, be free to put his son or daughter to learn letters at any school in the kingdom', but the affirmation cannot be taken too literally. Serfs had to seek permission from their lords and pay a licence to set their children to school. Though serfdom was fast disappearing in the fifteenth century, payments of this sort are recorded into Tudor times. Then there were school fees, accommodation expenses and lost earnings. Tuition at grammar schools averaged around 8d a quarter, the equivalent of two days' wages for most workmen. A number of schools did offer a few free places, and boys living in the vicinity of a generously endowed school were thus well favoured. The real costs of education were, in any case, the costs of accommodation and wages forgone. The advantage lay with townspeople living close to a grammar school: their sons could continue to live and, possibly, work at home. For people sending their sons away, board might amount to between 8d and 1s a week. The costs of fees and accommodation expenses at major centres like Oxford or London would have been quite considerable. Even for the middling ranks of rural and urban society, educating children was a financial struggle, and school expenses are

---

[11] F. J. Furnivall (ed.), *Early English Meals and Manners*, EETS 32 (1868), p. 25.
[12] Fortescue, *De Laudibus*, pp. 18–19.

the dominant theme of letters between parents and children.

Despite the obstacles, boys from the lowest strata of English society were certainly able to gain an education. A surprising number of prominent churchmen in the later middle ages were from obscure and wholly undistinguished backgrounds. Thomas Bekyngton, bishop of Bath and Wells, and William Wainfleet, bishop of Winchester, are just two prelates of low birth but high academic distinction. Presumably there were ways and means of finding assistance, connections to be mobilized and opportunities to be taken. Many rural families had kinsfolk in town where a son could be billeted while he attended school. Young men fit for 'clerisy' would be placed as servants in the household of churchmen known to the family. Some would go to Oxford or London as companions to the sons of lords of the manor, often specifically to do the homework of their privileged schoolfellows. In a great many cases, perhaps, the initiative came from individual churchmen sponsoring apt boys of their acquaintance. Notwithstanding concern about people of servile stock entering the priesthood, the church remained a career open to all the talents.

Entering the priesthood or a religious order cannot in itself be regarded as a form of secular advancement. It implied, in theory at least, lifelong celibacy and the renunciation of worldly concerns. The basic grounding in Latin grammar essential for priesthood, though, had a demonstrable value in the secular world. Most of the boys attending schools, including monastic and cathedral schools, probably had no intention of seeking ordination or pursuing a career in the church. While youths destined for lesser trades did not tarry long in schooling, a growing number of young men destined for careers in business, administration and the law not only completed grammar school but even proceeded to Oxford or Cambridge. Even among the scholars actively seeking degrees, a sense of calling to the priesthood may have been the exception rather than the rule. There was a tendency to value the arts degree as a preparation for clerical and administrative rather than pastoral work, and to delay ordination until preferment to the church benefices made it necessary. Given the costs of actually taking out degrees, graduates were almost by definition careerists, men seeking to capitalize on their qualifications. Masters of arts might progress, too, to the higher faculties. The study of canon and civil law was the high road for advancement in both the church and the royal service.

If formal education began with the need to train clergymen, it assuredly did not end there. The network of schools, once established, naturally assumed a larger educational role. A major feature of the later middle ages, a consequence as well as a cause of educational expansion and development, was the emergence of lay professions: scriveners, gentlemen-bureaucrats and, above all, lawyers. Grammar schools met the needs of would-be estate-managers and lawyers quite as well as would-be priests, and indeed some might even have served them better. In Oxford and Cambridge, as well as in London itself, there developed a number of what have been termed 'business schools'. The school at Oxford run by Thomas Sampson is the best known, not least because he produced a book of model letters designed to publicize his enterprise. In a typical letter a father wrote advising his son in Oxford that a nobleman was about to offer him employment, and that he should leave off his university course and seek instruction from Sampson in dictamen and accountancy. From the fourteenth century it was a common practice for would-be students to spend a few years at the schools in Oxford or Cambridge prior to attending the courts at Westminster. The later middle ages likewise saw the increasing formalization of legal education centring on the Inns of Court. Sir John Fortescue, surveying the scene around 1470, depicted a well-developed system of legal education.

In late medieval England many people certainly viewed education as a route to advancement. Somewhat paradoxically, the best evidence of this attitude is to be found in contemporary criticism of careerist ambition and social mobility. Hostility to people of base stock advancing in social scale was deep-rooted, and in the wake of the Black Death there was a rash of legislative concern for the maintenance of the social order. The Statute of Labourers in 1351 sought to bind people to their former employment. In 1391 the Commons unsuccessfully petitioned that serfs should be prevented from setting their sons to school. In 1406 a statute was passed which sought to prevent parents worth less than 20s per annum from securing apprenticeships for their children. In his eulogy of the Inns of Court, Sir John Fortescue wrote approvingly of their high fees and social exclusiveness, but his comments, especially if applied to legal training generally, seem more the product of wishful thinking than objective description.

Evidence of conscious careerism in the lowest strata of society is admittedly hard to obtain, largely because their arrangements went wholly undocumented. While a number of churchmen did rise from total obscurity to the heights of their profession, their achievement might be more attributable to sponsorship than to family ambition: bright boys like Bekyngton and Wainfleet probably owed more to the pull of a discerning patron than to the push of enterprising parents. Still, complaints about rustics and tradesmen setting their sons to school presumably indicate that, as far as the gentry and many pious laymen were concerned, a disconcerting number had the ambition and the means to do so. Thus the author of *Piers Plowman's Creed* wrote with evident distaste:

> Now must each souter [cobbler] his son set to school,
> And each a beggar's brol [brat] on the book learn . . . [13]

The underlying concern of such writers was that low-born careerists were necessarily avaricious and corrupt: the 'beggar's brat' becomes, a few lines later, a worldly bishop. In his sermon *Defensio Curatorum*, Archbishop FitzRalph likewise testified, in a curiously backhanded way, to the manner in which parents saw the education of their children as a material investment. He alleged that many of them had become fearful of sending their sons to Oxford, preferring them to be tillers of the earth than to be seduced into joining the orders of friars.[14]

The interest of the middling ranks in education is better documented. Yeomen and tradespeople had the experience of the world, the connections and the capital to see

---

[13] Furnivall (ed.), *Meals and Manners*, p. xiv.
[14] A. J. Perry (ed.), *Trevisa's Dialogus inter Militem et Clericum*, EETS 167 (1924), p. 56.

the opportunities and to exploit them. Many of them clearly saw education as an investment, and were willing to make the necessary sacrifices to have their son set to school, to an apprenticeship or to serve in a household where skills might be imparted. The scale of their ambition is attested by the countless young men of modest provenance establishing themselves in trade in London and graduating from universities. One measure of their success is that so few members of such elite groups as aldermen of London, bishops and judges had noble or even knightly backgrounds. Unfortunately the end points of successful careers are usually better recorded than the hopeful beginnings. The circumstances which led John Chaucer, vintner of London, to secure a place for his son in a noble household are, despite their momentous consequences for the history of English literature, wholly obscure. Happily, the educational plans of another vintner, William Tonge, are recorded in his will: one son was set to the study of the common law, while another had the option of an apprenticeship or going to university.[15]

Significantly, many successful careerists acknowledged their debt to learning through their own educational benefactions. Merchants, lawyers and churchmen all figure prominently among founders of grammar schools, often in their home towns, in the fifteenth century. Among London merchants, William Sevenoaks showed the way, endowing a free school at Sevenoaks, Kent, in 1432. In the last decades of the fifteenth century, two lord mayors of London were responsible for the establishment of the first grammar schools in east Cheshire: Sir Edmund Shaw at Stockport and Sir John Percival at Macclesfield. William Sevenoaks's provision that the schoolmaster should not be a priest was not followed, but the statutes of a growing number of new schools reflected secular concerns. In 1459 Simon Eyre, a draper of London, sought to establish a school at the Leadenhall in London which would teach drafting and conveyancing as well as grammar. Interestingly enough, the fullest recognition of the need to broaden the curriculum to include more technical training is to be found in the statutes for two schools founded by churchmen in Yorkshire in the 1480s. Archbishop Rotherham's foundation at Rotherham in 1483 is especially significant. After endowing a grammar master and a singing-teacher, he continued:

> In the third place, because that county produces many youths endowed with the light and sharpness of ability, who do not all wish to attain the dignity and elevation of the priesthood, that these may be better fitted for the mechanical arts and other concerns of this world, we have ordained a third fellow, learned and skilled in the art of writing and accounts.[16]

Education was not only a means to wealth but also a means to break through the all important divide between 'gentle' and 'common'. Successful careerists invested their fortunes in landed property, and set their children to learn 'gentility'. There was a

---

[15] Thrupp, *Merchant Class*, p. 205.
[16] Leach (ed.), *Educational Charters*, pp. 424–5.

natural tendency for the lower orders to seek to emulate their social superiors. Many country gentlemen and merchants set great store on acquiring the technical accomplishments and behavioural mores which were, in theory, the preserve of the nobility. It was sometimes a matter of pure observation: the behaviour of a gallant knight fresh from court would come under close scrutiny in a provincial household, as was Sir Gawain's at Hautdesert in the poem *Sir Gawain and the Green Knight*. The reading of courtly literature and, more prosaically, 'courtesy books' was increasingly central to this informal curriculum. Works like *How the Good Wife Taught her Daughter* and *How the Wise Man Taught his Son* were designed to help bourgeois parents teach their children Christian morality and genteel manners. Thus the daughter should be taught modesty and deportment, not to laugh too loud, not to toss the head or wriggle the shoulders. When it came to being accepted as a gentleman or gentlewoman, literacy could count for more than breeding. John Russell, who was gentleman-usher to Humphrey duke of Gloucester, claimed to have learned his *métier* by reading some treatise akin to his own *Book of Nurture*.[17]

The education of the aristocracy was less exclusive than might be supposed. The 'nurseries' of chivalry and courtesy were the households of the king and leading magnates, but they were rarely for the sons and daughters of the house alone. Princes shared their lessons with the sons of lords and knights, young squires with the sons of newly rich lawyers. The laws of wardship played some role in establishing this custom. It made sense, in any case, to draw into the family circle, for company and service, promising youngsters drawn from a wider and less privileged cousinage and clientele. Placements at court or in noble households, which could bring useful connections as well as the right sort of education, were eagerly sought by ambitious families. The Pastons of Norfolk placed sons and daughters in the households of the king and several peers in the late fifteenth century. For the gentry and would-be gentry who were unable to find places for their children, 'finishing schools' were an option. According to Fortescue, the Inns of Court provided education of this sort: 'In all the Inns there is beside a school of law, a kind of academy of all the manners that nobles learn. There they learn to sing and to exercise themselves in all kinds of harmonies. They are also taught there to practise dancing and all games proper for nobles.'[18]

The practice by which English people sent their children to be educated away from home was noted by foreigners. According to an Italian visitor around 1500 the English followed the custom because they were naturally mean, declining to share their comforts with their children, and preferring to be served by strangers whom they could discipline more effectively.[19] In England, though, the practice was rationalized in educational terms. Most basically, perhaps, another adult would discipline the child better. More positively, Sir John Fortescue saw great virtue in the custom by which 'the

[17] Furnivall (ed.), *Meals and Manners*, pp. 32–52, 197–8.
[18] Fortescue, *De Laudibus*, pp. 118–19.
[19] Furnivall (ed.), *Meals and Manners*, p. xiv.

sons of the nobles of England cannot easily degenerate, but will rather surpass their ancestors in probity, vigour and honesty of manners, since they will be trained in a superior and nobler household than their parents' home'. Fortescue's observations on the social consequences of this form of household education could be taken further. Encouragement to emulate was in some measure an incitement to compete. As the Dominican friar Robert Holcot (d. 1349) observed: 'We commonly see that the sons of the rich and powerful will not learn, while the sons of simple poor men reach the highest ecclesiastical dignities by their character and science.'[20] In the classroom, on the dance-floor or in the lists, the established social order might be temporarily in abeyance, and princes and lordlings might be outshone by their social inferiors. Chivalry and courtesy acknowledged virtue as well as birth. 'Nobility' itself could be seen as an educational accomplishment.

In the past there has been a tendency to disparage the achievements of the later middle ages. The process began in Tudor England, not least among humanist scholars and Protestant preachers, the pundits of the Renaissance and Reformation. With regard to education, the picture of the fifteenth century as a rude and barbarous age, devoid of real achievement, was already well entrenched by the Age of Elizabeth. In this picture schools were few and far between, and schoolmasters were ill-educated clergy or, worse still, obscurantist monks who taught bad Latin badly. Modern historical scholarship has challenged many elements of this picture, even perhaps to the point of overstating the achievements of the 1400s.

The main burden of this revisionism has been to show the fifteenth-century roots of the 'educational revolution' of the Tudor Age. A marked growth in lay literacy in the later middle ages is now assumed, and the advances of the sixteenth century correspondingly scaled down. Recent studies have added impressively to the tally of known schools in the later middle ages, and levels of educational provision, especially in relation to population, can be shown to be far less inadequate than previously assumed. The wave of grammar school endowments in the late fifteenth century makes it possible to argue that even before 1500 there had begun 'to emerge a system of education in the modern sense in the place of forms of upbringing designed to fit men for different estates of society'.[21] It has been assumed, of course, that the spirit of education was somehow different. Stress has been laid on clerical control and the traditionalism of the curriculum prior to the early sixteenth century. John Colet's refoundation of St Paul's School, London, in 1518, with its lay board of governors and its humanist programme has usually been presented as the start of the new era. Yet the contrasts have been overdrawn. Lay involvement was evident before 1500, and in some respects clerical direction increased rather than declined in the Reformation. Similarly, the transformation of the grammar school curriculum was a more protracted

---

[20] B. Smalley, 'Robert Holcot O.P.', *Archivum Fratrum Praedicatorum* 26 (1956), 94.
[21] J. Simon, *Education and Society in Tudor England* (Cambridge, 1979), p. 4.

and uneven process than is often supposed, and owed as much, if not more, to grammarians and school founders of fifteenth-century England than to Renaissance influences from the continent.

The foundations laid in the later middle ages are expressive of a quiet revolution in terms of people's experience of and attitudes to education. All the signs seem to be that the proportions of people who were becoming literate, who were undertaking schooling and who were engaged in the founding of schools were increasing in the 1400s. Even the number of students at Oxford and Cambridge, possibly as many as 3,000 in the early fifteenth century, seems quite impressive in a total population of only two and a half million. The view that it was a worthy goal for all parents to seek an education for their children, and that there was even a public interest in extending educational provision, was ever more clearly articulated. A monastery's claims to an educational monopoly in Gloucester in 1411 were repudiated by the common lawyers: it could not be right to restrict teaching, 'which is a virtuous and charitable thing to do, helpful to the people'.[22] In a similar case at Coventry the city fathers argued that reason demanded that everyone 'be at his free choice to set his child to school to what teacher of grammar he liketh'.[23] In the motives of school founders, generalized philanthropy became more evident in the later fifteenth century. If in earlier provisions the weight was on the functioning of the chantry, with schoolteaching a sideline, in later times the emphases seem wholly reversed.

Careerism played a large role in the increasing interest in and material commitment to education. England in the later middle ages was an unusually fluid society, and education was seen as the key to mobility. In a startling passage in his *Book of Nurture* John Russell gave eloquent expression to the promise of education:

> Now, son, if I thee teach, will thou anything learn?
> Will thou be a servant, ploughman or a labourer?
> Courtier or a clerk, merchant, or mason, or an artificer?[24]

Among the intelligentsia, at least, there was a general endorsement of the potential of education. The Aristotelian view that a child was disposed neither to virtue nor vice was generally affirmed, and his comparison of a young mind to a clean slate on which a teacher could write was generally endorsed in the fifteenth century.[25] Sir John Fortescue likewise cited with approval the old adage, 'What a vessel takes when new it tastes of old.' More strikingly, he claimed that it would be for 'the good of the realm' if the sons of burghers and freeholders were brought up in the households of men of higher condition.[26] The lower orders probably, it would seem, had a shrewder assessment of the value of education than the nobility. Richard Pace

---

[22] *Ibid.*, p. 24.
[23] M. D. Harris (ed.), *The Coventry Leet Book* II, EETS 135 (1908), p. 190.
[24] Furnivall (ed.), *Meals and Manners*, p. 119.
[25] Fortescue, *De Laudibus*, pp. 18–19.
[26] *Ibid.*, pp. 110–11.

lambasted the attitude of some nobles that schooling was for 'the sons of rustics', and pointed to the humiliations which an uneducated noble would experience at court.[27]

The growing importance attached to education placed considerable emphasis on the role of the teacher, and throughout the fifteenth century there was considerable concern about the number and quality of teachers. Sadly, an appreciation of the importance of the work did not translate into an increase in remuneration. For many clerks, teaching, when not a phase of life, was a part-time occupation. Still, though it remained the humblest and most poorly rewarded of callings, there are signs of professional development in the later middle ages. The universities introduced a new degree, the master of grammar, which served to certify practising teachers. It is possible to identify a growing number of 'professional' schoolmasters, some of whom were creative and committed teachers and text-book writers. It was a time when serious thought was given to problems of teaching. In preparing a programme of Christian education for laymen, for example, Bishop Pecock opined that it was necessary to relate what was taught to people's capacity for understanding, that the teacher must 'see to the capacity of the learners, whether they be at the first able to receive the teaching'.[28]

A consideration of attitudes to education in fifteenth-century England would not be complete without some reference to the attitudes of the children themselves. For all the 'revolutions' in educational thought and practice over the centuries, however, it would appear children's responses to the constraints of formal schooling have changed remarkably little:

> On Monday in the morning when I shall rise,
> At six of the clock, it is the gise
> To go to school without avise
> I have lever go twenty mile twice!
> What availeth it me though I say, nay?
>
> My master looketh as he were mad:
> 'Where hast thou be, thou sorry lad?'
> 'Milked ducks, my mother bade.'
> It was no marvel though I were sad!
> What availeth it me though I say, nay?
>
> My master peppered my arse with well good speed:
> It was worse than finkle [fennel] seed
> He would not leave till it did bleed –
> Much sorrow have he for his deed!
> What availeth it me though I say, nay?

---

[27] Furnivall (ed.), *Meals and Manners*, p. xiii.
[28] E. V. Hitchcock (ed.), *Pecock's Folewer to the Donet*, EETS 164 (1924), p. 12.

> I would my master were an hare,
> And all his books hounds were,
> And I myself a jolly hunter:
> To blow my horn I would not spare!
> For if he were dead I would not care.
> What availeth it me though I say, nay?[29]

Of course, it cannot be assumed that this song and other similarly expressive pieces were actually written by schoolboys. Since such items tend to appear in grammatical miscellanies, it might well be that they were the work of teachers. If so, they offer striking testimony of adult interest in the experience of childhood, and evidence of teachers' attempts to see themselves from their pupils' points of view. In their own fashion, they reflect a significant pedagogical breakthrough.

---

[29] R. T. Davies (ed.), *Medieval English Lyrics* (1963) no. 178.

6

INFORMATION AND SCIENCE

Peter Murray Jones

There is no escaping the fact that fifteenth-century England was not distinguished by achievements that would be regarded as landmarks in the history of science and technology. Even in English terms, comparisons with the first half of the fourteenth or the second half of the sixteenth, both marked by significant advances in theory or in technique, only emphasize an apparent poverty of invention in the two centuries that lie between. A number of reasons have been canvassed for this lack of achievement, with varying degrees of plausibility.

Some have sought to blame the Black Death for casting a pall over philosophic speculation of all sorts at the English universities after 1350. It may be that the appalling events of the visitation of 1348–50, succeeded at intervals by outbreaks hardly less severe in their effects, did have an immediate effect in depopulating the universities, and a longer term effect in causing a retreat to spirituality, an obsession with sin and death, although this latter hypothesis is often stated without any attempt at proof. The numbers of those attending Oxford and Cambridge in the fifteenth century were actually surprisingly buoyant, given the overall stagnation and perhaps decline in population. Cambridge went from 400–700 members in the 1370s and 1380s to around 1,300 by 1450, and though Oxford suffered comparatively for its reputation for Lollardy and heresy, it certainly did not decline in student population.[1] Sometimes the call to spirituality could have unforeseen effects too. King's College, Cambridge, was founded in 1441 as the College of St Nicholas and the Blessed Virgin Mary, explicitly to fill gaps in the parochial clergy decimated by plague, and to fight heresy – not at first sight a promising environment for the flourishing of science and medicine. Yet ten out of the first twenty doctors produced by the College were medical doctors, and one King's College doctor of medicine, William Hatcliffe, was even associated with a

---

I wish to thank Faye Marie Getz and Linda Ehrsam Voigts for their helpful comments on an earlier version of this chapter. They are in no way responsible for any errors that remain.

[1] Anna Campbell, *The Black Death and Men of Learning* (New York, 1931), pp. 146–80; William J. Courtenay, 'The effect of the Black Death on English higher education', *Speculum* 55 (1980), 696–714; Alan B. Cobban, *The Medieval English Universities: Oxford and Cambridge to c. 1500* (Aldershot, 1988), p. 392, says that the universities could not evade an 'outlook of morbidity and preoccupation with death'.

petition of 1461 for a licence to practice alchemy (forbidden in England since the reign of Henry IV).

Yet though the teaching of natural philosophy (which largely consisted of commentary on Aristotle's works on cosmology, physics and biology) as part of the arts degree, and the teaching of medicine as both a part of the study of arts and as a doctoral degree in its own right, seem to have continued to flourish in Oxford and Cambridge in the fifteenth century, we look in vain for a continuation of the originality and speculative interests of the Oxford calculators of the early fourteenth century. The Merton school – Walter Burley, Thomas Bradwardine, William of Heytesbury, Richard Swineshead and others – had then applied a refined scholastic logic to a variety of natural philosophical problems, the laws of dynamics, the concept of a vacuum, the measurement of intensity of qualities, and many more. The manuscript evidence which survives for the fifteenth century suggests by contrast very little interest in the more speculative areas of natural philosophy, but instead a practically oriented medicine, and a new interest in the occult science of alchemy. None of the major academic figures at Oxford and Cambridge seems to have been willing to do more than the perfunctory essentials in arts teaching (which included natural philosophy), so far as we can tell.

Outside the universities, we might look to court patronage for an explanation of the absence of achievement in science and technology. When English kings patronized science it seems to have been the occult sciences that attracted their attention.[2] We know of court astrologers like Lewis of Caerleon, but not even military technology or navigation seems to have enjoyed support at court, as it was to do spectacularly in the reigns of Henry VIII and his daughter Elizabeth. Of course English kings of the fifteenth century had plenty of other, perhaps more pressing, matters to concern them, including periods of war with France, and more damagingly, wars for the throne in England. Humanism had its patrons among the English nobility and leading clergy – John Tiptoft, earl of Worcester, and bishops like William Gray, George Neville and John Shirwood brought Italian humanist scribes and scholars to England, as well as creating libraries of humanist books. But little if any interest was shown by these men in natural philosophy or medicine.

The greatest single patron of art and science in fifteenth-century England was, of course, Humphrey, duke of Gloucester. One of his protégés was Gilbert Kymer, chancellor of Oxford University, and the man responsible for presenting the books of Duke Humphrey to Oxford University. Kymer was a doctor of medicine, with a library of his own containing works on science and medicine – but only one of their authors lived in the fifteenth century. Kymer employed at least one scribe, Hermann Zurke, who wrote out a number of scientific texts, including some of continental origin on medicine and alchemy. But this interest seems to have borne little fruit in terms of

---

[2] For a description of the courtly character of astrology in England in the fifteenth century, see Hilary M. Carey, *Courting Disaster: Astrology at the English Court and University in the Later Middle Ages* (1992), chapters 7–9.

13   An alchemist's laboratory

original work in these fields. We know that Kymer, with William Hatcliffe and others, applied to the crown successfully for a licence to practise alchemy in 1461 (alchemy was forbidden by law without a licence), but we do not know what he and his colleagues may have achieved in their researches.[3]

It is of course true that achievements in the occult or experimental sciences are unlikely to be recognized by the modern historian. Alchemy and astrology, like the practice of medicine, have practical and not theoretical ends, and the successes or

---

[3] F. M. Getz, 'The faculty of medicine before 1500', in J. I. Catto and Ralph Evans (eds.), *The History of the University of Oxford*, vol. II: *Late Medieval Oxford* (Oxford, 1992); D. Geoghegan, 'A licence of Henry VI to practise alchemy', *Ambix* 6 (1958), 10–17.

failures of their practice leave no mark on the historical record, unlike the writings of the natural philosopher. Who can now say what Gilbert Kymer and his colleagues may have succeeded in doing in their alchemical experiments? Or what Lewis of Caerleon may have successfully prognosticated in his consultations on astrology? These are only pseudo-sciences in the eyes of the historian, but it is as well to remember that the condescension of modern historians of science is founded very much on ignorance about the results of their practice. The division between science and pseudo-science, which comes so easily to us, is not one that would have made any sense to contemporaries; but they would have recognized that alchemy and astrology had practical ends, whereas natural philosophy did not.

It is not my intention here to argue simply that fifteenth-century England was notable for the practice of alchemy and astrology rather than 'true' sciences or technological advance. I do want to argue that after about 1375 attitudes to science both within university and court circles and, more importantly, outside those circles, underwent significant change. Instead of regarding science as primarily a body of knowledge about nature, to be understood as part of God's providential dispensation to man, many fifteenth-century English men and women regarded science primarily as a source of written information which would help them achieve practical results in the world. The key word here – the Latin word used at the time – is *opus* or *operatio*, the performance of practical tasks in ways prescribed by written authority. Each of the sciences with a practical end – like medicine, alchemy or astrology, but also husbandry, warfare or hunting – had its own *opus*, the controlling principles of which could be laid down in written form (though practice was of course required to perfect oneself in performance).

There is an interesting comparison to be made here between attitudes to information in the fifteenth century and our own times. The last forty years have seen the invention and popularization of the terms 'information technology' and 'information society'. These terms signify our awareness of the way in which the marriage of communications technology and computers has helped to give enormous significance to the idea of information. Information is now commonly seen as the currency of our economic, social and cultural exchanges. In the fifteenth century, by contrast, the great technological breakthrough of printing with movable type came after rather than before the development of new attitudes to written information – in fact the successful exploitation of the new invention may have owed a lot to the changes in attitude to written information that I am going to try to describe in this chapter. What is common to both eras is that value attaches itself to the very idea of information, because it is seen as a means of expanding control over our natural and social environments. Of course in the fifteenth century they could not have expressed this notion in similar terms, but there is strong evidence to support the thesis that written information came to be of increasing value to men and women who sought to exploit it for just those practical purposes.

It is not easy of course to measure this shift in attitudes. One rather crude index of the spread of interest in science and medicine outside the university context to which it had belonged hitherto is the number of manuscripts containing written information on these subjects which were in circulation in the fifteenth century. Starting it would seem in the last quarter of the fourteenth century, manuscripts written for practical rather than academic purposes began to be produced in great numbers, catering to a much wider demand for such information than had existed in previous centuries. So one measure of this development is simply the number of such manuscripts produced. Unfortunately the fact that the older a book is the more chance that it will be lost or destroyed in time inevitably makes measuring book production more difficult. Fourteenth-century books will survive in any case in smaller numbers than those from the fifteenth century because of these accidents of time and use. But even after allowing for this factor there is evidence that production of books of information and science took off quickly after 1375. One invaluable source of such evidence is the handlist of scientific manuscripts in the British Isles dating from before the sixteenth century compiled by Dorothea Waley Singer, which deals with an estimated 30,000 to 40,000 written texts. Although no scholar has yet found the patience and stamina necessary for a precise count it is clear from sampling that the proportion of texts surviving from the fifteenth century compared to those from the fourteenth century is at least six to one.[4]

The subjects included as headings in the Singer index amount to more than forty. Not surprisingly the largest single category of manuscripts is that concerned with medicine and related subjects, including anatomy, surgery, herbal medicine, blood-letting, gynaecology, regimen and diet, hospitals, bestiaries and lapidaries, ophthalmology, pestilence, prognostication, recipes and drugs, charms, diagnosis by urine and by pulse, and veterinary medicine. Many of the texts in the large categories of astrology and alchemy are also clearly concerned with diagnosis, prognosis and means of healing. Taken together, the numbers of texts and manuscripts dealing with medicine and related subjects amount to more than all those dealing with the remaining subjects. But natural philosophy as taught at the universities is also well represented under the headings of Aristotle, astronomy, cosmology, fermentation and generation, mathematics, physics and science. Irrespective of subject area, the numbers of post-1375 manuscripts in all categories, but especially the medical, vastly outweigh all those written before that – rather arbitrarily chosen – dividing line. The great expansion in the number of such manuscripts in circulation after 1375 runs contrary of course to what we might predict as a consequence of the population decline as a result of epidemics of plague from the Black Death of 1348–50 onwards. It is also plain that, even allowing for the surprising buoyancy of university matriculations in the fifteenth century, most of the demand for these manuscripts must have developed outside the universities, amongst people with no stake in purely academic knowledge of science and medicine.

Another index of changing attitudes to science and medicine is the appearance of

---

4 The slips on which the handlist was compiled are filed on cards in subject order, and then date order within subjects. The cards are held in the Department of Manuscripts at the British Library and (incomplete) at the Warburg Institute Library in London. Microfilm copies are held at Cornell University and the Library of Congress.

large numbers of manuscripts containing texts on science and medicine in Middle English. In a study of book production in England from 1375 to 1500 Linda Voigts has demonstrated the multilingual nature of fifteenth-century manuscripts, which contain Latin, Middle English and Anglo-Norman texts on medicine and science very frequently within the same booklet. Behind this output of texts must lie enormous labour in translating texts out of the traditional Latin language of learning into the vernaculars. For it turns out that the vast majority of texts in Anglo-Norman and Middle English are not original writings in those languages but translations from Latin. In the course of translation the technical vocabulary of Middle English expanded enormously in this period, both by forming words directly based on the Latin equivalent – for instance 'derivation' to describe the process of taking blood from a part of the body near to the site of an ailment is clearly based on the Latin term *derivatio* – and by coining new terms which owe more to colloquial English usage ('swoon' for Latin *cincopacio*, for example – although the latinate 'syncope' is also found).

Just very occasionally we can see the translation process in close-up, when we see a translator actually at work putting Latin texts into Middle English. Two manuscripts in the British Library present us with the Latin manuscript which the translator (working in the last quarter of the fifteenth century) had in front of him, and the Middle English manuscript which he produced in his own hand (Harley MS 3371 and Sloane MS 76 respectively). We can see the translator hesitating over the translation of a word or phrase, and trying out more than one solution, or correcting his own earlier translation with a better effort. He leaves gaps in the text where he cannot think of an English equivalent of the Latin. The texts he chose to translate in the Latin manuscript were extracts from the writings of the English fourteenth-century surgeon John of Arderne, an anonymous plague treatise which begins *Dilectissime frater* (most beloved brother), a note on the secrets of women (gynaecology), extracts from Roger of Parma and others on wounds of the head, and miscellaneous remedies for a variety of named complaints. None of these texts was new when it was translated – in fact they were all written in Latin in the fourteenth century or earlier. But they were all sources of very practical information, and the translator obviously felt that they could usefully be rendered into Middle English, enabling them to be used by a readership who had no Latin, or preferred to read in English.[5]

These translators often felt no inhibitions in tailoring their translation to suit the needs of the English reader. Since practicality was valued more highly than faithfulness

---

[5] Peter Murray Jones, 'British Library MS Sloane 76: a translator's holograph', in Linda L. Brownrigg (ed.), *Medieval Book Production: Assessing the Evidence* (Los Altos Hills, Calif., 1990), pp. 21–39). The prologue to the compendium in Cambridge, Gonville and Caius College MS 176/97 was written by Austin, the translator into Middle English for the London barber Thomas Plawdon. Austin says that the translation was made in order to 'enter better into the methods of medicine at a time when wise physicians are lacking' – presumably he meant that learned physicians trained at Oxford and Cambridge were in short supply, even in London. See Linda E. Voigts and Michael R. McVaugh, *A Latin Technical Phlebotomy and its Middle English Translation*, Transactions of the American Philosophical Society, 74 part 2 (Philadelphia, 1984), pp. 14–16, 24, 25.

to the intentions of the original Latin author it is not surprising that Middle English versions often differ markedly from the Latin originals. For instance the translator of the great compendium on practical medicine of Gilbertus Anglicus (Gilbert the Englishman) had no compunction in dropping all the passages to do with women's ailments, and in leaving out the long sections on fevers, and the more theoretical material describing the nature of diseases. Perhaps the translation was intended for a monastic community – hence the leaving out of women's ailments – and the translator evidently thought that his readers were not interested in academic disquisitions on such tricky points as the differentiation of fevers or the precise academic definition of whatever ailment the practitioner might be faced with. This characteristic of leaving out the more theoretical material and concentrating on the immediate practicalities is typical of much fifteenth-century translation of medical and scientific texts, whose value lay not in completeness or theoretical rigour so much as in the information they contained.[6]

So we have two broad indices which can serve as a measure of the extent to which medicine and science spread out beyond university walls in the fifteenth century, and the extent to which consumers of written information on science and medicine looked to practicalities rather than theory. These indices have their value, but they can only take us so far in appreciating the distinctive attitudes which lie behind statistics about book production or translation activity in the fifteenth century. What we really want to know is how the individual made use of information for his own practical purposes. There is at least one case – an autograph manuscript – in which we may feel we can get closer to an individual's attitudes to written information than almost anywhere else. Thomas Fayreford was a medical practitioner in the west of England during the first half of the fifteenth century. His practice was far-flung, with a number of patients named as coming from the Bridgwater area in Somerset, Tiverton in Devon and the north Devon coast from Porlock in the east to Barnstaple in the west. The scattering of these patients suggests that Fayreford travelled widely in the course of his practice.[7] He owned at least one book, which contains a number of texts on medicine and science in other hands, but he also decided to add to this book a number of texts written in his own hand.[8]

---

[6] Faye Marie Getz, *Healing and Society in Medieval England: A Middle English Translation of the Pharmaceutical Writings of Gilbertus Anglicus* (Wisconsin, 1991), Introduction.

[7] The other rural practitioner for whom a list of patients has survived, John Crophill, travelled much less. He was bailiff of Wix priory (Essex) from 1455 to 1477, and all his patients lived within twenty miles of the small house of Benedictine nuns which he served. See James K. Mustain, 'A rural medical practitioner in fifteenth-century England', *Bulletin of the History of Medicine* 46 (1972), 469–76.

[8] For Fayreford, see Charles H. Talbot and E. A. Hammond, *The Medical Practitioners in Medieval England: a Biographical Register* (1965), p. 343, where he is wrongly placed in the fourteenth century; Tony Hunt, 'The "Novele cirurgerie" in MS London, British Library Harley 2558', *Zeitschrift für Romanische Philologie* 103 (1987), 271–99; Peter Murray Jones, 'Harley MS 2558: a fifteenth-century medical commonplace book', in Margaret Schleissner (ed.), *Manuscripts and Medieval Medicine* (New York, forthcoming).

These writings of his own include a list of the cures he had performed in his medical practice, an alphabetical herbal, the *Modus medendi* (Method of healing) of a thirteenth-century French author Pontius de Sancto Egidio, a long *Practica* or treatise on medical practice and a surgery 'collected by Fayreford', as the title tells us. With the exception of the work by Pontius, the other texts are compiled or collected by Fayreford himself, though he acknowledges many different sources for the information he includes. The herbal, *Practica* and surgery show clear signs of having been compiled like a commonplace book. Pages, or sections within pages, have been given headings, and underneath each heading material has been added at different times, as can be seen from changes in the colour of the ink, and gaps left unfilled in various sections. So Fayreford must have compiled these texts in his own hand as he came across information he wanted to include.

Fayreford obviously hoped that these writings would not only be useful to other practitioners but would make his reputation too – hence the list of patients he had cured, and the way in which his own name is written large in gold letters within a cartouche at the beginning of the *Practica*. The sorts of information he saw fit to record and pass on to his readers came from several different kinds of source. First, there were the 'authorities' or 'doctors', as he calls them. Sometimes he names them, sometimes not. The first section of the *Practica* on *dolor capitis* (headache) is a précis of corresponding passages in the *Practica* written in the thirteenth century by Roger Baron – but then Fayreford goes on to add other material from other sources, and he never credits Roger by name. He does cite by name well-known works on practical medicine like the *Lilium medicine* of Bernard of Gordon, the compendium of Gilbertus Anglicus, the *Thesaurus pauperum* of Petrus Hispanus, the surgery of Lanfranc and writings of John of Arderne. He also makes use of Arab authorities – Avicenna, Rasis, Abulcasis, Serapion, Mesue, etc. – and the standard university texts deriving originally from the famous medical school of Salerno. What emerges here is that Fayreford's knowledge of his Latin sources was extensive. We know that at one time in his life Fayreford must have been at Oxford, and it may be that much of his information is based on access to books there. It is very unlikely that he would have owned all these texts himself.

Although Fayreford does occasionally quote his authorities on the definition and diagnosis of ailments, the bulk of what he copies from them is therapeutic. He ascribes particular remedies to them, citing the name of his authority presumably because he felt it would give the remedy additional prestige with his readers. In effect he trawls his written sources for information which he thinks will be of value to himself and to his readers, disregarding the theoretical context of what he copies.

But Fayreford's borrowing from others did not stop at copying from books. He also attributed many individual recipes to physicians and surgeons of his own and earlier times, men who were not medical authors. For instance he mentions Nicholas Colnet, the Oxford physician who is best known as the doctor who accompanied the Agincourt campaign of 1415. Colnet is mentioned as curing one Hugo the apothecary of Oxford of hectic fever in a case described as if Fayreford were present at the time. Other names mentioned belong to earlier generations, like Nicholas Tyngewick, another royal physician who died in 1339. Some will probably only ever be known to us because Fayreford cited their names in connection with a particular recipe – Master Walter Bolle for example, who is mentioned more often than anyone else. It would seem that word of mouth or observation of the medical practice of others played a considerable part in Fayreford's collecting of information. Here what is recorded is not copied from the writings of others, but probably written down for the first time in recognition of its potential value as information.

There are a large number of prescriptions in Middle English scattered at random through Fayreford's mainly Latin writings. These of course are just as likely to derive from Fayreford's reading as the Latin prescriptions, since by the first quarter of the fifteenth century there was already a considerable medical literature in Middle English, with surgery and recipe collections particularly well represented. There is no real difference in kind between the material in Latin and that in Middle English – charms for instance come in both languages. In Latin we are told that whoever will wear the name of Nichasius will not see spots before his eyes; in Middle English that certain sacred words must be written on the patient's cheek for toothache, and orisons said to saints Apollonia and Nichasius (again).[9] But it does seem as if one or two of the Middle English remedies were definitely learnt by Fayreford in the course of his travelling practice – what he titles the *operacio* of Lady Ponynges is a recipe for *demigreyne* (a migraine), written in Middle English. This must be the same Lady Ponynges who is the first on Fayreford's list of cures (she suffered from suffocation of the womb, which caused her womb to press on other organs), and she must have passed on the recipe for *demigreyne* to Fayreford. Another Middle English recipe for *demigreyne* comes from a friar John, one of the white friars (Carmelites) of London, but perhaps not at first hand. Finally one of the most intriguing remedies is a recommendation to take a green frog that leaps in the trees and anoint any tooth that you wish to fall out (ordinary pond frogs are not so good for the purpose) – this curious remedy is described as 'one of my secrets (*privities*) that barbers have given me silver for'. Here information literally has its price, and we can imagine Fayreford as the fancied possessor of secrets which others will pay to have access to.

Another layer of information which can be disinterred from Fayreford's writings is that based on his personal experience of healing. The *Practica* and surgery contain a number of case histories which reflect his own medical practice. One of the cures mentioned in the list is that of a youth of Tiverton in Devon who lost the sight of his eye and recovered it with application of swallow's blood and betony. In the section headed *de oculis* (on eyes) in the *Practica* we find the following:

---

[9] Probably Nichasius or Nicasius, bishop of Rouen and martyr, who had an English cult, rather than his better known namesake, the bishop of Rheims; see *Bibliotheca Sanctorum* 9 (Rome, 1967), cols. 858–9. For Apollonia, patron saint of dentistry, see David Hugh Farmer, *The Oxford Dictionary of Saints* (Oxford, 1987), p. 24.

there was a boy from Tiverton in Devon about twelve years of age who lost the sight of one eye after a blow to it, so that he could not see at all with the other eye closed. Twice daily I put in the affected eye swallow's blood and he drank daily betony mashed up with ale, and within fifteen days he recovered his sight by the grace of God. And certainly in many cases I have discovered betony to be effective in getting rid of all fleshy growths in eyes when drunk in this fashion, and after bathing with rosewater as mentioned elsewhere.

Fayreford himself points out that the use of betony in such cases is recommended by Macer (Odo of Meung, the text of whose poem *de viribus herbarum* – on the powers of plants – is found written by a fourteenth-century scribe in the same manuscript). In this way Fayreford integrated his recollections of the ailment suffered by this particular boy in Tiverton with his understanding of therapy for eye diseases based on his reading of medical authorities. Such case histories present information which comes with the additional recommendation of having been tried and tested by Fayreford himself.

Fayreford also went to a lot of trouble to make his writings user-friendly for those readers looking for practical help. At the beginning he supplied tables of contents for the *Practica* and surgery, to help readers to go straight to the section they wanted. The texts themselves have been given folio numbers in Fayreford's hand to speed up the process of looking up information. Fayreford also makes use of cross-references within the text, so that readers can move between related ailments – for instance syncope is associated with suffocation of the womb, and there is a cross-reference from one to the other, using tiny symbols in the margin to speed the process up. Where words are not adequate to the description of an ailment, a plant mentioned, or a plaster or bandage, Fayreford has included little diagrams to help make his meaning clear. All these devices come into their own in an age which valued ease and speed of reference.

The sorts of attitude which lay behind Fayreford's information gathering and packaging for his readers were not restricted to country medical practitioners like him. Unfortunately documents like Harley MS 2558 are comparatively hard to come by. However there are pieces of evidence which suggest that men from different backgrounds, and practising in very different spheres, shared those same attitudes. In the case of John Cokkes of Oxford we are lucky enough to have preserved one of the few attested writings based on lectures on medicine and science given by academics in the fifteenth century. King's College, Cambridge, MS 16 part 2 contains lectures given in Oxford by Cokkes at some time after he took the Bachelor of Medicine degree there in 1450. Cokkes was already a beneficed priest when he began his studies in Oxford in 1447, and he continued to live in Oxford and to practise medicine there until his death, which had occurred by April 1475. On one occasion Cokkes was summoned to chancery to answer for having withheld evidence relating to the death of one of his patients, John Walweyn (between 1467 and 1472). Cokkes never went on to take a degree as doctor of medicine, but evidently he lectured at Oxford while a bachelor.

Revealingly he refers at one point in his lectures to the *archana* or secrets of his profession which he proffers to his pupils. The lectures do not take the form we might expect from the degree regulations for medicine, that is to say a commentary on the texts of the *articella* (the core curriculum in medicine, texts assembled originally at Salerno). Instead his pupils were offered a digest of information culled from Salernitan and other sources, and interspersed with the occasional case history. After an introductory session on prognosis, the bulk of the lectures is taken up with information about different types of medication. An Oxford manuscript (Bodleian Library, Ashmole MS 1432) also contains recipes ascribed to Cokkes, including a drink for the stone 'proved uppon hymselff', another for dropsy, others for palsy, bad sight, *fleuma* and various pains. These are just the same sort of secrets for which Thomas Fayreford was offered money by the barbers, and their willingness to give currency to such 'irrational' remedies reveals very similar attitudes in the two practitioners, despite the academic environment in which Cokkes gave his lectures.[10]

Another academic physician and churchman, but this time one who mixed in the highest court circles, was John Argentine (b. *c.* 1442, d. 1508). Although a fellow of King's College, Cambridge by 1461, he seems to have gone to Padua for his medical training, and to have acquired an MD there by 1465. If, like Cokkes, he ever lectured in medicine, he has left no trace. We do know that he put together a library of books on medicine and of a humanistic sort, many of them acquired in Italy. In 1473 he was ordained acolyte, the beginning of an ecclesiastical career which gained him a whole string of benefices. His career as physician also took him to the top – he was physician to the princes in the Tower in the reign of Richard III, and later became physician and dean of chapel to Arthur, prince of Wales, under Henry VII. In 1501 he was appointed provost of King's College, a post he retained until death, when he left substantial legacies to the College. Argentine thus reached the highest pinnacles to which the practice of physic could bring an academic.

The only medical work he left was his *loci communes seu liber de morbis et medicinis, ordine alphabetico dispositis* (commonplaces or book of diseases and medicines, in alphabetical order), now part of Bodleian Library, Ashmole MS 1437. As the name suggests it is a collection of recipe material ordered by alphabetical name of disease, with space left for additional entries. It is a rather more orderly equivalent of the commonplace book of Thomas Fayreford. The predictable references to academic authorities and written sources like John of Arderne (the author most frequently referred to) are balanced by what Argentine calls *experimenta*. These might be the *experimentum* of a certain woman near Ware (in Hertfordshire) who cured a friar from 'ciatica' in 1476, or of Argentine's King's College colleague William Ordew, who treated a forty-year-old rector near Cambridge suffering from hectic fever, or sometimes an *experimentum* of Argentine himself. These *experimenta*, whether cases of his own or other practitioners, are given equal weight with the prescriptions of written authorities.[11]

---

[10] Talbot and Hammond, *Medical Practitioners*, pp. 134–6; F. M. Getz, 'Medical practitioners in medieval England', *Social History of Medicine* 3 (1990), 265.

[11] Talbot and Hammond, *Medical Practitioners*, pp. 112–15; Getz, 'Medical practitioners', 263; Getz, 'Faculty of medicine', p. 395.

The examples of John Cokkes and John Argentine go to show that the attitudes which underlay Thomas Fayreford's writings are far from exceptional, indeed that they were shared by physicians of different background and status. The doctrinal writings on medicine of earlier authorities were to be treated as quarries of practical information, and remedies recommended by word of mouth, or tested by personal experience, were to be given equal value with them, to be written down in their turn for the use of further generations of practitioner. Of course looked at in a different light these activities are uncreative and derivative just because of their entirely practical bent – they are not likely to give birth to the sort of original academic contributions which would, in the standard perspective of the historian of science, distinguish a century of significant advance and achievement in medicine and science.

The way in which information could be boiled down from a long-winded academic format to something which could be used for reference purposes is most attractively demonstrated by the survival of fifteenth-century physicians' calendars. These manuscripts are written on parchment leaves folded so that each folio leaf is divided into three writing surfaces vertically, and two horizontally. Each folded section is then gathered up by a vellum tab at the top of the section, and sewn up with as many as seven other such sections. The whole can then be packed away into a carrying pouch carried at the belt, and brought out for consultation – each section is endorsed so that the physician can see at a glance the one that he needs to unfold. More than twenty of these folding calendars have now been identified as made in England in the fifteenth century, and many more were probably in circulation. Typically they contain short texts on the solar calendar, canons of eclipses of the sun and moon, tables of planets, rules for bloodletting and for diagnosis from urine. Together these add up to a brief conspectus of the essential information needed by the medical practitioner for diagnosis, prognosis and surgical treatment. These manuscripts are also illustrated spectacularly, with a zodiac man – showing the parts of the body and the star signs with particular influence over them – a set of twenty urine glasses showing the different colours to be found, a bloodletting man showing veins, as well as eclipse diagrams and a decorated calendar. Only the better off sort of physician would have been able to afford such a handy and beautiful reference tool as he travelled to visit important patients.[12]

All of these examples of the information culture of fifteenth-century England have been taken from the area of medicine, and it has been implied that what was true of medicine was also true of a range of other scientific subjects. But of course there is one significant difference between medicine and other branches of science. While alchemy or astronomy could be combined with the practice of medicine, the other sciences were not the basis for earning a living, as medicine was for Fayreford, Cokkes or Argentine (although the last two combined medical and clerical careers). Choosing these medical examples is nevertheless justifiable. An interest in practical information in written form

---

[12] C. H. Talbot, 'A medieval physician's vade mecum', *Journal of the History of Medicine and Allied Sciences* 16 (1961), 212–33; Peter Murray Jones, *Medieval Medical Miniatures* (1984), pp. 67–9 and figs. 27–8.

was not restricted to men who made a profession of physic – on the contrary the vast numbers of fifteenth-century manuscripts on medicine testify that this interest extended to lay men and women. They shared a practical concern for their own health, and that of their families and households, in the same way as, for instance, they shared a concern with aspects of household management which similarly could become the subject matter of practical science (for instance animal husbandry, warfare, dyeing, hunting and fishing and cookery). It is not surprising that these practical subjects are very often found alongside medical texts in manuscripts (Argentine's manuscript includes a Middle English 'Boke of Marchalsi' – a text on the management of horses).

Medicine also shades off into a wider concern with prognosticating the future. The same sorts of information required by the medical practitioner trying to forecast the outcome of a case, or to judge the appropriate time for treatment, were required by others for equally practical purposes. Not surprisingly in such an uncertain world, threatened by plague, war and political turmoil, to say nothing of the common accidents of life, fifteenth-century England had an insatiable appetite for the sorts of information that might enable individuals to foretell the future, or even to control it by occult means. Prognostication might be necessary for predicting the weather in its effects on the outcome of a journey or the planting of a crop, for casting a horoscope or for divining the future of any human enterprise by onomancy (using the letters of a name) or geomancy (using lines and patterns formed by chance). Similarly diagnosis as a medical tool was very closely related to the reading of character by physiognomy or chiromancy (using the hand). Many of the Latin and Middle English chiromancies are illustrated with diagrams of the hand, showing the principal lines and the general proportions of hands, nails and joints. Small fingers denote a person who is 'envyus, proud, hardy, and bold', for instance. Short texts on all these matters circulated in abundance, and very often in conjunction with medical material.

Calculations based on astronomical information also linked the medical and non-medical. Calendars and almanacs were of use to both the doctor and the layman. The more elaborate almanacs might contain a month by month calendar with columns indicating the length of daylight and shadow scales, tables and figures of both solar and lunar eclipses, the ascendants and beginnings of celestial houses, the reign of each planet over hours of the day, tables of movable feasts, the motions of the sun and dignities of the planets (situations in which a planet's influence is heightened by its position in the zodiac and its aspects with other planets), which sign the moon is in each day, and finally canons or rules explaining how these things are established. As we have seen, astrology was of central interest to medical men, but not to them alone. The calendars of Nicholas of Lynn, William Rede or John Somer, which circulated widely, were in the majority of cases not owned or used by medical men.

Perhaps the most common shorter form of calendar is the lunary, consulted according to the position of the moon. This could be calculated either by the cycle the moon makes throughout its twenty-eight to thirty mansions or days, or by its zodiacal cycle through the twelve signs, beginning with Aries. The moon was held to have a more direct influence over human affairs because of its closer position to the earth. Lunaries are found in Latin, Anglo-Norman and Middle English versions. John

Metham, in a Middle English prose lunary dating from *c.* 1448, from a manuscript compiled for and dedicated to his patrons Sir Miles and Lady Stapleton of Norfolk, provides a number of detailed prognostications linked to the lunary. They are qualified by such remarks as 'yt ys gode that day to take vyage over the see yff the wynde will serve', or 'the .vi. day off the mone ys lukky for hem that will go an-huntyng and hawkyng, yff the wedyr be temperat'. He concludes with a warning that the lunary must be used with 'dyscrecion and resun'.[13]

So just as it is anachronistic to assume that the boundaries of medicine as a science in the fifteenth century were as sharply defined as they are today – in fact medicine could almost be thought of as *the* science of the time, embracing as it did then so many of the key intellectual and practical concerns – so it is equally anachronistic to assume that medicine was the property of a professional elite. The practical outlook that was so characteristic of medicine in the fifteenth century was certainly not confined to medicine, but manifested itself in other sciences and amongst lay men and women even more emphatically than amongst the university-trained doctors of the time.

The fifteenth century can then be fairly described as an information age – an age in which science as a body of knowledge about the natural world was valued chiefly for what it could provide in the way of guidance in practical matters. It was also an age in which written information was valued and used by many outside the narrow elite who had pursued university courses in natural philosophy and medicine at Oxford and Cambridge. For the first time in the middle ages a medical practitioner out in the shires might have thought it worth while to assemble useful therapeutic advice in writing, and to record his own observations for the use of others. Of course Thomas Fayreford and his like were constrained by the limitations of a culture in which writing was still writing by hand, so that books had to be copied laboriously one at a time.

Since these practical interests seem to have been so widely shared it is not surprising that they created a demand for writing which scribal resources must have been hard-pressed to fill. We are beginning to learn something of the extensive community of manuscript book artisans who flourished in London in the fifteenth century, though our knowledge of similar communities in York, or Norwich, Oxford, Cambridge or Exeter is very scanty.[14] But given the limitations imposed by copying by hand, and the numerous separate processes which had to be gone through before the book was complete, it is not surprising that demand exceeded supply for writing. It was hardly simply by chance that the printing press arrived on the scene, and the new technology's role was to help relieve a bottleneck created by the slowness of scribal labour in the face

---

[13] John Metham, *The Works*, ed. Hardin Craig, Early English Text Society, orig. series 132 (1916), pp. 149, 150, 156; Laura Braswell, 'Utilitarian and scientific prose', in A. S. G. Edwards and Derek Pearsall (eds.), *Middle English Prose: Essays on Bibliographical Problems* (New York, 1981), pp. 346–7; Laurel Means (ed.), *Medieval Lunar Astrology* (Lewiston, New York, 1993).

[14] C. Paul Christianson, *A Directory of London Stationers and Book Artisans, 1300–1500* (New York, 1990). An early example of 'mass-produced' manuscripts containing medical and alchemical texts is discussed in Linda Ehrsam Voigts, '"The Sloane Group": related scientific and medical manuscripts of the 15th century in the Sloane Collection', *British Library Journal* 16 (1990), 26–57.

14   A doctor studies the stars before making a diagnosis

of an ever-growing demand for information. The information revolution in England was already in full swing before the arrival of the printing press with William Caxton, and indeed created the conditions in which the press might flourish. By the end of the century printing was beginning to make significant inroads into manuscript culture even in England, and the appearance of printed almanacs, plague and bloodletting treatises testify to the lucrative market for printers in information and science. No landmarks in the history of science and technology in the fifteenth century it is true – but in England as elsewhere information and science in written form had made an impact on far greater numbers of people than ever before.

7

WOMEN

P. J. P. Goldberg

Women in fifteenth-century England could hold land, bring lawsuits, make wills, be admitted to the franchise, engage in trade in their own right, take apprentices, hold guild office, run households, manage estates, even, in respect of Lollard women, administer the sacraments. Most did not. Custom, law and scripture tended to limit the opportunities open to women far more than was true of men. The dominant culture was indeed an essentially patriarchal culture. The political, demographic and economic vicissitudes of the time tended only to reinforce these patriarchal values as the century wore on. Associated with hardening patriarchal attitudes was an intensification of oppositional images of women as, on the one hand, virtuous wives and, on the other, whores. In a society searching for stability, the consolidation of gender distinctions, the subordination of women to men, daughters to fathers, wives to husbands, was seen as a necessary and laudable goal.

The principal authority upon which thought about women was based was scripture. The patriarchal order was thus a divinely sanctioned order and women's questioning of that order was consequently an affront to God and, as at the Fall, the cause of perdition. The Genesis account was reinforced through the teaching of Paul. Whereas man was created in God's image, woman was made from man to be his helper. Because woman was first tempted by the serpent, she was to be subject to her husband. It followed that women were to keep silent in church and were not to teach. Peter similarly referred to women as the 'weaker vessel' and urged them to sobriety of dress and chastity of person. The Proverbs likewise contained contrasting images of the model wife, devoted to the material needs of her husband and her household, charitable and industrious, and of the harlot, 'loud and wayward', whose 'feet do not stay at home'.[1] Many later medieval notions about women can be traced back to these texts. Thus when John of Ely was presented before a London court in 1422 for farming his office of keeper of the assay of oysters to a woman, the court ruled that it was not 'worship to this city that women should have such things in governance'. Likewise when Margery Nesfeld attempted to sue for legal separation from her husband, Thomas, on grounds of cruelty, his defence was that he used only reasonable

---

[1] Genesis 1.27, 2.18–24, 3.1–6, 16; 1 Corinthians 11.7–9, 14.34–5; 1 Timothy 2.11–15; 1 Peter 3.1–7; Proverbs 7.10–12, 31.10–31. The Vulgate has *garrula et vaga . . . nec valens in domo consistere.*

15   The temptation of Eve: the serpent has a woman's shape

force to chastise her 'rebellion' expressed in her unwillingness to abide within the home.

Medical science also helped shape prevailing attitudes. Medieval medical knowledge owed much to the Hippocratic doctrine of the four humours. Woman was held to be by nature colder and moister and thus inferior to the hotter, drier and consequently more active man. Various physiological observations were believed to follow from this. Women menstruate because they are normally unable to produce sufficient heat to burn up or otherwise transform superfluous matter. A fifteenth-century English gynaecological handbook explained 'that women have lesse hete in here bodies than men have and more moistnesse for defaute of hete that shuld dryen her moistnesse and her humors, but netheles of bledyng to make her bodies clene and hoole from syknesse'.[2] As a consequence of menstruation, it was argued, women do not grow bodily hair which in the male is produced from this same waste matter. They tend to have more fat than men and to have broader hips, but narrower shoulders since they lack heat to generate sufficient energy to drive matter higher up the body. More importantly, women were thought to have better memories and more imagination than men since their humours were both more pliable and more mutable. The negative side of this was that women were believed to be fickle or even unfaithful. This vice was compounded by the supposed influence of the uterus. To quote Aristotle, 'woman is more compassionate than man, more easily moved to tears, at the same time is more jealous, more querulous, more apt to scold and to strike'. A late fifteenth-century lyric likewise ascribed three qualities to women, namely spinning, weeping and deceit. This Aristotelian view, repeated by Bartholomew Glanville, seems to have been a common-place of late medieval thought and accords with the scriptural view of woman as 'the weaker vessel'.[3]

Law and custom were similarly influenced by theology. Though Paul, reiterating the Genesis account, taught that man and woman joined in matrimony were one flesh, it was the husband that had authority over his wife.[4] It followed that in law a married woman was expected to be represented or at least be supported by her husband and that the husband alone might be held answerable for his wife's actions. In terms of statute law a married woman was only permitted to bring an action in her own right for rape or the murder of her spouse. Borough law often made some allowance for women to engage in trade in their own right and even to pursue or answer for debts in their own person. Thus at Hastings in the later fifteenth century it was ordained that if a married woman 'be ympledyd in courte of dette, or covenaunt broken, or ells cattell withholden, yf she be reputyd and taken as a merchaunt, she may be putt to answere in absence of her husband'. Married women who were not recognized traders,

---

[2] B. Rowland (ed.), *Medieval Woman's Guide to Health: The First English Gynecological Handbook* (Kent, Ohio, 1981), p. 58.

[3] I. Maclean, *The Renaissance Notion of Woman* (Cambridge, 1980), p. 42; R. T. Davies (ed.), *Medieval English Lyrics* (1963), no. 135.

[4] Genesis 2.24, 3.16; Ephesians 5.22–3, 31.

however, were treated as dependants of their husbands and could neither bring nor defend an action without their husbands' support. The borough ordinances of Ipswich, for example, which date to 1291, provided that 'the husband shall answer in the court . . . to every plea of debt that his wife owed before their spousals, and for debt that she may have incurred after their spousals'.[5] Canon law seems to have placed least impediments in the way of women and even permitted married women to make their own wills so long as they had their partners' consent. In practice this right was questioned by the common lawyers and a marked decline can be observed over the course of the century in the numbers of married women leaving wills.

The consequence of the convention that married women were often regarded as infants before the law was that wives are often invisible in written records. This invisibility may blind the modern historian into believing that women's position in late medieval society was more marginal than would have been apparent to contemporaries. Thus lists of persons fined for breach of the assize of ale, that is for brewing for sale, may record mostly the names of married men and not those of their spouses who were actually doing the brewing. Similarly when married men were admitted to the franchise, and were thus permitted to set up trade independently and engage apprentices, or were made masters within the guild, it is implicit that their wives were understood to be associated with them in the privileges so acquired. Women are consequently found trading as members of the franchise and as independent 'masters' in the craft after their husbands' decease although not recorded by name in the registers of freemen and not explicitly provided for in surviving guild ordinances. A London widow, Maud Holbeck, for example, chose to defend herself in an action for detinue of goods as a 'freewoman of the city', and Margaret Burton, a York widow, described herself as a citizen in her will of 1488. The names of a few women, presumably widows, are likewise found endorsing the ordinance of craft guilds in York.

The attitude of craft guilds towards women may have been less negative than the evidence immediately suggests, but guilds nevertheless played their part in maintaining the patriarchal status quo. Women only had a voice in guild affairs as the widows of master artisans. So long as their husbands were alive, their participation in guild affairs does not seem to have extended beyond the annual feast. Marion Kent achieved her position on the council of the elite mercers' guild of York as a widow, not as a wife. Wives and daughters are only noted in guild ordinances in their capacity as assistants, though it is implicit that the guilds assumed that wives would so assist their husbands and, in consequence, be sufficiently skilled in the 'mystery' as to be able to direct servants in their husbands' absence or indeed to take over the running of the workshop on his death. This is precisely what the eponymous Goodwife taught her daughter in a didactic verse that appears to have achieved some popularity in the fifteenth century. 'And if thin hosbonde be from hoome,' she advised, 'lete not thi meyne goon ydil.'[6]

---

[5] M. Bateson (ed.), *Borough Customs* (2 vols., Selden Soc. 18 and 21, 1904–6), II, pp. 224, 228.

[6] T.-F. Mustanoja (ed.), *The Good Wife Taught her Daughter* (Helsinki, 1948), p. 200 (line 99).

Another observation that has often been made concerning women's relation to guilds is that there were no exclusively female guilds in late medieval England. This is in contrast to the pattern found, for example, at Cologne in the fifteenth century or Paris in the late thirteenth. Thus the London silkwomen enjoyed a considerable group solidarity, reflected in their petitions to parliament, but apparently no formal guild structure. Likewise, though women alone were spinsters, midwives, laundresses or even prostitutes, these groups enjoyed no guild structure. From this it has been argued that 'most "women's work" in medieval towns was either too low-skilled or low-status to merit a gild'.[7] The case of the highly skilled London silkwomen is perhaps less anomalous than at first appears. Most silkwomen were married to members of the major London guilds and would thus be associated with their husbands in those guilds. A guild of silkwomen would only have served to create a conflict of loyalties that could not have been tolerated by a city government made of men who were themselves associated with these same major guilds. In the case of other kinds of 'women's work' the issue was probably not one of skill, but of status. Guilds were collectivities of independent artisans who possessed their own workshops, employed labour and worked for profit, i.e. they were employers' organizations concerned with the regulation of labour. Laundry work, spinning, midwifery and prostitution, in contrast, were conducted on an essentially piece-rate basis by women who were neither independent artisans nor employers of labour in their own right. Spinsters, for example, worked for, and were regularly exploited by, textile entrepreneurs who provided the raw wool and paid by the weight for spun yarn. Civic authorities could thus no more tolerate their forming guilds than they could journeymen or other employees.

'Women's work' seems to have been characterized more by its diversity and flexibility than by its remoteness from 'men's work'. Women as daughters or servants would have contributed both to such household tasks as washing, cooking and child-minding and to the economic activities of the household. Married women likewise combined domestic duties with the responsibilities of the workshop or family holding. Their work identity was thus very fluid, a fact recognized by an act of 1363 which exempted women from the provision that all artificers confine themselves to a single craft. Women were regularly associated with a range of by-employments, such as carding and spinning or brewing, but they were also conspicuous as petty retailers or hucksters. In rural society women appear to have been responsible for much of the brewing and baking. Mak's wife pointedly asked her husband in the Wakefield Second Shepherds' pageant, 'Who brewys, who bakys?' and in the ballad of the tyrannical husband the wife declared, 'I bake, I brew, yt wylle not elles be welle.' Women also weeded crops, made hay, participated in the grain harvest, tended poultry, sheared sheep, looked after livestock, milked cows and sheep, made butter and cheese, spun yarn, prepared flax and wove cloth. Only ploughing and mowing, which involved the

---

[7] M. Kowaleski and J. M. Bennett, 'Crafts, guilds and women in the middle ages: fifty years after Marian K. Dale', *Signs* 14 (1989), 475.

use of a scythe, were specifically male preserves. Most of these are tasks noted by the tyrannical husband's wife and they are also found in Fitzherbert's *Boke of Husbandry*. Fitzherbert further directed under the head 'what works a wife should do in general', that women should 'go or ride to the market, to sell butter, cheese, milk, eggs, chickens, capons, hens, pigs, geese, and all manner of corns, . . . to buy all manner of necessary things belonging to the household, and to make a true reckoning and accompt to her husband'. When, therefore, Mak accused his wife of doing 'noght bot lakys and clowse her toose' [plays about and scratches her toes], it is not difficult to concur with his wife's response, 'Full wofull is the householde / That wantys a woman.'[8]

The eponymous tyrannical husband similarly complained to his wife that, whilst he was hard at work in the fields, 'Thou goyst to thi neybores howse, . . . / and syttes ther janglynge with Jake an with John.' In this particular verse the husband is again shown to be unjust in his criticism, for, as has just been seen, his wife presents herself as ever concerned with the welfare of her household and industrious after the manner of the virtuous wife of Proverbs 31, but it serves to illustrate a common enough weapon in the anti-feminist armoury. Women's supposedly insatiable desire for 'gossip' was frequently a matter of comment and even friction. The Goodwife advised her daughter not to go into town from house to house 'for to seke the mase'. Noah's wife in the Chester miracle cycle made herself the object of ridicule by refusing to enter the ark since it meant leaving behind her gossips and was consequently unceremoniously carried aboard by her three sons.[9] Her disobedience was, of course, not merely in respect of her husband, but of divine authority. These examples demonstrate that the dominant culture equated the desire for 'gossip' with an unwillingness on the part of women to be confined within the private sphere of the home, symbolized in this last instance by the ark. Paul had warned of the young widows 'gadding about from house to house, and not only idlers but gossips'. Didactic literature reinforced the point. The daughter in *The Good Wyfe Wold a Pylgremage* was told, 'rene thou not fro hous to house lyke an Antyny gryce', and the Goodwife bluntly advised, 'wone at hom, doughtir'.[10] Giles of Rome, whose writing was known in aristocratic circles, likewise stressed the importance of confining daughters to the home. Mary, according to one vernacular sermon, was found by Gabriel 'in a pryvy chambre and nought stondynge ne walkynge by stretys'. Judith was likewise represented a virtuous widow who 'held hir priveliche in clos in hir hous with hir women and wolde noght goon

---

[8] Wakefield Second Shepherds' pageant, in A. C. Cawley (ed.), *The Wakefield Pageants in the Towneley Cycle* (Manchester, 1958), p. 54 (lines 414, 416, 420–1); 'The ballad of the tyrannical husband', in T. Wright and J. O. Halliwell (eds.), *Reliquae Antiquae* (2 vols., 1841–3), II, p. 197 (line 57); A. Fitzherbert, *The Boke of Husbandry*, in C. H. Williams (ed.), *English Historical Documents, 1485–1558* (1965), p. 924.

[9] Wright and Halliwell (eds.), *Reliquae Antiquae*, II, p. 197 (lines 39–40); Mustanoja (ed.), *Good Wife*, p. 199 (line 58); P. Happé (ed.), *English Mystery Plays* (Harmondsworth, 1975), pp. 125–7.

[10] 1 Timothy 5.13; Mustanoja (ed.), *Good Wife*, pp. 173 (line 8), 199 (line 73). A Tantony piglet (Antyny gryce) proverbially trotted to and fro behind other people.

out'.[11] In this respect, as in so many others, most women are believed to have fallen short of the scriptural ideal.

Women might be expected to stay at home, but men were not so confined. The point was graphically made in the *Ludus Coventriae* pageant of Joseph, for the play commences with Joseph's return from work. The door of his home is locked and his dutiful wife opens it from within. This particular aspect of the public/private dichotomy was, as we have seen in the case of Margery Nesfeld or the fictional wife of the tyrannical husband, open to challenge. It may be, however, that the prescriptive ideal had some bearing on social practice. The attitude of male authorities has a depressingly familiar ring to it; maids who, like Dinah the daughter of Jephthah, would rather roam the streets than abide at home risked rape. This was a very real fear that confronted Margery Kempe when travelling unaccompanied and it is probable that she gives rare voice to a more general fear. The woman who went about unaccompanied was, like the harlot of Proverbs, thus considered of ill repute. Such a concern for reputation would further explain the desire of husbands such as Thomas Nesfeld to curtail their spouses' freedom of movement outside the marital home. The issue, however, was probably more one of enforcing patriarchal authority than of curtailing women's movement outside the domestic sphere; the nature of the familial economy ensured that women were not confined to the home. Had not, as the Knight of La Tour-Landry observed, 'the serpent avised her tyme, whanne Eve was from her husbonde alone'?[12]

Patriarchy was also concerned to limit women's voice in the public sphere. Here again scripture provided the necessary authority. As the good Knight explained, Eve sinned in giving answer to the serpent 'with-oute counsaile of her husbonde . . . for the ansuere longed to her husbonde, and not to her'. When in 1496 Alice Wade was presented before the court of the archdeacon of Buckingham as a 'chatterer in church at the time of divine worship' she was in breach of Paul's injunction that women should keep silent in church.[13] Talking during divine service was thus a gender-specific sin and the subject of much anti-feminist comment. The grinning image of Tutivillus, for example, the demon who wrote down the conversations of women in church, appears frequently in church art. The Pauline prohibition was complemented by Peter's direction that wifely virtues lay not in speech, but in submissive action. According to a contemporary proverb, 'a mayde schulde be seen but not herd'. Aristotle likewise had identified silence as a specifically female virtue and this was one of the virtues associated with the Virgin Mary. Indeed according to contemporary tradition, the Mother of God spoke only four times in her life.[14] Didactic writings reinforced this

[11] G. R. Owst, *Literature and Pulpit in Medieval England* (Oxford, 2nd edn, 1961), p. 119.

[12] T. Wright (ed.), *The Book of the Knight of La Tour-Landry*, Early English Text Society (hereafter EETS) 33 (1906), p. 55.

[13] Wright (ed.), *La Tour-Landry*, p. 56; E. M. Elvey, *The Courts of the Archdeaconry of Buckingham*, Buckingham Record Soc. 19 (1975), no. 254.

[14] Maclean, *Renaissance Notion of Women*, p. 23; Luke 2.19; Owst, *Literature and Pulpit*, p. 387; T. Erbe (ed.), *Mirk's Festial*, Part 1 EETS extra series 96 (1905), p. 230.

point. 'Doghter, temper well thi tonge', was the mother's advice in *The Good Wyfe Wold a Pylgremage*. The Knight of La Tour-Landry in like manner wrote that one 'good thinge that may be in a woman, to be in a littel speche' and warned that young women who spoke too freely might be spurned as potential marriage partners.[15]

If silence was a womanly virtue, it followed that failure to bridle the tongue was particularly a vice of women; together with the magpie and the jay, woman was one of the three 'clatterers'. Though the ideal woman, according to Bartholomew Glanville, was 'wary in speaking', yet 'no man hath more woe than he that hath an evil wife, crying and jangling, chiding and scolding'. There is indeed a whole genre of literature warning that 'women list to smater' and are incapable of keeping counsel. One late-fifteenth-century lyric noted ironically that women were 'not liberal in language but ever in secree' and would 'lever go quik to hell' than reveal to their neighbours matters told in confidence. Several of the Knight of La Tour-Landry's chapters likewise warned of evil women who told their husbands' secrets to their 'gossips' with inevitable dire consequences. Noah, in the Wakefield pageant, consequently advises men regarding their wives, 'whyls thay ar yong / If ye luf youre lifys, chastice thare tong.'[16]

The problem was not merely that women's supposed love of 'gossip' took them, as we have seen, outside the confines of the home. It was that women's speech was also potentially subversive. The harlot of Proverbs was *garrula*, but her words posed a threat to the moral order; her lips 'drip honey, and her speech is smoother than oil; but in the end she is bitter as wormwood' and her mouth 'is a deep pit'. The ordinance concerning scolds at Hereford, dated 1486, observed that 'through such women many ills in the city arose, viz. quarrelling, beating, disturbing the peace of the night, discord frequently stirred between neighbours, as well as opposing the bailiffs, officers and others'. Again it is worth observing that scolding was a gender-specific transgression, although one that, according to Aristotle, women were by nature given to. Such sentiment helps explain the presentment of women in both borough and manorial courts both for gossiping and for scolding. Women so convicted at Hereford were to be exhibited barefoot and with their hair hanging down in the cuckingstool and afterwards imprisoned until they paid a fine, a form of punishment designed to shame and humiliate.[17]

Moderation in speech may have been an integral element in the construction of femininity, but it would appear that women were more likely than men to employ verbal as opposed to physical violence in response to disputes. On one level this must reflect a greater social abhorrence of physical violence perpetrated by women than by men. On another level it may simply indicate that where men were assaulted by women they were unwilling to seek redress through the courts. Certain kinds of verbal violence,

---

[15] Mustanoja (ed.), *Good Wife*, p. 174 (line 43); Wright (ed.), *La Tour-Landry*, pp. 18–19, 126–8.

[16] R. Steele, *Medieval Lore from Bartholomew Anglicus* (1905), pp. 57–8; Owst, *Literature and Pulpit*, pp. 4, 386–7; Davies (ed.), *Medieval English Lyrics*, no. 123, cf. no. 125 (lines 397–8); Cawley (ed.), *The Wakefield Pageants*, p. 24 (lines 397–8).

[17] Proverbs 5.3–4, 22.14; Bateson (ed.), *Borough Customs*, II, pp. 79–80.

the use of defamatory words, may, however, have been an especially effective weapon for women to use against other women since a woman's standing in society was so much a matter of reputation, particularly in matters of sexuality. Indeed, according to litigation evidence, defamatory words directed against women frequently had sexual connotations. For a woman to be called a whore by her neighbours could also bring about the sort of discord feared by the authorities at Hereford. When Emma, the wife of John Lylle, called Agnes Popilton variously 'old monks' whore', 'friars' whore' and 'old rank tainted thief' as the congregation was leaving Sunday vespers in Holy Trinity, King's Court in York, the initial response of the victim's husband was to disown his wife and drive her from his home.[18] Litigation was the one means open to women to restore their injured reputations. Women are thus frequently noticed involved in litigation concerning sexual slander.

Single women seem to have been especially vulnerable to such slander. It was, for example, alleged in a matrimonial cause of 1432 that Isabel Henryson and Katherine Burton, who shared a house together in Bootham, York, 'were and are still common fornicators and adulteresses'.[19] Medieval authorities seem to have been particularly suspicious of single females. Parents or masters had a moral duty to exercise very strict supervision of their daughters or maids, but in practice not all unmarried women were subject to this discipline. Such ungoverned females were perceived to pose a direct threat to the social order through their twin association with unregulated sexuality and with criminality. The attitude of civic and manorial authorities seem to have hardened by the latter part of the century, probably because economic recession pushed more and more single women the wrong side of the law. This is, however, not how contemporaries understood what was perceived to be a moral disintegration. Far from being victims of circumstance, women were regarded as active agents of the devil whose actions provoked divine displeasure in the form of economic malaise. The prevailing mentality is reflected in the response of the civic authorities to Coventry's worsening economic situation in 1492. A comprehensive series of ordinances designed to restore the moral order were issued. These included provisions that civic officers guilty of sexual misconduct be deprived of office and that guild priests dutifully discharge their office 'in encreasyng of dyvyn service', but they culminate in three clauses specifically directed at single females. Coventry folk were forbidden to let rooms to 'eny Tapster, or Woman of evell name', nor were such women to receive any servants or apprentices. Most draconian of all it was ordained that 'no senglewoman, beyng in good hele & myghty in body to labour within the age of l [fifty] yeres, take nor kepe frohensfurth housez nor chambres to them-self . . . but that they go to service till they be married'.[20] Through marriage the patriarchal order was thus re-established, but it is appropriate here to consider the role played by education in first instilling patriarchal values.

---

[18] Borthwick Institute of Historical Research, York (hereafter BIHR), CP.F.153.
[19] *Ibid.*, CP.F.104.
[20] M. D. Harris (ed.), *The Coventry Leet Book*, EETS 134–5, 138, 146 (1907–13), pp. 544–5.

16   St Anne teaching the Virgin Mary to read

All too little is known about the education of girls in an era which saw a proliferation of grammar school provision for boys. There is some evidence that elementary education of both sexes up to the age of about seven was regarded as women's responsibility. Formal secondary education seems to have been provided only for boys and was provided exclusively by male tutors and schoolmasters. Very few female schoolmistresses are recorded, although a *magistra scholarum* is noted at Boston in 1404, a usage that prompted Eileen Power to suggest that here at least some girls may have been taught Latin.[21] Although nunneries appear to have provided some education for children of good families, most girls must initially have been instructed at home, perhaps by their mothers. The Goodwife offers no advice on this score save that unruly children should be soundly beaten, but the poem depends upon the notion that it was the mother's role to instruct her daughters. The image of St Anne teaching her daughter, the Virgin Mary, to read was widely popular and may reflect practice at least within comparatively well-to-do households, though such a literal interpretation of contemporary iconography is problematic. Books were, however, as much a symbol of as a practical aid to feminine devotion. There is good evidence for women as book owners and even, in a few cases, patrons. Primers or service books in particular are sometimes noted among the possessions of women testators. Significantly, these were usually bequeathed through the female line and it was from such books that infants were first instructed in the rudiments of the alphabet.

It may well be that we have here a further expression of the public/private dichotomy. Women may sometimes have been taught to read, but their knowledge of Latin need not have extended beyond an ability to pronounce the words of the Paternoster, Ave Maria and Creed or perhaps the other material contained in the primer. Despite the example of the learned St Catherine, the Knight of La Tour-Landry advocated the education of girls, but only 'to lerne vertuous thinges of the scripture, wherthorugh thei may the beter see and knowe thaire sauvement, and to duell and for to eschewe al that is evel in manere'.[22] Unlike boys, they were probably not generally taught Latin grammar, and thus the facility to read Latin with understanding, or the mechanical skill of writing, at least in any formal manner. The implications of these observations are that most women were effectively denied access to literature in Latin beyond that learned by rote for devotional purposes and were largely unable to communicate through the written word save by means of an amanuensis. Perhaps this last was, for those like the Paston women who could afford such assistance, not such a handicap, for Margery Brews even trusted her secretary to write her a valentine, verses included, to her sweetheart, John Paston. There was, however, a parallel between the scriptural injunction against women teaching and the effective constraint upon women writing. According to the *Dicts and Sayings of the Philosophers*,

---

[21] E. Power, *Medieval Women*, ed. M. M. Postan (Cambridge, 1975), p. 84.
[22] Wright (ed.), *La Tour-Landry*, p. 117.

Socrates said to a young woman who had learned how to write, 'multiplie not evil upon evil'.[23]

Formal academic education was apparently limited because inappropriate for a girl aspiring to marriage and the demands of running a household. Training in deportment was, however, an integral part of women's education. A woman, the Goodwife taught, should maintain a sober expression and neither laugh too loud nor yawn too wide. The young woman who 'beheld every man in the face' was castigated for 'her shamles boldnesse'. The well-mannered woman was taught instead to walk with straight head, but eyes cast down to the ground before her. The Goodwife instructed her daughter 'whan thou goist in the way, go thou not to faste, / Brandische not with thin heed, thi schuldris thou ne caste.' Similarly, Bartholomew Glanville described the model wife as 'mannerly in clothing, sober in moving, wary in speaking, chaste in looking, honest in bearing, sad in going, shamefast among the people'. Again the purpose was to discourage women from catching the eye of lustful men. For similar reasons the Goodwife advised her daughter, 'Go not to the wrastelinge, ne to schotynge at cok, / As it were a strumpet.' She also advised against drinking to excess; to be too often drunk was a cause of shame. A woman was taught to greet a man 'swiftli' and thus not be detained in his company. Kissing was discouraged. The Knight of La Tour-Landry, through the persona of his wife, warned that 'kyssynge is nyghe parente and Cosyn unto the fowle faytte or dede'. Nor was a woman to take gifts of a man. If a man spoke of love she was to leave his company or call somebody else to hear him speak. She should on no account sit or stand alone with him for, as the Goodwife warned, 'a sclaundre reisid ille / is yvel for to stille'.[24]

Related to deportment and a matter of equal concern to didactic writers was the question of dress. The late northern Gothic ideal of feminine beauty placed much emphasis on a slender body, small high-set breasts and an unusually prominent belly. This was the model for the virgin martyrs so frequently depicted in church art with their rosy complexions and long golden hair. Their conventional good looks only emphasized their desirability to men and thus their virtue in defending their virginity. For lesser mortals dress was used to emphasize or create the illusion of a fashionable, and thus more attractive figure. Didactic writers and preachers decried such vanity which was perceived to be a vice particularly of women. William Staunton's vision of Purgatory included 'the women with gowns trailing behind them a great space, and some others with gay chaplets on their heads of gold and pearls and other precious stones'.[25] Elaborate headdresses, which were designed to suggest greater height and,

---

[23] C. F. Bühler (ed.), *The Dicts and Sayings of the Philosophers*, EETS, orig. series 211 (1941 for 1939), p. 102.

[24] M. A. Manzaloui (ed.), *Secretum Secretorum: Nine English Versions*, EETS 276 (1977), p. 45; Mustanoja (ed.), *Good Wife*, pp. 198 (lines 26–7, 50–1), 199 (line 71); Steele, *Medieval Lore*, p. 58; Wright (ed.), *La Tour-Landry*, p. 185.

[25] Quoted in F. E. Baldwin, *Sumptuary Legislation and Personal Regulation in England* (Baltimore, 1926), p. 78.

accompanied by the plucking of hair on the eyebrows and temples, to help accentuate the forehead, low necklines and tight-fitting garments were regularly castigated. The Knight of La Tour-Landry warned women against wearing clothes that were too revealing and described how a woman was tormented after death by a devil who stabbed her face where in life she had plucked her hair and another who applied burning pitch, oil, tar and boiling lead where she had used paint. The character of Tutivillus in the Towneley Domesday pageant mocked the women whose vanity had condemned their souls to damnation:

> If she be never so fowll a dowde   with hir kelles and hir pynnes,
> The shrew hir self can shrowde   both hir chekys and hir chynnes;
> she can make it full prowde   with iapes and with gynnes,
> hir hede as hy as a clowde   bot no shame of hir synnes
> Thai fele;
> When she is thus paynt,
> she makys it so quaynte,
> She lookys like a saynt,
> And wars then the deyle [devil].[26]

The moralists' attack on women's dress probably embraced a number of concerns. On the one hand expenditure on clothes had to be justified against other needs. The Goodwife warned her daughter 'make not thin husbonde poore with spendinge ne with pride' and the Knight of La Tour-Landry, addressing a more affluent, aristocratic audience, advised that it was better to have fewer garments than that the poor should lack. The Knight did, nevertheless, allow them to wear their best clothes to church out of respect to God. Bartholomew Glanville likewise praised the wife who sought to please her husband 'with virtues than with fair and gay clothes', an observation derived from the scriptural injunction 'let not yours be the outward adorning with braiding of hair, decoration of gold, and wearing of fine clothing, but let it be the hidden person of the heart with the imperishable jewel of the gentle and quiet spirit'.[27] On the other hand the woman who showed too much interest in fashion threatened the moral order. To wear the very latest fashions was to undermine the social hierarchy of which dress was an important indicator. This was the concern that underpinned the sumptuary legislation of the period. To wear fine clothes and to use artifice to enhance one's physical appearance was, moreover, to attract the attention of men and lead them to sin. Tutivillus in the Towneley pageant boasted that 'ilka las in a lande / like a lady nerehand, / so fresh and so plesande, / makys men to foly'. One preacher, with true medieval logic, used the example of how Judith dazzled Holofernes by her beauty and fine array to illustrate the point. On a more mundane level the prostitute used dress to gain clients and thus other women who dressed immodestly or beyond their station were morally no better. It is pertinent to remark here that an ordinance of c. 1439

[26] G. England (ed.), *The Towneley Plays*, EETS, extra series 71 (1897), p. 372 (lines 260–8).
[27] Mustanoja (ed.), *Good Wife*, p. 202 (line 165); Steele, *Medieval Lore*, p. 58; 1 Peter 3.3–4.

demanded that prostitutes wear distinctive clothing so as to distinguish themselves from other women. The Knight of La Tour-Landry related a sermon to the effect that Noah's Flood was divine punishment for the lechery that was a consequence of 'the pride and disguysinge that was amonge women'.[28]

The education of women was thus more about shaping gender identity, such that they would make men good wives, than providing the skills by which they might challenge that identity. When Brian Roucliffe wrote to Sir William Plumpton, concerning his new daughter-in-law Margaret Roucliffe, that she 'speaketh prattely and french and hath near hand lerned her sawter [psalter]', he probably reflected male pride in such a well-accomplished young lady who would do them both credit (and make a good wife for his son) rather than enthusiasm for the higher education of women. Giles of Rome, whose *De Regime Principum* was still read in aristocratic circles in the fifteenth century, advocated that girls be secluded, restrained in speech and kept from idleness. He advocated sewing, spinning and working with silk as especially suitable occupations just as in later times girls were given samplers to work. Aristocratic girls were, however, given practical training in running a household, in addition no doubt to instruction in proper manners and deportment, as a consequence of their going into service in other aristocratic households. Ideally a daughter would be placed with a family higher up the social hierarchy in the hope, as Margaret Paston made explicit in a letter to her son, that her prospects, not least in respect of marriage, might be advanced.[29]

It was not only daughters of the landed aristocracy that passed some at least of their adolescence as servants in other households. Numbers of girls of more humble birth spent time in service, particularly in artisan and urban households. For these girls and young women, as for their brothers, servanthood was a stage in growing up. Just as a Paston daughter might be urged to aspire to becoming the wife of a knight, so a young woman in service to a draper or a baker might herself come to be the mistress of a house and workshop with servants of her own. This specifically was the expectation of the Goodwife's daughter. Service provided training in household skills; female servants were probably expected to assist with the care of young children, draw water, go to market, prepare food, make beds, light fires, fetch candles and all the other domestic tasks. Service also provided a craft and commercial training. Women servants assisted in their masters' workshops and helped to market their goods. It is even probable that many female servants gained some basic skills in numeracy in the course of their work. We can, for example, glimpse from a debt case of 1430 the women servants employed by Robert Lascelles, a York merchant, weighing and costing merchandise, carrying a particularly large purchase to a customer's home and visiting a customer to demand payment.[30] A young woman who had gained experience as a servant of the discipline of the household and the workshop, and acquired a range of marketable skills in the

---

[28] England (ed.), *Towneley Plays*, p. 372 (lines 256–9); Wright (ed.), *La Tour-Landry*, p. 62.
[29] T. Stapleton (ed.), *Plumpton Correspondence*, Camden Soc., old series 4 (1839), p. 8.
[30] BIHR, CP.F.174.

process, may thus have enhanced her marriage prospects. To this end, to judge from probate evidence, employers sometimes provided their female servants with household utensils and bedding.

Marriage as a sacrament fell within the jurisdiction of the church and canon law. The canon law of marriage, which dated back to the twelfth century, insisted that the essence of matrimony was consent. A canonically binding marriage could thus be contracted by simple exchange of words of present consent, viz. 'I take you to be my husband/wife', or of words of future consent, viz. 'I will marry you', followed by intercourse. Sexual relations alone could not make a marriage, but in this instance were deemed to demonstrate present consent to a future contract. Witnesses were not necessary, although the church courts required a minimum of two witnesses in the event of one of the parties disputing the contract. Marriages made against the will of one or both parties were thus invalid. That will, moreover, could only be exercised by young persons who had achieved canonical majority, itself tied to supposed age of puberty, viz. twelve for girls and fourteen for boys. In this respect canon law was at odds with the implications of the decalogue, for a daughter might in theory make a binding marriage without the approval of her parents. The celebrated case of Margery Paston's marriage to the Paston bailiff, Richard Calle, demonstrates that this was sometimes also true in practice. Examined before the bishop of Norwich, Margery stoutly refused to unremember the binding words of present consent despite the bishop's pointed urging to think of how her family might reward her if she were obedient and to consider her pedigree. This last, given the Pastons' humble and probably servile origins, was a particular irony. Elena Couper of Welton near Hull, observed in a disputed marriage case of 1491, was similarly determined that parental disapproval would not undo her contract to John Wystow to whom she was lawfully 'handfast'. She told her father, 'I desire no more of your goods but your blessyng.'[31]

Probably few women were prepared to stand up to parental authority and to sacrifice material gain to get their own way in marriage after the manner of Margery Paston or Elena Couper. Prescriptive literature tended to back parents and undermine the opportunities open to daughters for unsupervised courtship. The Knight of La Tour-Landry advised, through the persona of his wife, that if a man attempted to talk of love to a young woman, she 'shalle voyde and breke his talkynge'. Elsewhere he advised, 'doughtres, be ware, as ye wol kepe youre honoure and worshippe both, bethe never allone with no manere of man'. The Goodwife likewise directed her daughter to consult her friends, i.e. family, before responding to any offer of matrimony, but also to shun too close contact with a lover lest her reputation be thus besmirched. Peter Idley, writing for his son, cited Paul as an authority for the dangers inherent in men being alone with women and elsewhere warned women that men will privately promise marriage in order to seduce them. The duty of a virtuous daughter was to obey her parents and to preserve her reputation, implicitly understood in sexual terms and

---

[31] *Ibid.*, CP.F.280.

predicated upon the supposed frailty and thus vulnerability to seduction of woman as the daughter of Eve. When William Shirwod of York was asked if he would permit his daughter to marry Walter Lematon to whom she was already handfast, he replied, 'She shall never be maried bot wher me list.'[32]

Other daughters correctly made their consent to contracts of marriage conditional upon the approval of their fathers or guardians. Thus Agnes Fraunceys said of Andrew Kellum, 'I Will have hym to my Husband if my Fadir will assent' and Agnes Ruke agreed to marry John Porter if he were able to obtain her uncle's goodwill. Godfrey Grene likewise wrote to Sir William Plumpton that his sister, whose hand was sought by a London mercer, told her mistress 'that of her selfe she could nott ne wold nothing do without the advise of you and her freinds, but whatsoever my lady thought she shold do, she wold do it unwitting you or any of her freinds'. Paternal authority was even given symbolic expression in the giving of the daughter in marriage. When in 1474 Elizabeth Pereson of Cawood contracted Adam Pryngill in her parents' home, it was her father who took her by the right hand and gave her away.[33]

The daughter who deviated from this normative ideal was akin to the prostitute. The mother of Elena Couper addressed her as 'thow filth and harlot' when she heard of her engagement. Margaret Paston's language is unlikely to have been any more restrained. What is especially difficult to assess, however, is the attitude to marriage formation that this normative ideal tends to conceal. Most daughters probably accepted that they had some responsibility to consult their parents about their choice of marriage partner just as most parents who would have preferred to have arranged their daughters' marriages probably would have backed down in the face of actual hostility; although it is likely that the more families were concerned with issues of succession, the descent of property and the forging of dynastic alliances, the more they would have demanded compliance from their daughters. This may have been especially true of gentry and aristocratic families, but also of substantial peasant families. This was the social order that an essentially aristocratic text like *The Book of the Knight of La Tour-Landry* was designed to uphold. Where daughters left home to work or take up positions as servants, they were able to engage in courtship free from parental supervision and appear thus to have enjoyed a greater initiative in terms of courtship and ultimately marriage. It is in reaction to this potentially subversive freedom that *How the Good Wijf taughte Hir Doughtir* was written. Had the Goodwife's daughter really been at home with her mother, the cosy formula adopted by the (presumably male?) author, then the text would have been redundant.

Marriage was justified, following Paul, in terms of the need to contain carnal desire within lawful bounds. It was also justified as a means by which children might be begotten. The theory of reproduction derived from Galen held that both the male and the female produced sperm. This followed from the belief that the female reproductive

[32] Wright (ed.), *La Tour-Landry*, pp. 57, 78, 176; BIHR, CP.F.261.
[33] BIHR, CP.F.84, 176, 256A; Stapleton (ed.), *Plumpton Correspondence*, p. 11.

organs were essentially analogous to the male, but were internal as a further consequence of the lesser heat associated with the development of the female. Thus the womb was likened to an inverse penis and the ovaries were then referred to as the female testicles. It was these female testicles that were believed to produce sperm that was transmitted to the uterus through the Fallopian tubes. Conception was thought to result from the mixing of the male and female sperm ejaculated during intercourse. It followed that, since sexual pleasure was necessary to stimulate the emission of seed for both women and men, conception could not occur unless the woman took pleasure from the act of coitus. The implications of this were mixed. If the church pursued the line that the principal purpose of marriage was the begetting of children, then medicine dictated that pleasure in love-making for both parties was essential to conception. On the other hand, a woman was thought to be unable to conceive as a consequence of rape; a woman who became pregnant following an alleged rape would not be believed. Similarly it was argued that prostitutes rarely conceived since they engaged in sex for money and not for pleasure.

The female seed was naturally colder and thus less active than that of the male. The sex of the child thus conceived would be determined by the heat of the combined seed. Galen associated heat with the right side of the body and cold with the left. The blood reaching both the left testicle and the left part of the womb was believed to be less pure, and hence colder, than that which came direct from the liver and supplied the right testicle and right part of the womb. A female child would thus be conceived from seed drawn from the man's left testicle and mixed with the woman's seed deposited in the left half of the womb. Knowledge of contraception or abortifacients certainly existed, but was regarded as contrary to the purpose of marriage and hence sinful. Prolonged breastfeeding, which was the normal practice among women below the rank of the aristocracy, probably provided a more effective means of limiting fertility. According to Paul, however, 'woman will be saved through bearing children' and for the Knight of La Tour-Landry childbirth was the greatest reward of a good wife. He cites the Biblical examples of Elizabeth, Sarah, Rebecca, Leah and the paradigm Mary, 'the most meke and humble of all creatoures', as women whose piety was rewarded in childbirth.[34] Depictions in church art of the families of Anne, Mary Salome and Mary Cleophas provided a positive image of motherhood, but may have been provided by male patrons to just this end. If may thus be easy to be deceived by the maternal imagery associated with the cult of the Holy Family; it is hardly possible to know how women themselves regarded childbirth. For Margery Kempe at least it was not a happy experience. Childbirth was, however, one of the few areas of women's lives over which women had effective control. Midwives were exclusively female and the mother was attended only by women at her delivery.

According to the Knight of La Tour-Landry, Rachel lost her child because she failed to give God due thanks. A proper sense of piety was instilled from an early age. It has

---

[34] 1 Timothy 2.15; Wright (ed.), *La Tour-Landry*, p. 110.

17   Childbirth

already been seen that an integral part of women's education was the learning of 'vertuous thinges of the scripture'. The first thing the Goodwife taught her daughter was to 'love god and holi chirche' and to 'go to chirche whanne thou may'. The notion that women were by nature more given to piety than men can be found in some high medieval sources. Paul taught that wives could convert their husbands by their example. Charity, which was central to late medieval pious practice, seems to have been an attribute particularly associated with women. Aristotle, as already noted, thought women by nature more compassionate than men; the Knight of La Tour-Landry observed by way of corollary that 'a woman that is not humble and pitous she is mannishe and not womanly, whiche is a vice in womanhode'. Didactic writers, however, saw concern for the poor, the sick and the homeless more in terms of a womanly duty. The Knight of La Tour-Landry wrote that 'the plesaunce of all goode women aught to be to visite and fede the pore and faderles children, and to norshe and clothe yong litell children . . . '. The Goodwife likewise taught her daughter to give of her own goods to the poor and the bedridden. The virtuous wife of Proverbs who 'opens her hands to the poor, and reaches out her hands to the needy' was again the model to which women were taught to aspire, though other models were provided by a number of women saints. Two who enjoyed particular popularity in the fifteenth century were Anne, the mother of Mary, and Zita of Lucca, the servant saint, known locally as Sitha. Anne, who seems to have had a particular following among well-to-do householders, was said to have helped her husband Joachim divide their income such that a third went 'to widows and childer fadyrlesse and other pouer at lay'.[35] St Sitha, whose gift of bread to the poor miraculously turned to flowers upon being challenged by her master, commemorated in her attribute of a loaf turned to flowers, probably enjoyed a following among female servants and householders.

Female householders seem to have been particularly associated with the giving of alms, often in the form of a dole of food or drink, at the door of their homes and in offering shelter for the destitute. Women also provided fuel to poor neighbours. Agnes Grantham, for example, a devout York widow, was said to have provided 'alms to the poor by bringing them wood, fuel and other necessaries'.[36] It may also be that some women comforted and nursed sick friends and neighbours out of charity. Margery Kempe seems to have practised this form of piety and on one occasion helped a woman recover from post-natal psychosis. These forms of charity are extensions of the roles women were expected to perform as householders; women were providers of food and fuel and they were also expected to nurse sick members of the household. Though women were effectively excluded from academic medicine, knowledge of the healing properties of herbs and of a variety of remedies may have been expected of women householders. In some instances women may even have possessed medical texts; the English translation of the gynaecological treatise known as *Trotula* was specifically aimed at a female audience. Women also found more formal employment as sick nurses or in hospitals.

This brief survey of fifteenth-century English attitudes in relation to women has necessarily been very much concerned with (primarily aristocratic and bourgeois) male attitudes, but it is evident that these did much to shape women's lives. If on the one hand women were believed to be more malleable, easier to instruct, then on the other they were easily led, fickle, liable to go astray especially in sexual matters. Fathers and husbands alike believed that they had a moral responsibility to exercise a high degree of supervision over the lives of their daughters and wives to keep them virtuous and

---

[35] Mustanoja (ed.), *Good Wife*, p. 197 (line 2); 1 Peter 3.1–2; Wright (ed.), *La Tour-Landry*, pp. 29, 117, 136; R. E. Parker (ed.), *The Middle English Stanzaic Versions of the Life of St Anne*, EETS 174 (1927), p. 2 (lines 44–5).

[36] BIHR, CP.F.36.

dutiful. This took the form not just of legal subordination, economic dependence or physical chastisement, but the more insidious constraint of reputation. Once again, reputation was understood in terms of sexuality. Reputations were fragile and could be broken by mere slander. The binary polarity of the virtuous wife and the whore allowed little middle ground and thus the fall from virtue was swift. Ideology was, however, challenged by experience. The earlier fifteenth century especially allowed some women an unusual freedom to support themselves in employment and to make their own decisions regarding marriage. Only with economic recession later in the century were patriarchal values most forcefully articulated and most strongly felt. It was against this background, for example, that the weavers of Hull excluded women from the craft in 1490 and the civic authorities in Coventry attempted to force single women into positions of dependency in 1492.

□
8
□

URBAN SOCIETY

D. M. Palliser

In 1483, writing his account of Richard III's usurpation, Dominic Mancini concluded with an interesting if largely irrelevant account of London for the benefit of his readers: 'she is so famous throughout the world', he said in justification. In 1497 another Italian, writing an account of England for the Venetian Senate, also stressed the wealth and importance of London, but was curt about other towns – there were 'scarcely any towns of importance' except Bristol and York.[1] It is understandable that Italians should have paid respect to London but to few other towns: at that period about eleven Italian cities (including Venice) boasted over 40,000 inhabitants, but in England only London qualified. Yet if England was less urbanized and less commercialized than northern Italy, its towns were by no means insignificant. Perhaps one in forty of the English population lived in London, and one in ten in towns as a whole, and they had in any case an importance out of proportion to their size. Politically, London in particular played a decisive role in coming to terms with new monarchs – in 1461, 1483 and 1485 – and even Coventry and York proved worth wooing during the dynastic struggles. Economically and socially also, the towns played an important part in the life of the nation.

In 1972 the fifteenth century was called 'the Dark Age of English urban historiography', and attention was drawn to the scarcity of work on provincial urban society in particular.[2] Though much work has since been published, it has been largely on the economic, rather than social, history of towns. Yet, as Susan Reynolds rightly put it in writing of the earlier middle ages,

> The problems of when and why towns started to grow and what they lived off are not only economic ones. They are also social. What sort of people formed urban communities and what sort of communities did they form? How far did townspeople, their communities, their way of life, and their values, differ from those outside? Medieval records are more or less inadequate to answer such questions, which require accurate and full statistics on the one hand and plenty of personal papers on the other, but unless we make some attempt to consider them our talk of such subjects as urban liberties and the policies of

---

[1] C. A. J. Armstrong (ed.), *The Usurpation of Richard the Third* (Gloucester, 1984), p. 101; C. A. Sneyd (ed.), *A Relation, or rather a True Account, of the Island of England*, Camden Soc., old series 37 (1847), p. 41.
[2] P. Clark and P. Slack (eds.), *Crisis and Order in English Towns 1500–1700* (1972), pp. 8, 44 (n. 29).

town governments, as well as of townspeople themselves, will sink into a morass of unexplored assumptions about the communities which won the liberties and made the policies.[3]

For the fifteenth century sources are less inadequate than for earlier periods, even though not as full as might be wished, and it is at least possible to attempt to answer some of her questions. In particular, it is important to ask who formed urban communities, and how far those communities were distinct from rural ones. These are issues of some disagreement at present. Reynolds herself has said that an 'essential attribute of the town is that it forms a social unit more or less distinct from the surrounding countryside', while Maryanne Kowaleski states that 'Towns differed physically, economically, *socially*, and legally from the rural and feudal worlds.' On the other hand, Michael Lynch and others have recently expressed scepticism about Reynolds's 'social unit' definition, at least for Scottish towns, while Rosemary Horrox has argued for England that 'town and country were not separate worlds, between which a choice had to be made, but integrated elements of a single society'.[4] Before attempting to consider these alternative judgements, however, it may be helpful to review briefly the basic nature of English towns in the fifteenth century.

I

London itself was one of the great cities of Europe, as the Italian visitors conceded, with a population of 40,000–50,000, judged by the poll tax returns of 1377. The same returns, however, suggest only some 15,000 in York, the next largest, and altogether only about thirteen towns with over 5,000 people, and another twenty-seven with between 2,000 and 5,000. Even those, small by our standards, were the *large* towns of England; below them were well over 500 small market towns with populations of perhaps 500 to 2,000, which collectively comprised perhaps as much as half of the urban population. However, comparing their sizes to modern towns and deciding that they were scarcely urban would be erroneous. The larger towns were often as crowded as modern ones, if not more so, partly because their inhabitants chose to live close together within protecting walls. Keene has calculated that the heart of Winchester (the aldermanry of High Street) had a density of eighty persons per acre around 1400, about double the density of present-day Chelsea or Kensington, while, even more startlingly, one central York parish had a density of eighty *taxpayers* per acre, which would have given it about four times the Chelsea density.[5] Furthermore, even the small market towns were larger than contemporary villages, and more complex in their social and

---

[3] S. Reynolds, *An Introduction to the History of English Medieval Towns* (Oxford, 1977), p. 66.

[4] *Ibid.*, p. ix; M. Kowaleski, 'The history of urban families in medieval England', *Journal of Medieval History* 14 (1988), 58; M. Lynch *et al.*, *The Scottish Medieval Town* (Edinburgh, 1988), p. 1; R. Horrox, 'The urban gentry in the fifteenth century', in J. A. F. Thomson (ed.), *Towns and Townspeople in the Fifteenth Century* (Gloucester, 1988), p. 36.

[5] D. Keene, *Survey of Medieval Winchester* (2 vols., Oxford, 1985), I, p. 370; M. W. Beresford and J. K. S. St Joseph, *Medieval England: An Aerial Survey* (Cambridge, 2nd edn, 1979), p. 176.

economic structure. Towns differed from villages in that a significant proportion of their inhabitants did not work in agriculture, and in acting as centres for their rural hinterlands via markets, fairs and shops, providing goods and manufactures in exchange for foodstuffs and raw materials. Nor should we neglect their administrative and cultural facilities: towns were centres of royal and ecclesiastical government, of medicine and education, of pilgrimages and processions, of plays and pageants, and, for that matter, of prostitution.

These combined activities meant that towns influenced the whole population of England in one way or another. Many countryfolk came regularly to town, and even the smallest places with a market – dubbed 'market villages' rather than towns by some historians – were temporarily transformed one day every week. In the larger towns day visitors and temporary residents also played a major role. London and Westminster were periodically swollen by visitors attending the royal court, law courts or parliaments; while Oxford and Cambridge had of course their seasonal inflows of students. The Stonor, Cely and Paston letters abound with requests to relatives to make use of London visits for shopping. A rare statistical measure is provided by York in 1537, preparing for a royal visit. This city of some 8,000 souls (it had shrunk by nearly half since 1377) had available 1,035 beds for visitors and stabling for 1,711 horses, over and above accommodation in the ecclesiastical liberties and in the homes of aldermen and merchants.[6]

Nor was it only a matter of short-term visitors. Most towns probably had an unhealthy 'natural deficit' of births over deaths, so that immigration on a considerable scale was needed to keep them stable in size. Towns may have had higher 'normal' mortality rates than the countryside, especially the larger towns with populations crammed inside walls, and living conditions in their centres may have been as crowded, uncomfortable and insanitary as in the worst periods of the Industrial Revolution. There was, in addition, epidemic mortality, which may also have been worst in the towns, especially the frequent outbreaks of bubonic plague. The consequences of epidemics included, as in Tudor and Stuart times, flight to the countryside by the prosperous. Richard Cely reported in 1479 that 'the sekenese ys sore yn London werefor meche pepyll of the sete [city] ys yn to the contre fur fere of the sekenese'.[7] This must have been more than counterbalanced, however, by the rural inflow *after* epidemics, as dead men's (and women's) shoes were filled.

Towns varied considerably in their government as well as in their size and their economy, and this is not without relevance for a consideration of their social life. Most of the larger centres had acquired some measure of self-government by 1400, usually involving a privileged class of burgesses or freemen who chose annually elected officers

---

[6] *Letters and Papers, Foreign and Domestic, of the Reign of Henry VIII* (22 vols., 1864–1922), XII (2), no. 22; Addenda I (I), no. 1192; D. M. Palliser, *Tudor York* (Oxford, 1979) p. 166 and n.

[7] H. E. Malden (ed.), *The Cely Papers*, Camden Soc., 3rd series I (1900), p. 16. A London chronicler reported 'an huge mortalyte' in 1479–80: S. L. Thrupp, *The Merchant Class of Medieval London* (Chicago, 1948), p. 201.

18   An urban street scene

and councillors. A common pattern was a mayor and twelve aldermen, usually assisted by a junior council. From 1345 some of the most important towns received royal grants of incorporation, while from 1373 a very few were made counties corporate, being exempted completely from interference by the sheriff and justices of the peace of the surrounding county. On the other hand, some quite important towns, and many small market towns, acquired little or no independence, especially those 'mesne boroughs' which had a lord other than the king. Salisbury and Beverley were largely under the thumb of bishops, and St Albans and Bury St Edmunds under abbots, while Manchester and Birmingham remained under the control of rural manor courts. Furthermore, even large cities did not always have jurisdictions that coincided with their built-up areas. Lincoln, Norwich and York all received crown grants of rural manors within their urban liberties, but conversely all three had areas within their walls exempt from the jurisdiction of their corporations – in each case the castle was controlled by the county sheriff and the cathedral close by the dean and chapter, while the monasteries and friaries were also exempt from city jurisdiction. All of these varied jurisdictions affected social life, groupings and loyalties: townsmen and women without self-government developed fraternities and guilds to by-pass the power of their lords, while townspeople in a city honeycombed with exempt liberties could use them as sanctuaries and loopholes beyond the reach of the city fathers. In York, for instance, the cordwainers' journeymen tried meeting in friaries to avoid the power of their masters, and in the troubled 1470s one alderman moved with his whole household into the Dominican friary for protection against a rival faction.

II

What sort of people lived within these very varied urban communities? Perhaps the first point to note is that many were probably first- or second-generation immigrants. Sylvia Thrupp calculated that London's aldermen and merchants were barely able to maintain their numbers by natural replacement, especially in the period 1377–1437, and although her figures have been questioned in detail, there is no reason to doubt her conclusion that the class could not have maintained its numbers without immigration – and this class was, of course, among the better-off and better-nourished part of the population. There are, unfortunately, no surviving London freemen registers to confirm the extent of immigration, but comparable records do survive for a few towns. The Romney jurats' accounts, for instance, give the birthplace of all freemen, and although nearly half came from within a radius of five miles, others were drawn from all parts of east Kent and about one quarter came from over fifty miles away. Larger towns would tend to draw over a wider distance. The less precise evidence of surnames, for the previous century, suggests that about half of all migrants into York and Norwich came from over twenty miles away, and for London the figure rises to half from over forty miles. More precisely, although for a limited group, an amazing 46 per cent of London skinners' and tailors' apprentices in the 1480s and 1490s came from the north of England. Similarly, men of all social levels except noblemen and paupers seem to have taken up apprenticeships in London. If Richard Whittington was – despite later legend – the third son of a knight and lord of a manor, there were many others whose fathers were yeomen, husbandmen, craftsmen and even villeins. That London companies often took poor-born apprentices is suggested by the city's opposition to a statute of 1406 which made it illegal to take apprentices from families with less than 20s annual income from lands or rents.

The extreme case of immigration was that of the aliens – foreigners from overseas – who were a permanent feature of English town life, especially in London. They ranged from well-to-do Italian and Hanseatic merchants to artisans and servants, and we can estimate their numbers because in 1440 the crown instituted a tax on aliens. Sporadic returns survive from 1441 to 1484, the only national surveys of immigrants that survive for any European state from such an early period. Taking London, Westminster and the suburbs together, there were about 2,200 (excluding married women) in 1441, most of them 'Dutch' (Germans and Netherlanders), and perhaps 3,000 men, women and children in 1501. Other towns also had significant colonies: Winchester's aliens, for example, may have comprised 3 per cent of the city's population in 1440.

It should be stressed that a continuous influx of immigrants did not prevent urban societies from cohering as social units. On the contrary, so far as can be seen, immigrants were quick to intermarry with established urban families, while many immigrants were related to those already living in the towns. The evidence chiefly relates to the merchants and leading craftsmen, but it does clearly suggest that population mobility did not prevent urban communities cohering through ties of marriage and kinship. Thus in London, 'The country line of the virile family of Frowyks twice reared three sons . . . and each time one of the three entered the mercers' company',[8] while for York, Hull and Beverley complex genealogies have been traced linking many of the main merchant families through marriage and remarriage.

This is not the place to discuss the changing population totals of fifteenth-century towns, and their relationship to economic prosperity or decline, thorny issues which have been the subject of vigorous debate. It is clear, however, that population totals did vary widely, with considerable social as well as economic consequences. Thus Colchester seems to have grown from below 3,000 around 1350 to a peak of over 8,000 around 1414; it then fell by at least one third over the following century. Similarly, Coventry may have reached 10,000 or more by the 1430s, but a census of 1523 recorded only 5,699. One consequence of such fluctuations may well have been changes in the status of women. P. J. P. Goldberg, drawing on evidence from northern towns and particularly York, has noted that the demand for labour in the early fifteenth century, especially for female servants, allowed women to choose paid employment instead of early marriage, whereas after the mid-century economic recession both narrowed their economic opportunities and encouraged men to try to exclude female competition for jobs. In consequence, by the end of the century, more women were marrying and probably at younger ages.[9] York was perhaps untypical in the degree of its economic decline, but Goldberg has extended his analysis to a wide range of towns and found the same pattern.

---

[8] Thrupp, *Merchant Class*, pp. 231–2, 342–3.

[9] P. J. P. Goldberg, 'Female labour, service and marriage in the late medieval urban north', *Northern History* 22 (1986), 18–38; *idem*, 'Marriage, migration, servanthood and life-cycle in Yorkshire towns of the later middle ages', *Continuity and Change* 1 (1986), 141–69. Since this essay was written P. J. P. Goldberg's book on medieval women has appeared: *Women, Work and Life Cycle in a Medieval Economy: Women in York and Yorkshire c. 1300–1520* (Oxford, 1992).

The basic unit of society, whether in town or country, was the household, consisting of those living together in one dwelling – sometimes a single person or simple family group, but in other cases including lodgers, apprentices or living-in servants. The urban household may have been smaller than its rural counterpart, whether because of mobility, late marriage or high mortality. The Coventry census of 1523 shows that mean household size was under four, and although that city was perhaps exceptional in its degree of decline and depopulation, the figure is in line with those for continental cities of the fifteenth century. The Coventry census also reveals that household size usually correlated with wealth, from 7.4 among the merchants down to 2.6 for cottagers and 1.8 for paupers.

Coventrians drew a clear distinction between householders and cottagers, assuming 'that a household comprised a larger entity than that living in a cottage, basically because the former included, or could include, either in-servants or out-servants'. Cottages were often one-roomed, whereas houses included at least a hall and solar, and often a workshop fronting the street.

> There was thus a fundamental division, not often commented upon by historians, between . . . those whose dwellings were deserted daily by the menfolk, and probably any others of their families who were old enough to go out to work; and . . . those homes where the inmates both lived and worked together with, in some cases, daily outside additions . . . The living and working areas of houses had . . . to be larger to accommodate more people.[10]

In other words, just as towns experienced daily fluctuations in their populations, with the influx of visitors to markets, courts or pageants, so too did houses within the towns experience daily fluctuations in their inhabitants.

It has already been remarked that the population densities in at least the larger towns could be very high indeed, especially when town walls restricted expansion, and the crowding called for different approaches to housing from those necessary in villages. Pantin's pioneer analysis of late medieval town-house plans drew attention to the way in which many houses were built at right angles to the street to economize on valuable frontages, while even the more spacious plots with halls parallel to the street often incorporated commercial premises to let along the street frontage. The considerable research on medieval urban housing over the past thirty years has refined but not essentially changed that picture. In addition to crowding more buildings on to plots, houses in the larger towns were often extended upwards; at York, for example, most fourteenth-century houses were of two storeys, whereas in the fifteenth century three-storey framed buildings became very common. It is true that not all towns conformed to this crowded pattern. In Colchester and Durham houses remained little different from those in surrounding villages, mainly small, single-storey and thatched. Yet in

---

[10] C. Phythian-Adams, *Desolation of a City: Coventry and the Urban Crisis of the Late Middle Ages* (Cambridge, 1979), pp. 80, 81.

either case towns were affected by the freedom of their burgesses to buy, sell and bequeath property freely, which made for a more complex pattern of landholding than the rural norm.

The household, to say it again, was the basic unit of the social, political and economic structure. The 'householder' (usually a man, but widows could also head households) was answerable to his or her neighbours, fellow-craftsmen or town councillors for his or her dependants. It was not a patriarchal system; the norm, then as now, was a conjugal family, and when a father died the children did not go to his kin, but accompanied their mother on her remarriage and became step-children to a new 'father'. Much of this applied equally to urban and rural society, but what was distinctive about many self-governing towns was that borough law deviated considerably from common law, often over what we would now call family law: inheritance customs, widows' rights and so on. For example, burgages could be freely devised by will and did not have to pass to the eldest son, while in many boroughs partible inheritance gave daughters equal rights of inheritance with sons. Some towns maintained separate courts of orphans to safeguard the estates of burgess families. However, it is not clear to what extent such borough law applied only to full citizens or property owners. That leads on to another major difference between town and country: the institutional difference between burgesses and the rest of the urban population.

III

Some 600 towns were called boroughs in late medieval England, and most of them were distinguished by a privileged group of inhabitants called burgesses (or, in cities, citizens) holding their dwellings by burgage tenure: a tenure with a fixed money rent and the right to bequeath or sell them freely. In the self-governing towns, the burgesses usually had exclusive political and economic power, often under the alternative name of freemen. They normally had a monopoly of running businesses or shops as merchants or master craftsmen; they alone could take part in elections and in borough government. All other inhabitants, as well as countryfolk coming into town, were called foreigns or foreigners, and were restricted in trading and in politics. At Canterbury, for instance, only freemen could by custom 'come to the council of the city and there speak and be heard', and at Leicester from 1466 only freemen could 'enter the guild hall . . . at any common hall held there'.[11] This division between burgesses and 'foreigns' was perhaps the most fundamental in urban society – more fundamental even than the undoubted inequality of men and women – and is reflected in the fact that many towns kept careful records of those admitted to the franchise. Freedom was both an obligation and a privilege: those eligible were expected to take it up, usually by one of three recognized routes (inheritance, apprenticeship or purchase), especially so as to take their share of the financial burdens of running the town. They had also to be

---

[11] A. R. Myers (ed.), *English Historical Documents 1327–1485* (1969), pp. 569–70, 575.

careful not to forfeit their privileged status by defying the town council or flouting its regulations.

The freeman class should not, however, be thought of as a small minority dominating an unfree majority. Freemen in London and York numbered perhaps one in three of all adult males, and in Coventry they were in a majority of four out of five. Nor should we envisage a monolithic freeman 'class' in most towns facing resentment from the excluded 'foreigns', since most freemen had loyalties to craft guilds or companies which were often divided from one another.

That is not to say that there were not real divisions among townspeople, based on wide inequalities. By and large, one can generalize about a twofold or three-fold division into powerful, middling and lesser townsfolk – not by imposing modern viewpoints but by reflecting contemporary perceptions. Thus Lynn's municipal records speak consistently of the *potentiores*, *mediocres* and *inferiores*. Between 1411 and 1418 the hold of the *potentiores* upon government and finance was challenged, and eventually the *mediocres* (although not the *inferiores*) achieved a share of power. At Lincoln, similarly, townsmen were characterized as great, middling (*secondarii*) and lesser. At Beverley, however, the townsmen were conventionally divided into two. The bitter struggle there in 1381–2 was described as one of the *menes comunes* against the *potentiores* or *bones gentz*, while in the more orderly circumstances of 1411 an agreement on Corpus Christi pageants was made 'for the peaceful union of the worthier and lesser commons'.[12] Such groups have often been interpreted as economic class divisions – between, say, merchants and independent craftsmen, and dependent craftsmen or labourers – but towns varied greatly in the proportions and importance of merchants and craftsmen, and it may be better to view such distinctions as distinctions of wealth and status rather than of occupation.

At the apex of urban society were usually two overlapping groups, merchants and gentry, who formed the core of the *potentiores*. Merchants by this period had come to signify wholesale traders in mixed goods, usually but not exclusively overseas traders. London was dominated by up to eleven merchant companies; most provincial towns had only one, though a few other groups of prosperous traders and craftsmen, notably drapers and goldsmiths, might be counted as equal to merchants in status. The greater merchants were often treated as equivalent in status to rural gentry; when one London chronicler wrote of 'many ryche marchaunts and comeners' he seemed to mean that the wealthier merchants were gentle and not commoners. There were also, as Rosemary Horrox has emphasized, true urban gentry by this period, whether genuinely landed gentry choosing to live in towns, or an emergent class of bureaucrats and professional men.[13] Of thirty-two bailiffs of Colchester between 1460 and

---

[12] Humberside County Record Office, BC II/3, fol. 12v; A. F. Leach (ed.), *Beverley Town Documents*, Selden Soc. 14 (1900), p. 34.
[13] Thrupp, *Merchant Class*, p. 294; Horrox, 'The urban gentry'.

19   Loading a ship at the quayside

1499, five were gentlemen with no involvement in commerce. The greater part of town councils was made up of men described as merchants, with a leavening of gentlemen and craftsmen; to such an extent that the government of towns is often described as a 'mercantile oligarchy'. Some recent writers have described merchants as forming a distinct 'class' which dominated society and government of the towns, but that may be misleading. Fifteenth-century townsfolk seem to have stratified themselves largely by wealth and not by occupation; 'more able' and 'less able' described the ability to pay taxes and to support the town financially. It is true that the majority of the rich in the larger towns tended to be merchants, but in the smaller towns they were often craftsmen, and even wealth was no more the sole yardstick than occupation. Other factors like blood and respectability played a part; some towns explicitly debarred adulterers from office, while some debarred men like innkeepers as having occupations which were not sufficiently respectable.

IV

Given the enormous inequalities of wealth, status and privilege within towns, and the close links between townspeople and countryfolk, how far can the towns be regarded as separate communities? How far did townspeople regard themselves as distinct from countryfolk, and how far did they create a sense of shared identity within the town? At one level, that of urban gentry and greater merchants, it is indeed valid to think of town and country as 'not separate worlds . . . but integrated elements of a single society'. That is the level described, for early modern England, by Peter Laslett, in which a nation-wide class of gentlemen co-existed with separate local communities of commoners; for the leading merchants and town gentry were not typical members of urban societies. Those urban societies were, in the fifteenth century, often sharply divided, but coherent urban communities can still exist despite serious internal divisions.

The larger towns were certainly controlled by minorities of citizens and freemen, but they were often large minorities. Large crowds of citizens could take an active part in decision making, at least on special occasions. In London such assemblies were apparently limited by the size of the Guildhall, and the largest attendance recorded was 528 in 1340; but then London, with its unique size, had its structure of local wardmotes in which many other citizens could take part. In other towns substantial proportions of the adult male population could gather in a single place to ratify important decisions – 239 named persons, for instance, at Lincoln in 1421.[14] Even so, to integrate the whole population of a town into feeling part of the community required further mechanisms: households, craft fellowships, guilds, councils, social strata, extended families and geographical groupings. They were particularly important for women, who could frequently, through them, play an active part in their communities. Two levels can perhaps be distinguished: small geographical sub-divisions of towns, and those associations straddling the town as a whole.

At least in the larger towns, the geographical sub-divisions were generally the parishes, which were remarkably numerous – over a hundred in London, over fifty in Norwich and forty in York. If we regard them socially and not only ecclesiastically, they look like urban villages, and it may be that in a large urban community men and women could feel socially at ease only in village-sized sub-divisions. The localism of towns-people is clear from many instances: in York one witness from Petergate claimed not to know others dwelling in Bootham or St Sampson's parish because they were 'remote', while a rich widow left money for a funeral feast for 'my nebours from Stanegait ende to Bothome bar'.[15] Such neighbours could worship and organize together through their parish churches, as well as meeting in one another's homes. One characteristic late medieval institution was the parish guild or fraternity, whose

---

[14] Lincolnshire Archives Office, White Book of Lincoln, fols. 2v, 3.
[15] J. S. Purvis, *A Mediaeval Act Book* (York, n.d.), p. 27; D. M. Palliser, 'Civic mentality and the environment in Tudor York', *Northern History* 18 (1982), 112.

members met in the church and which acted as clubs or friendly societies as well as providing masses. They could serve as a vehicle for the humble as well as the powerful; indeed the guild of St Michael on the Hill at Lincoln was explicitly founded by 'common and middling folks' and its statutes required it to admit applicants of the same rank (*ejusdem status*) as the brothers and sisters who founded it.[16] The parish guilds played a vital part in the strength of late medieval communities, in towns as well as in the countryside.

Confusingly, the term 'guild' and 'fraternity' were used very widely – so much so that the term 'guild' means little more than the late medieval equivalent of 'committee'. In addition to parish guilds, urban examples included at least two different types with membership town-wide: the economic crafts and the socio-religious fraternities, although the same sort of language could be used to describe either; for instance, Henry VI incorporated the London drapers as the Guild or Fraternity of the Blessed Virgin Mary. Crafts were associations of traders and craftsmen with an ostensibly occupational basis – merchants, tailors, brewers, bakers and so on – and have usually been seen as having primarily economic aims, although Heather Swanson has suggested that they were often arbitrarily grouped together by town councils for political control rather than economic organization. There is some truth in this – certainly in London and the large towns crafts were not confined to men dealing in one commodity – but either way the crafts also formed *social* organizations, since they encompassed activities beyond the economic. It was usual, for instance, for crafts to require members to attend each other's weddings and funerals.

Beyond these, there were growing numbers of socio-religious fraternities which drew members from all occupations. In Coventry, for instance, the leading guilds were those of Corpus Christi and Holy Trinity, which organized processions and banquets as well as religious services. In general, Corpus Christi was the preserve of wealthy young craftsmen and older middling craftsmen; the wealthiest tended to gravitate to the Trinity Guild in mid-career. These are exceptional cases from a major city, but in most towns guilds required at least a degree of economic independence and social respectability; even the 'poor people's guild' in St Augustine's parish, Norwich, was not open to all. It could therefore be argued that many urban guilds, while welcoming recruits from virtually all occupations, both sexes or most social levels, were divisive within the towns. In compensation, they often helped to create bonds between a market town and its region; thus Stratford's Holy Cross Guild numbered many members from surrounding villages, and guild membership gave them a recognized status in Stratford when they came there to trade. Indeed, one might go so far as to say that these men and women thereby became part of Stratford's urban society.

---

[16] Lucy Toulmin Smith (ed.), *English Gilds*, Early English Text Soc., orig. series 40 (1870), p. 178 and n.; F. Hill, *Medieval Lincoln* (Cambridge, 1965), p. 298; Myers (ed.), *Historical Documents*, p. 1068.

D. M. PALLISER

V

Town communities, therefore, were bonded together in all kinds of ways which made them more than collections of individuals. They were also *aware* of themselves as urban communities, in some important ways separate from their rural hinterlands and often self-consciously proud of themselves. The evidence for this pride and self-awareness is abundant, especially for the larger towns with self-government and chartered rights. For one thing, although the leading towns had often enjoyed some degree of self-government since the twelfth or thirteenth centuries, and had generated administrative records to cope, it was often only in the late fourteenth century, and especially the fifteenth century, that they compiled more self-conscious records which codified their liberties and reflected on how they should be governed: sources like London's *Liber Albus*, *Ricart's Kalendar* at Bristol, Northampton's *Liber Custumarum* and the custumal compiled by a former mayor of Lincoln about 1480. Colchester and Bristol even copied London in producing town chronicles – a commonplace in Italy and the Empire, but a rarity among the smaller towns of England. Furthermore, many towns strove to acquire privileges and liberties by charter, or to extend those they already had, often taking advantage of the weakness of the crown between the 1440s and 1480s to do so. The coveted status of formal incorporation, first claimed by Coventry in 1345, was awarded to only ten towns by 1440, but to another thirty by 1490. In a few of these cases kings were persuaded to add the ultimate privilege of making the town or city into a 'county corporate', separate from its county. Henry VI granted this to Hull (1440), Southampton (1447), Nottingham (1449) and Coventry (1451); Edward IV to Canterbury (1461); and Richard III to Gloucester (1483) and even to Scarborough (1485), although the last was not confirmed by Henry VII.

Towns also advertised themselves in public building as well as in charters and chronicles. It is well known that many built or rebuilt a town hall ('Common' or 'Guild' Hall) in this period, from London, York and Norwich down to Thaxted or Stratford. 'Most of the evidence at present available', notes R. B. Dobson, 'points to the first fifty or sixty years of the fifteenth century as a time of a veritable boom in the building or rebuilding of town halls', and he characterizes the boom, at least for the larger towns, as 'the material expression of that late medieval transition from urban community to urban corporation'.[17] A great stress was also laid on town walls, not just for military purposes but as symbols of pride; they featured on many urban seals, and they might be completed (as at Coventry) well after threats of real disorder had receded, simply because a major city was expected to have an imposing circuit. In most walled towns a clear distinction was made between the 'town' or 'city' proper and the extramural suburbs, and when a monarch was received on a formal progress, as Henry VII was at York in 1486, he was welcomed ceremonially at the city gate as well as at the city boundary.

---

[17] R. B. Dobson, 'Urban decline in late medieval England', reprinted in R. Holt and G. Rosser (eds.), *The Medieval Town* (1990), p. 272.

It has already been noted that there was no sharp distinction between town notables and rural gentry; nevertheless, the rulers of towns could, in the event of a clash with rural or national notables, stand on their dignity on behalf of their separate urban communities. The mayor of London was, within the city, second only to the king. When one mayor, invited to a legal feast, found that the earl of Worcester had been given the place of honour, he promptly withdrew, and had an even more magnificent banquet served in his house. When a local gentleman contemptuously described a York alderman as 'a carle . . . comen lightly up and of smale substance and wilbe maid glade shortly to knawe his neghbours for his better', the mayor retorted that 'I and my Brether and all this Citie knaweth that he wurshipfully hath been and born the charge as the Kyngs lieutenant within this Citie.'[18] It is true that the increasing invasion of borough seats in parliament by gentry, lawyers and crown officials might be interpreted as subservience by townsmen to gentry, but it could equally be interpreted as an arrangement of mutual interest.

Urban self-awareness was to some extent a consequence of sheer numbers, because towns' packed yet heterogeneous populations (including many first-generation immigrants) called for a different approach from any needed by agricultural communities. Borough law and custom developed separately from common law, and most boroughs became corporate in fact if not always in legal theory. Maitland put it well: 'The borough community is corporate; the village community is not. This is a real and important difference. In the fifteenth century it stands out in the clear light . . . Corporateness came of urban life.' A major reason was the numbers involved; a quantitative difference *can* become qualitative. To cite Maitland once more:

> I can not see the English village of the remotest days as populous . . . and I think it no paradox but a very simple truth that the fewer our numbers, the further we are from any constitutional unity. It is the crowded town that is one . . . When there is no longer any hope of continuous agreement, then comes the demand for and the possibility of an organic union, a permanent habit of agreeing to differ and yet to be permanently one.

And, he adds significantly, 'Mere numbers are important . . . *There are some thoughts which will not come to men who are not tightly packed.*'[19]

What are those thoughts? The first, perhaps, was the realization that densely populated settlements could generate quarrelling and disorder, and that this had to be averted. One thirteenth-century writer had pointed out that Londoners, being 'housed close together' and more crowded than countryfolk, were at more risk of killing one another if they quarrelled 'at their drinking or elsewhere'.[20] This awareness of the

---

[18] J. Gairdner (ed.), *The Historical Collections of a Citizen of London in the Fifteenth Century*, Camden Soc., new series 17 (1876), p. 222; A. Raine (ed.), *York Civic Records* (8 vols., Yorks Archaeological Soc. record series, 1939–53), II, p. 156.

[19] F. W. Maitland, *Township and Borough* (Cambridge, 1898), pp. 18, 22–4 (my italics).

[20] M. Bateson, 'A London municipal collection of the reign of John', *English Historical Review* 17 (1902), 720.

increased risks of faction and fighting produced, in the larger towns, not only rudimentary policing, but also complex constitutions with careful arrangements for interlocking councils and elections to office. Another result was the gradual acceptance of disunity through voting. Here again Maitland pointed the way, showing how in towns the early medieval demand for unanimity in decisions gave way to counting heads or hands. (The chronology of this change has yet to be worked out: elections of mayors or aldermen by open majority voting are not recorded before 1512 at Lincoln and 1522 at York.) And yet another result was the widespread acceptance of separate borough law and custom, as noted earlier.

Fear of disorder in crowded towns led many councils to detailed supervision of daily life, a phenomenon which has been characterized as 'paternalism' or 'social control'. Townsmen were in some respects freer than countryfolk (especially in the areas of personal freedom and the transfer of property), but in other ways, paradoxically, they were far more tightly controlled. One is accustomed to town bylaws regulating in detail food supplies, prices, the carrying of weapons, refuse disposal and so on; but it is still possible to be pulled up short by the sheer degree of social engineering which was enacted, if not necessarily enforced. Thus in 1492 the city fathers of Coventry forbade any 'sole woman' under the age of fifty to set up house by herself, an age limit later reduced to forty; while a little later (1540) Chester forbade women aged between fourteen and forty to keep alehouses. More positively, some towns at least were already taking an active part in areas like poor relief for which the sixteenth century is better known. Thus Southampton was in 1441 paying £4 2s 1d weekly to poor men and women, which may represent 1d a day subsistence for 140 poor people.

The corollary to all this, as leading merchants and craftsmen would have retorted, was *noblesse oblige* (or *bourgeoisie oblige*?) – if towns had to be controlled and organized *they* had to do it, and in ways not necessary in the countryside; and this pressure on the elites grew. As Britnell puts it in his fine study of Colchester, there was by the early sixteenth century a direct correlation between a man's wealth and the number of times he was elected bailiff: 'Because of the greater demands of the community [and] the heightened emphasis on sharing the burdens of administration . . . it was harder to opt out than it had been in the fourteenth century. A rich man who wanted to enjoy his wealth without pageantry was better off living in a country village.'[21] And the pressure for close regulation which could make civic office burdensome was increased by pressure from the crown in times of disorder. The king expected to have tight policing, and was ready to threaten the withdrawal of civic liberties if this basic condition was not met. In 1495 Henry VII told the mayor and aldermen of York to their faces that 'I may not see the Citie go in utter ruyne and dekaye in defaute of you that shuld rewle for rather of necessite I most and woll put in other rewlers that woll rewle and govern the Citie according to my lawez.'[22] The size and complexity of towns also meant that

---

[21] R. H. Britnell, *Growth and Decline in Colchester 1300–1525* (Cambridge, 1986), p. 235.
[22] Raine, *York Civic Records*, II, p. 115.

public works might have to be carried out by what was, in effect, the forced labour of the whole community. At Nottingham 'booners' – the burgesses or their substitutes – repaired the streets until a paid paviour was appointed. At Hythe the townsmen had to help with harbour works on a rota basis, and at Sandwich the jurats and councillors had to provide labourers for the harbour, while all other townsmen either had to work there themselves or provide substitutes.

Most town councils tried hard to cultivate a sense of civic harmony and unity among their heterogeneous populations. One obvious channel for such efforts was the church, with cohesion through special civic masses, intercessions and fraternities. A related area was civic pageantry, much of it connected with ecclesiastical festivals when civic officers, or guildsmen and craftsmen, might march in order of procession. Coventry and York both held such processions on the feast of Corpus Christi. Many towns also staged miracle plays, often also at Corpus Christi, which were performed by the laity, usually on a craft basis; the well-known examples of Chester, Wakefield and York are merely those with surviving texts. Both the plays and the processions of Corpus Christi had, among other aims, the explicit purpose of fostering civic harmony. In particular, they provided a framework by which the changing role and importance of crafts and occupations could be peacefully absorbed. Overlapping with them were more purely secular festivities, perhaps very ancient and even pagan in origin, like the bawdy Hocktide play at Coventry and the apparently equally bawdy Yule Riding at York. London, Bristol and Coventry all celebrated midsummer by civic processions and bonfires on the eves of St John (24 June) and Sts Peter and Paul (29 June), in what Phythian-Adams has termed the climax of a 'ritualistic' half year between Christmas and Midsummer.[23]

History and myth were also employed, both by city rulers and by ordinary towns-people, to bolster a sense of civic pride and unity. At Coventry the Hocktide revels were seen as re-enacting a victory of the citizens over the Danes, while the Godiva story was already popular as the legendary explanation for the city's freedom. Earl Leofric was said for love of her to 'make Coventre tol-free', and rebellious citizens in the 1490s appealed to this tradition against a new toll on wool and cloth:

> Be it knowen & understand
> This Cite shuld be free & nowe is bonde.
> Dame good Eve made it free;
> & nowe the custome for woll & the draperie.

Grimsby displayed on its seal the legendary Grim, founder of the town in Viking times; while Southampton made much of Bevis of Hampton, a common legendary figure appropriated by the town: effigies of Bevis and his giant counterpart were set up over Bargate in 1522 to welcome the Emperor Charles V. Towns with a greater claim to

---

[23] C. Phythian-Adams, 'Ceremony and the citizen: the communal year at Coventry 1450–1550', in Clark and Slack (eds.), *Crisis and Order*, pp. 57–85.

antiquity plumped for Roman or pre-Roman founders, especially if they could find one in Geoffrey of Monmouth. Thus, when Henry VII made his progress in 1486, he was greeted at York by the figure of King Ebrauk and at Bristol by King Brennius (both appear in Geoffrey, but although he attributes the foundation of York to Ebrauk he does not associate Brennius with Bristol). Bath likewise cultivated King Bladud, Colchester King Coil ('Cole') and Oxford King Mempricius. Not all figures, however, were so far-fetched; Henry VII was also greeted on his 1486 progress by King Ethelbert at Hereford, and at Worcester by Sts Oswald and Wulfstan, all of them real figures with genuine local connections.

The clearest example of the importance of this searching for antiquity is the correspondence of Mayor Shillingford as he pursued a lawsuit with the dean and chapter of his city of Exeter. He and his colleagues argued that Exeter was already a city before the Romans, and held the town in fee farm of the king before there was a cathedral. The bishop, dean and chapter quite rightly retorted that there 'was no mayer ne fee ferme' until the reign of Henry III. It typifies the way in which large towns appealed to historical myth as the ultimate customary precedent. 'The late-medieval sense of history', notes Phythian-Adams, 'thus seems to have been selective; relevance was restricted to origins and unity . . . The welfare and the dignity, "the welth & worship of the *hole* body" was the ideal.'[24] London, interestingly, made little of either its Galfridian founder (Brutus) or of King Lud, but then London did not need to impress other towns with its history and importance.

All of this could be interpreted as evidence of *disunity* in the late medieval town, the use of pageantry and myth being seen as desperate attempts to fabricate unity and a sense of community. It could also be argued, however, that such celebrations were so successful because the message fell on receptive ears. Rich and poor shared a common view of mutual responsibilities; political power and consultation were diffused *relatively* widely in most of these towns; the combination of high mortality and high immigration led to much social fluidity and some upward social mobility; and the cheek-by-jowl mixture of rich and poor households in physical proximity made for some social mixing. As Reynolds suggests, 'Whatever the economic interests of a town's leading inhabitants, the conditions in which they and their inferiors lived created both solidarity against outsiders and conflicts within. The conflicts in turn . . . bound them together as well as divided them.'[25]

Reynolds's conclusion on social cohesion seems worth restating: 'Perhaps . . . unity was less fragile than the abundant evidence of dissension allows us to see. Though contemporaries worried about the divisiveness of subordinate associations, the way that households, workshops, crafts, fraternities, parishes . . . enmeshed so many people in a mass of associations may rather have helped to bind populations of

---

[24] S. A. Moore (ed.), *Letters and Papers of John Shillingford*, Camden Soc., new series 2 (1871), pp. 75–6, 95–6, A. S. Green, *Town Life in the Fifteenth Century* (2 vols., 1894), I, pp. 342–3; Phythian-Adams, *Desolation of a City*, pp. 173–4.

[25] Reynolds, *Medieval Towns*, p. 67.

immigrants into communities.'[26] This seems to have been borne out by London, far and away the largest town, and the one most at risk of social breakdown through its size, crowding and disorder. Yet Sylvia Thrupp depicts a fourteenth- and fifteenth-century capital in which social cohesion prevented anarchy, and in which other loyalties competed with rank and class: 'The emotion that was evoked by religious teaching and festivals and neighborhood loyalties, growing up around the parish churches, did much to keep friendships open between families that otherwise moved in different social spheres.' Dr Rosser has recently come to a similar judgement over Westminster, where problems of urban cohesion were even more acute than in the City of London, owing to the weakness of local government. He concludes that 'not continuously . . . but periodically . . . a significant proportion of the population of Westminster perceived itself as belonging to a single community', whether regularly in rituals, or irregularly when public needs like water supply called for common action. 'The population of medieval Westminster, despite its diversity and frequent fluctuations both in size and in composition, did develop effective strategies for communal behaviour.'[27]

The Reformation, however, marked the beginning of the end for many of the common cultural assumptions which bound together the late medieval urban community. Phythian-Adams writes of 'Medieval mirrors shattered' in his fine study of Coventry, and argues that 'If the Reformation represented a line drawn under the long and evolving tradition of medieval urban community, it also signalised a final disruption of cultural assumptions.'[28] That may be to emphasize too sharp a break, for if many rituals connected with the old church had to be abandoned in the 1530s and 1540s, other customs and attitudes lingered on. Yet if the Reformation is seen as a long-drawn-out process of readjustment to a new world of assumptions, then Phythian-Adams is surely right. The traditional concept of order in the late medieval towns, based on ceremonial, myth and ritual

was suited to a localised society in which hierarchy, together with obligation to those below and deference to those above, made sense of people's lives. This mental world did not suddenly collapse at some point during the period between 1500 and 1800 but, in face of changes in thinking about man, God, science and the natural environment, it was slowly being dissolved.[29]

---

[26] S. Reynolds, *Kingdoms and Communities in Western Europe, 900–1300* (Oxford, 1984), p. 213.
[27] Thrupp, *Merchant Class*, p. 38; G. Rosser, *Medieval Westminster 1200–1540* (Oxford, 1989), pp. 225, 247–8, 325–7.
[28] Phythian-Adams, *Desolation of a City*, p. 275.
[29] A. J. Fletcher and J. Stevenson, *Order and Disorder in Early Modern England* (Cambridge, 1985), pp. 2, 3.

$$\boxed{9}$$

RURAL SOCIETY

Mark Bailey

INTRODUCTION

Historians know relatively little about the lives of the mass of fifteenth-century Englishmen, and less still about their attitudes towards their own experiences and existence. This is partly due to a lack of research, for the later fifteenth century has tended to be something of an historical no-man's land between the medieval and early modern periods. Yet even when this research is completed, our knowledge of medieval peasant life will still be constrained by a lack of evidence. Lay literacy may have increased in the fifteenth century, but the majority of the populace remained illiterate and so there are no written records composed by the peasantry themselves. Much of our information has to be culled from manorial court rolls, but this is highly selective material which reflects the administrative priorities of the landlords who held the courts. Despite these limitations some admirable accounts of village life in the middle ages have been constructed, but many of these concentrate on the period 1270–1450, when court rolls were most detailed and accurate. Building bricks without straw is an occupational necessity for the historian of rural England in the later fifteenth century.

The terms 'landlords' and 'peasantry' have been used as if they were homogenous and easily defined classes in the fifteenth century. In practice, of course, this was not the case. Not only did these groups incorporate fine gradations of status and wealth, but English society underwent great changes in the century after the Black Death (1348–9), and to generalize about its structure without risking oversimplification is difficult. Among landowners, the great ecclesiastical magnates rivalled the dukes, earls and barons in wealth and standing. Dukedoms were bestowed upon immediate members of the royal family, and barons were defined as those who received personal summons to attend parliament. Below them stood numerous lesser abbeys and priories, and a variety of lay landlords. Notable among the last were the knights. The chivalric and military credentials of knighthood had been eroded by the fifteenth century, and knights were now those men whose income, mainly from land, placed them just below the barons. Next in the hierarchy was a class of lesser but emerging

Dr Richard Britnell, Dr Duncan Bythell, Dr John Hatcher and Dr Rosemary Horrox provided stimulating comments on an earlier draft of this essay.

landowners, the esquires and gentlemen, men of local importance who – along with the lower ranks of knights – have been collectively dubbed the gentry.

Among the peasantry, the classic and conventional distinctions between the various forms of free and unfree peasants (such as freemen, sokemen, mollmen; and villeins, bondmen, serfs) are mainly associated with the period *c.* 1100–1400. The majority of peasants were unfree, and as such owed a range of heavy personal and financial obligations to the lord of the manor. However, with the decline of serfdom in the later middle ages, these descriptions became less common and were gradually replaced by new ones, such as yeomen, labourers, husbandmen and servants. Hence fifteenth-century nomenclature tended to be based more on an assessment of a peasant's economic or landholding position, rather than his personal status. At the apex of peasant society were the yeomen, a small group of wealthy villagers who each possessed land totalling upwards of forty acres. These holdings were constructed from a variety of different land tenures, and often included substantial leases of the lord's own manorial arable and pasture lands. They produced a surplus for the market, often with the help of hired local wage labourers or live-in servants. They were men of ambition and influence within the village, sometimes increasing their income and standing by holding senior administrative offices for the local lord. The yeomanry in this sense were the successors of the wealthier freemen of the high middle ages.

Below the yeomen were the more numerous husbandmen, who were peasants with holdings of around ten to forty acres. In this group were the lesser freemen and more prosperous villeins, who were described by William Langland (1370s) as sworn to 'swink and sweat and sow'. The scale of their commercial operations was modest, and few were able to increase their holding size substantially. Their economic position was limited by difficulties in securing capital, the high cost of labour required to run a larger farm and the depressed market for agricultural produce. In social standing if not wealth they were manifestly below the yeomen, and their ambition was limited to improving the security and status of their contracts with the lord. Yet it must be stressed that the family wealth of both the yeomanry and the husbandmen was often transitory, for mismanagement or a failure to produce direct heirs often prevented a family's survival for more than a couple of generations.

Smallholders, labourers, domestic servants and the village poor formed the lower ranks of village society. These represent the most poorly documented and least studied group. In some villages, the availability of land in the fifteenth century resulted in a decline in the number of smallholders and a rise in the ranks of husbandmen, a process readily observable in Stoughton (Leics). In many other villages, however, the number of smallholders did not decline substantially, and as a result there was a growing polarization of village society. These divergent patterns of landholding have yet to be explained properly, but the local availability of non-agricultural employment may have been an important factor because smallholders, and to some extent the lesser husbandmen, depended upon part- or full-time wage labouring. In rural East Anglia and the south-east, where opportunities for wage labouring were traditionally high, over half of the population were probably wage earners in the early fifteenth century. In the midlands, however, the figure may have been lower than one quarter.

Although the elements which constituted rural society were diverse and relatively fluid, it was still common for fifteenth-century administrators and poets to define the social hierarchy precisely and minutely, and to ascribe specific functions to each stratum. This practice had its roots in early medieval estates theory, in which warriors, clergy and peasants co-existed as three distinct groups in an harmonious, divinely ordained and interdependent society. Chaucer had satirized this concept in his *Canterbury Tales*, and its survival in an attenuated form in the fifteenth century says rather more about contemporaries' idealized view of the gradations in society than it does about reality. This idealism is reflected in the sumptuary law of 1463, one of a number in the late middle ages, which was designed to ensure that people dressed 'only according to their degrees', for clothing was supposed to be a visible confirmation of status. For instance, only the parliamentary peerage were permitted to wear gold, which was to set them apart from even the knights. In contrast, the yeomen were not to stuff out their doublets or wear shoes with long pikes, ostentations which presumably rendered them indistinguishable from the lesser gentry.[1] The law was ineffective, but it does reflect the aristocracy's dogged commitment to an outmoded social philosophy, and their belief that society should be ordered and well defined. Fifteenth-century England was still a status-conscious and, by extension, a deferential society.

LANDLORDS AND THEIR ESTATES

There can be few historical periods of greater economic contrast than the later middle ages. In the thirteenth century, landlords had gained at the expense of the peasantry. Seigneurial incomes swelled as land scarcity pushed rent levels upwards, and high profits in agriculture encouraged landlords to exploit their own (demesne) land directly. Yet this prosperity was not extended to many of the peasantry, who, burdened by a shortage of land and employment opportunities, led an increasingly precarious existence. In the fifteenth century, however, the situation was effectively reversed. Agricultural profits were severely depressed, many landlords chose to lease their demesnes in the hope of establishing a more secure income, and rent levels fell dramatically in many areas of England. As a consequence, it was not uncommon for lords to suffer a sharp drop in income. In contrast, the peasantry were able to obtain land cheaply, often leasing parcels of the lord's demesne, and could choose from a variety of well-paid employment opportunities. Their standard of living improved significantly, so that the fifteenth century has been dubbed 'the golden age of the peasantry'.

The main cause of these enormous changes in rural society was undoubtedly demographic decline. England's population had peaked at perhaps 6 million people in the early fourteenth century, but the Black Death of 1348–9 and subsequent epidemics had more than halved this figure by 1377. There has been some dispute over the

---

[1] *Statutes of the Realm*, II (1816), pp. 399–401.

demographic trend in the century after the 1370s, although most historians now agree that it was at best stagnant and at worst gently declining. Much of the fifteenth century was characterized by frequent and virulent plague outbreaks, and in some regions the disease had become endemic. Recent work has also suggested that low fertility rates contributed to the demographic decline, although this is an issue which warrants further research. It is often assumed that rising living standards resulted in larger families, but under the psychological impact of plague married couples may have preferred to defend their new-found affluence by limiting family size. There is also a suggestion that the epidemics of 1361 and 1369 particularly afflicted children and adolescents, thus reducing the reproductive capacity of the population in subsequent generations. This capacity may have been further reduced by prevailing labour shortages, which encouraged women to enter the labour market and hence delay marriage.

As population declined, so agricultural goods were in over-supply, and labour shortages inflated wage costs. Hence agrarian profitability fell but the purchasing power of labour improved significantly, and real wage rates doubled between 1300–40 and 1400–40. Most of these gains were made in the later fourteenth century, but rates remained high and constant throughout the fifteenth century, and only showed signs of a decline in the 1490s. In contrast, land values and the area under cultivation continued to fall, particularly between the 1430s and the 1470s when some agricultural rents fell by one third. Mills and farm buildings became dilapidated, and demesne lands were either abandoned or leased to tenants on easy terms. This period represents one of the most sustained and severe agricultural depressions in documented English history, and its implications were potentially worse for landlords than for the peasantry.

Of course, it would be too simplistic to assume that these images of rural economic decline and depopulation were universal. A few rural areas experienced industrial growth in the fifteenth century, which bolstered local rents and created pockets of economic prosperity for certain landlords. The booming textile manufacturing village of Castle Combe (Wilts) was a highly profitable source of income to its lord, Sir John Fastolf. A prominent commander in the French wars, Fastolf was also a shrewd entrepreneur who stimulated trade for his tenants by dressing his soldiers with livery made in Castle Combe. His military successes, notably at the battle of Verneuil (1424), also yielded considerable revenue and enabled him to purchase yet more estates. Nor would it be accurate to suppose that the lower orders of rural society were universally wealthy, for a seam of poverty and want persisted on the margins of peasant society. Life may have been easier for the peasantry but it was by no means easy, and, for all the sense of relative well-being, rural society was still vulnerable to severe harvest failure. The 1430s, for example, was a decade of extreme weather conditions and deficient crops, resulting in famine and high death rates.

The success of men such as Fastolf has prompted some historians to write optimistically about the financial position of fifteenth-century landlords, in spite of the prevailing agricultural depression. It is argued that although land values declined, many lords defended and even augmented their incomes with a mixture of skill and good fortune, through the fruits of war, patronage and political office, or prudent marriage. Yet for all the obvious successes, it is hard to escape the conclusion that economic conditions were simply too unfavourable for landlords to survive with impunity, and most faced financial difficulties. On occasions, these conditions fuelled magnate rivalries. Recent work on north-east England suggests that the feud between the Nevilles and the Percys in the 1450s had its roots in the acute economic crisis of the late 1430s.

Financial matters were a source of constant anxiety to fifteenth-century landlords. Indifferent management would have been ruinous in the prevailing economic conditions, and under the direction of an inexperienced bursar Durham priory suffered serious distress in mid-century. Similarly, the estate of the cellarer of Bury St Edmunds abbey recorded substantial losses in almost every year of the early fifteenth century due to high expenditure and taxation. Efficient management along the lines of modern businesses was not particularly evident, for medieval estates were social and adminis-trative units, reflecting power and status, and not strictly economic ventures. The better landlords balanced their declining incomes by prudent cuts in expenditure, by centralizing and streamlining their administration, by undertaking judicious but modest investment programmes on rural manors, and assuming a greater personal interest in the running of their estates. In the 1460s, for instance, John Paston I was actively involved in decision making on his Norfolk manors, even when he was in London, and administrative issues were frequently addressed in his letters. Even so, the Pastons were often hard-pressed for cash, and on occasions struggled to meet their wage bills: in 1469, it was thought 'better to selle som of [the corn] as the price gothe than for to lete [the work-force] be on-payd'.

LANDLORD AND PEASANT RELATIONS

Earlier in this essay, attention was drawn to the decline of personal status as the basis for peasant nomenclature, a trend which owed much to the gradual disappearance of serfdom after the late fourteenth century. From the 1450s, manorial documents distinguish between freemen or villeins infrequently, and by the 1490s the practical differences between them had been greatly eroded. Serfdom, one of the pillars of feudal society, gradually dissolved during the fifteenth century. However, the system's decline was a complex and uneven process, and some of its vestiges survived into the sixteenth century. So even though the old personal ties which bound a peasant to his lord had weakened inexorably by the 1490s, he was still tied to the land. The object of this discussion is not to chart the decline of villeinage, but to consider some of the forces behind it. Market forces – and in particular the scarcity of labour – certainly encouraged an improvement in the peasant's position and status in the fifteenth century, but to what extent did landlords' attitudes prove obstructive to this process, and to what extent did peasant attitudes facilitate it?

There is no doubt that the slack demand for land in the fifteenth century enabled the peasantry to secure substantial concessions over the nature of land tenures. This was an important development, because land tenure re-enforced personal status. Many thirteenth-century villein holdings were customary, in that they were inalienable and liable for a range of renders, payments and dues associated exclusively with unfree

20 Harvesting

status, such as death duties (heriots) and marriage fines (merchets). One of the most prominent, but onerous and unpopular, renders on unfree holdings was weekly labour services on the lord's demesne land. However, by the mid-fifteenth century it was uncommon for an unfree peasant to owe labour services, and their disappearance reflected a general movement from customary to contractual tenures. Many of these holdings had now been converted to alienable and hereditary copyhold tenures, which rendered to the lord a fixed cash payment, and sometimes a heriot and entry fine. As a result of these changes, the only bodily service now owed by a peasant to the lord was attendance at the manorial court. The copyhold system allowed the peasantry greater control over their own time and action, although it did not necessarily constitute the removal of all elements of arbitrary exaction. Heriots were often agreed between lord and tenant at the outset, but the entry fines payable on the accession to the holding of each heir were not fixed, and could be raised to excessive levels in the late fifteenth century.

Prevailing economic conditions provide a ready explanation for the evolution of contractual tenures and the overall decline in fifteenth-century rent levels. Yet the peasantry's own contempt for customary exactions, and their willingness and ability to exert constant pressure for change on landlords, was clearly another important factor. Peasant resistance to the excessive demands of their landlords can be traced long before the Black Death, but in the fifteenth century their actions became more coherent and insistent. Jurors on manorial courts often refused to compile new rentals in the fifteenth century, because such rentals would document their theoretical liability for the old customary dues. In response, lords threatened sizeable financial penalties but with little success. Where liability for feudal dues could be established, the peasantry often refused to pay them. Demands for recognition payments, due from unfree peasants on the election of a new bishop, were met with collective refusals on most of the bishopric of Worcester's manors throughout the fifteenth century.

Peasant recalcitrance was not confined to the payment of 'arbitrary' customary obligations. The peasantry's growing economic strength and self-assertiveness in the fifteenth century resulted in bolder displays of defiance in many of their dealings with landlords. Throughout England there were widespread refusals to repair dilapidated peasant houses, despite seigneurial offers of financial assistance. Non-attendance at manorial courts increased, and verbal outbursts and dissent in the court itself became more common. On occasions, peasants even declined to pay court amercements if they regarded them as 'unjust and without cause'. The decline in rental income on many estates was undoubtedly exacerbated by peasant rent refusals, and rent strikes were common throughout the west midlands. As a consequence, arrears of rent mounted steadily on some manors. It is important to emphasize that many rents and amercements, and some feudal incidents, *were* paid by the peasantry, especially by those occupying prime holdings. The essential point is that demands which were deemed excessive or arbitrary were increasingly disputed or rejected in the fifteenth century. Underpinning these refusals was a growing self-confidence among the peasantry, and – on occasions – a willingness to act collectively. It is also apparent that a concept of what constituted a fair payment, or a just exaction, had become widely established.

Fifteenth-century landlords had to compromise with their peasants to a far greater degree than had their predecessors. The very process of compromise inevitably gave rise to tension, but it would be wrong to suppose that the peasantry obtained concessions by constantly verging on open rebellion. English lord/peasant relations never came close to deteriorating into the class wars which ravaged Catalonia in the later middle ages, and there was nothing to compare with the mass uprising of 1381. The major revolts of the fifteenth century – notably Oldcastle's (1414), and Cade's (1450) – were essentially the result of religious and political disorders, and gained only limited support. Although Cade's rebellion did inspire sporadic rural uprisings, in most cases the political disruption was being used as a vehicle for local grievances, and it could hardly be described as a popular movement. Despite this, authorities in Kent were still fearful that the rebellion would spark mass peasant upheaval. This nervousness owed much to the profound psychological impact of the 1381 revolt, which for many landlords was 'a warnyng to be ware'. A precedent was created in 1381 which temporized landlords' attitudes thereafter.

Feudal lordship may have been less imposing and effective than in the thirteenth century, but – for all the changes described above – it was still operative. Indeed, many landlords found the growing wealth and assertiveness of the peasantry distasteful, an affront to the natural order of things. This enduring conservatism was captured by John Gower, himself from a gentry background, in *Vox Clamantis* (1370s). The peasantry, he wrote, had 'a rough, boorish nature', whose aspirations of social mobility were profoundly misplaced: 'it is not for man's estate that anyone from the class of serfs should try to set things right'. Such conservatism is also reflected in the attempt to distinguish sections of society according to their dress in the sumptuary regulations of 1463. These attitudes explain why peasant pressure for change was fiercely resisted on some estates, a policy which undoubtedly intensified local resentment of serfdom. For instance, serfdom was rigorously maintained on the East Anglian estates of the dukes of Norfolk throughout the fifteenth and sixteenth centuries. The consistency of this policy is remarkable when one considers the various changes in ownership of the Norfolk estate during the fifteenth century, and suggests that the conservative attitude of estate administrators was as important as that of the lord. Indeed, lords themselves were sometimes keen to blame the oppressive behaviour of estate and government officials as a source of tension with peasants, perhaps because it deflected attention from other issues. John of Gaunt suspected that the attacks on his rural properties in the revolt of 1381 were partly the result of heavy-handed management by his local officials, many of whom were recruited from the aspiring middle classes.

It is worth recording that not all of the upper estates possessed a philosophical aversion to the advancement of the lower orders, as the work of Sir John Fortescue reveals.[2] But whatever their thoughts about the advance of the peasantry, most landlords accepted the inevitability of some change in the fifteenth century, although they remained determined to protect their rights and incomes as skilfully as possible. For example, many lords came to regard rent refusals as a fact of economic life. Indeed, some treated them with a degree of sympathy, accepting that the larger peasant landholders, like themselves, were affected by depressed grain prices and occasional shortages of coin. The Pastons grasped the importance of continually reassessing rent levels, for 'if ye undo your tenauntes with overchargyng of your fermes it shall distroy your tenauntes and lordshepes'.[3] Put simply, it was better to accept a lower rent than to have no tenant at all. Harsh economic reality demanded flexibility, and a degree of paternalism, from landlords. John Hopton, a Suffolk gentleman, took some notice of the personal circumstances of his tenants, and was prepared to waive court fines accordingly. Westminster abbey preferred to accept lower rents from local tenants,

---

[2] Sir John Fortescue, *The Governance of England*, ed. C. Plummer (Oxford, 1885), pp. 138–40.
[3] R. H. Britnell, 'The Pastons and their Norfolk', *Agricultural History Review* 36 (1986), 137–8.

rather than grant land to acquisitive outsiders and urban dwellers. Lords had to maintain a healthy vigilance over their estates, although where they suspected that peasants were deliberately withholding rents, then the judicious use or threat of force could be important weapons in securing payment.

One suspects that many landlords regarded rent concessions and the movement towards copyholds as an unavoidable, yet tactical, compromise. These were practical responses to the shortage of tenants in the fifteenth century, but not a concession on the important issue of the personal status of unfree peasants, and many would have expected to recoup any concessions in better times ahead. There can be no doubt that personal status was regarded as an important issue by the peasantry themselves, and that the taint of serfdom carried a measure of social stigma. Although the general distinction between free and unfree peasants disappeared in the fifteenth century, some lords did continue to identify one sub-group of hereditary unfree peasants known as *nativi de sanguine* ('the serfs by blood'). Although not especially numerous, these serfs could be found on estates throughout England and were subject to a greater degree of feudal control than other classes of unfree peasants. They often tried to deny their status to manorial officials, and Richard Seveger of Kempsey (Warws) preferred to be known as a bastard rather than admit he was a serf. These denials represented more than just a crude attempt to escape financial liability for various feudal dues. They also reflect a deep-rooted and very real sense of social inferiority, for on occasions serfs were openly scorned and abused by other peasants. Henry Helay, a monk at Durham priory, launched a smear campaign against the sub-prior by accusing him of servile status, an accusation deemed sufficiently serious for the sub-prior to clear his name by an enquiry. One detects echoes of *Vox Clamantis* in Helay's slur: 'nothing is more troublesome than a lowly person when he has risen to the top, at least when he was born a serf.'[4] The Pastons, too, were not immune from allegations of unfree ancestry.

The distaste for serfdom by blood is marvellously illustrated by the case of Matthew Oxe of Staverton (Suff), who rose from a local family of serfs to gain his freedom. Matthew fled the manor for an unknown destination in the mid-1430s, perhaps entering the service of the duke of Norfolk at Framlingham castle. Then in 1455 he made a triumphant return to his home village, when he proudly displayed a charter of manumission dating from 1447 to the manorial court. He gleefully paid 6d to have a copy of the charter recorded in the court rolls, which noted that Matthew and all his heirs were now freemen, and that his surname had been changed to Groom. In those parts, the name Oxe must have been firmly associated with servile status.[5]

Manumissions, or the purchase of freedom, provided an obvious means of improving personal status for all unfree peasants. On most estates, the number

---

[4] Durham Cathedral Muniments, Misc. Charters 1055, 1066, 1487.
[5] Suffolk Record Office (hereafter SRO) (Ipswich) (hereafter I), HD1538/357, temp. HVI, mm. 53, 106.

of grants peaked in the period 1450–70, when the seigneurial need for cash, and the peasantry's resources, were greatest. Yet seigneurial attitudes to manumission varied and some lords were reluctant to grant charters, and so its importance should not be overstated. The grant of freedom to a villein represented an inalienable loss of jurisdiction to the lord, and consequently would only be granted at a price: on the Ramsey abbey estates manumission cost anything from £6 to £20, depending on the bargaining power of the villein. Hence the purchase of freedom was available only to the wealthiest husbandmen, or to those – such as Matthew Oxe – who had performed loyal service in a lord's retinue.

For those unfree peasants who could neither afford nor secure manumissions, effective freedom could be achieved by simply fleeing the manor in search of better pay or conditions. Villeins were required to obtain seigneurial permission to leave their home manor, but in practice there were many illegal departures and landlords were increasingly hard-pressed to control peasant mobility in the fifteenth century. Their attempts to do so provide valuable details about the migration of peasants. Towns attracted many rural migrants with their unparalleled range of employment opportunities, and the steady flow of workers demonstrates the strong links that must have existed between rural and urban societies. As the tale of Dick Whittington suggests, London's pull was particularly strong, and six villeins from the distant village of Warboys (Hunts) emigrated to London in the early fifteenth century. However, the majority of migrants settled within a ten-mile radius of their home village. Some were enticed by inheritance of land from distant relatives, whilst others sought marriage partners or temporary employment in servanthood.

THE VILLAGE COMMUNITY

Migration represented an individualistic response to the economic opportunities of the later middle ages. To some historians, such individual strategies undermined the solidarity and interdependence of both the later medieval village community and the family. They argue that before the Black Death the economic circumstances of want and scarcity, coupled with forceful manorial administration, created a strong cohesion and a highly refined co-operative spirit within English villages. Thereafter, however, it is held that private and independent interests and activities took precedence over those of groups. The evidence provided in support of this argument is varied. The institution of personal pledging, a form of mutual surety among peasants used to enforce decisions made in the manorial court, had fallen into decline by the early fifteenth century; the number of presentments for trespass between peasants increased in manorial courts; and the transfer of peasant land came to be dominated by the forces of supply and demand, rather than by familial or customary influences. It is also argued that there was a growing disregard for manorial interests, a point reinforced in many places in the fifteenth century. At Mildenhall (Suff) refusals to maintain communal waterways, roads and fenland drainage channels were all too evident. In 1462, the villagers refused to repair a dilapidated stretch of the main highway, and then in 1471 the court unsuccessfully attempted to enforce communal action by ordering that each tenant should provide 'one labouring man' to clean a common ditch.[6]

Another apparent manifestation of the breakdown in village society was the increase in physical violence between peasants. This trend was particularly evident in the immediate aftermath of the Black Death, but was still discernible in the fifteenth century. High levels of personal violence and a disturbing willingness to draw knives have been detected on the estates of the bishopric of Worcester. Much of this violence resulted from clashes of interest, and stemmed from a belief among the lower orders that this was an acceptable way of resolving disputes. The presence of newcomers and migrant labourers in villages could exacerbate social tensions, and an increasing number of attacks involving strangers are recorded in many rural areas in the later fifteenth century. In Isleham Hundred (Msx) between 1472 and 1495 there were many instances of fights involving outsiders, and a similar trend is observable in Havering (Ess).

It is sometimes supposed that the emergence of village guilds in the later middle ages also reflected growing divisions in village society. These guilds were essentially religious fraternities established around the worship of a particular saint, and by the late fifteenth century one or more had been established in almost every English parish. A key feature of guilds was the opportunity they provided for lay participation in religion, but they also offered agreeable company and financial assistance to members. However, some historians argue that their religious role was fundamentally opposed to that of the parish, and hence their very existence presented a potential source of friction and disharmony. For instance, it is argued that guild members assumed a priggish demeanour, and that membership was elitist, amounting to a 'certificate of moral qualification' among leading parishioners.

The argument for a breakdown in village cohesion is not, however, accepted by all historians. For instance, recent interpretations have stressed the substantial areas of common ground between guild and parish, with guilds contributing generous funds towards the refurbishment of parish churches. Some guilds operated almshouses for the village poor, and others were prominent in the running of the local market, all of which indicates a sense of their collective responsibility. The financial commitment of villagers to their parish churches is also reflected in testamentary evidence. Wills abound with bequests not only to the fabric of churches, but also to the parish poor and the repair of roads. Although these were essentially private acts, they also coincided with a public need, and so there is an element of community action and responsibility here which should not be overlooked.

Other historians have suggested that an illusion of disunity in fifteenth-century villages is sometimes created by the documents themselves. For instance, much of the evidence for disharmony is culled from court rolls, which – by their very nature – tend to emphasize elements of disunity and conflict in village society. It has also been shown

---

[6] SRO (Bury St Edmunds) (hereafter B), E.18/451/5.

that family influence in the land market did not necessarily decline after the Black Death; instead, family ties merely become much harder for the historian to trace in the sources. On matters of fiscal and legal procedure, and during rent strikes against landlords, villagers were quite capable of acting in a responsible and collective fashion. Likewise, the pronouncements of increasingly assertive bylaws, which recur in many late fifteenth-century court rolls, signify a positive communal response to agricultural issues. Individualism may have increased, but it is argued that communal solidarity was maintained by familial commitments and sustained resistance to the feudal lord.

There is clearly some disagreement between historians over the nature of village communities in fifteenth-century England. The 'special degree of harmony' which characterized pre-Black Death villages had certainly been displaced, but what had replaced it? One suspects that attempts to answer this question have concentrated too much on the search for an unchanging and composite village community throughout the middle ages. This approach implicitly assumes that village society was comprised of an amorphous mass of peasants, whereas in reality village society became increasingly polarized during the fifteenth century, if not in economic terms then at least in social standing. By the 1450s, a peasant elite had emerged in most villages, whose group interests coincided less and less with those of the lower orders (see below). As this elite possessed wealth and influence in the village, it is their activities, their priorities, and their sense of 'community' which emerges most clearly from the records of the later fifteenth century. Hence the attempts to employ manorial courts as an indicator of community cohesion are fraught with difficulty, because their business largely reflects the private and communal priorities of the elites who ran them, and not necessarily those of the whole village.

The evidence used by historians to make judgements about the village community is sometimes far more complex than is allowed. For instance, the flooding of ditches and waterways in Mildenhall was presented as an example of the growing and widespread disregard for community interests. Yet it was the prosperous yeomen farmers who were most inconvenienced by irregularities such as this, not the village servants or labourers. So is this really evidence of subversive individualism, as historians have alleged, or does it reflect little more than the failure of the lower ranks of village society to comply with the imposed priorities of the elite? The neglect of hedging, drainage and buildings is also explicable in terms of the prevailing agrarian depression, for it was scarcely worth maintaining such assets when profits were low. Disinvestment in agriculture had a powerful economic rationale, with little significance for individualistic attitudes. Historians need to be more cautious in interpreting the evidence for individualism from fifteenth-century documents. Arguments that the village community either disintegrated or remained cohesive seem too simplistic. More attention should be paid to the different priorities of emergent social groups within the village.

WORK AND LEISURE

If the ready availability of cheap land enabled the upper ranks of peasant society to construct larger agricultural holdings in the fifteenth century, what impact did high wage rates have on the life styles of the lower ranks, those who depended upon part- or full-time labouring? In order to answer this question, a distinction must be drawn between wages and earnings: wage rates may have improved, but how often did people work? There remains much work to be done on this subject, but it seems likely that earnings rose alongside wages in the period immediately after the Black Death, as opportunities in craftwork and industrial employment expanded rapidly. However, earnings rose less rapidly after the early fifteenth century, and eventually may even have reached a plateau. This is partly explained by economic factors; many sectors of the economy suffered from stagnation or contraction in output around this time, thus disrupting the regularity of employment opportunities. However, as real wages continued to improve steadily during the fifteenth century, so labourers were able to maintain their living standards without having to seek much extra work.

Changing attitudes to work may provide another important explanation as to why fifteenth-century labourers worked less frequently than did their fourteenth-century predecessors. There is evidence that workers had developed a preference for irregular – albeit well-paid – employment, a suggestion implied in their reluctance to commit themselves to long-term contracts. Not surprisingly, annual contracts of employment on seigneurial demesnes were especially unpopular, which forced landlords to entice workers with very high wages. Government legislation and moral tracts of the period noted with concern that many workers sought employment by the week or by the day, a tendency which was attributed to growing idleness and truculence. Gower complained that labourers 'are not willing to serve anyone by the year; one cannot retain them even for a single month'. The Statutes of Labourers were increasingly concerned that labourers 'would not serve for a long season', and attempted to force them to do so.[7] In one prosecution under the statute, Thomas Mellere of Essex was reported to have enjoyed profitable employment for two consecutive years, and was then accused of becoming a 'vagrant by reason of his excessive earning'.

The attitude of many labourers was to attain a comfortable income level with the minimum of effort. The desired income level was itself determined by their fixed annual outgoings, such as rent, tools and purchases of staple industrial goods, and their preference was to earn it at a gentle pace, often in jobs that were physically undemanding. Hence labour intensity was low, a fact illustrated in a contemporary description of the habits of building workers: 'they waste much part of the day . . . in late coming to work, early departing therefrom, long sitting at their breakfast . . . and longtime of sleeping afternoon'. Labourers preferred not to work unless necessary, and with feastdays and holidays it is possible that some were employed for less than a third of the year.

Unfortunately, there are problems with accepting the testimony of moral tracts at face value. Idleness and truculence undoubtedly characterized some labourers, but these are subjective sources prone to exaggeration, and provide no independent

---

[7] *Statutes of the Realm*, II, p. 57.

confirmation that such attitudes were commonplace. Labour shortages in the later middle ages must have made employers more sensitive to labourers who worked slackly or not at all. This sensitivity contributed significantly to an increase in moralizing about the way in which workers spent their time, particularly on evenings and holidays. The carping tones of moralizers seeped into legal pronouncements, where complaints about labourers' idleness were often closely tied to complaints about their demands for excessive wages. None of this evidence reveals a particularly clear understanding among contemporaries of the mechanics of the labour market, and, on its own, cannot provide a reliable picture of workers' attitudes. Legislative evidence and moral tracts are primarily a statement of *seigneurial* expectations of how workers should behave and how long they should work, and thus the image they create is blurred by a web of social prejudices, jealousies and ignorance about labourers. The prejudices were largely those of the landlords, but potentially extended to all employers of labour, including the yeomanry. The attitudes of fifteenth-century wage earners can only be properly determined by gleaning evidence from other sources.

One feature of the government legislation on labourers was the concern that they were devoting too much time to recreational pursuits. In 1390, parliament noted that labourers and servants 'keep greyhounds and other dogs, and on the holydays when good christian people be at church . . . they go hunting in parks and warrens and connigries of lords'. The statute banned them from doing so because this was 'gentlemen's game'.[8] Hunting was indeed a coveted seigneurial privilege, and the exclusive right of landlords to take small game was particularly resented by the peasantry. Significantly, the statute's content is confirmed by evidence from manorial courts, where peasants were increasingly presented for petty poaching offences from the late fourteenth century. In most cases, the targets for poachers were fish and lesser game, rather than deer. In part, the rise in manorial presentments reflects tougher enforcement of warren rights by landlords, as at Framlingham (Suff) where the court ordered that one foot should be amputated from all hunting dogs in the village. Yet the sheer number of offences also reflected a genuine increase in poaching activity by peasants. Four labourers from Hadleigh (Suff) were amerced £6 in the 1450s for poaching 'hares, rabbits, pheasants, and partridges' from a nearby warren. The hunting statute was responding to a real issue.

It is also probable that as poaching increased, so did the playing of games and pastimes. It had been common to play games on holidays during the thirteenth century, but an under-researched aspect of the later middle ages is the extent to which a leisure culture emerged among the lower orders of rural society. Such activities were not recorded as a matter of course in contemporary documents, yet – once again – parliamentary statutes become increasingly concerned to regulate participation in games in the fifteenth century. It was argued that games distracted men from perfecting military skills such as archery, but a determination to discipline the

---

[8] *Ibid.*, II, p. 65.

workforce must have been another, unstated, aim. In 1388 parliament ordained that 'servants and labourers shall have bows and arrows and use the same on Sundays and Holydays, and leave all playing at Tennis or football and other games'. This was repeated in 1409, and then replaced by a statute of 1477 which noted that 'many new imagined games are played . . . Closh, Kails, Half Bowl, Hand-in Hand-out, and Queckboard'.[9] Nor did games escape the attention of moralizers: Gower noted that the peasantry 'desired the leisure of great men', and preachers complained of dice-playing during their sermons.

Recent research has corroborated the impression that games and pastimes became increasingly popular in the fifteenth century. In East Anglia, references to communal recreation areas appear more frequently after 1450, especially those set aside for the playing of 'camping', a violent mixture of football and handball. Throughout rural East Anglia and in north-east England, football, handball and tennis are recorded more frequently after the Black Death. In one County Durham village, eighteen men were warned against playing football in 1383. Robert Cook, the rector of Martlesham (Suff), was described as a 'habitual gamester' and accused of playing 'tenys' in the market square at Woodbridge in 1431, while dressed only in his shirt and breeches. The playing preference was for handball at nearby Eyke in 1425, although in the late 1450s John Folkard was also amerced for 'sustaining diverse outsiders' who played tennis in his enclosure.[10] At Goldington (Beds) a coroner's report recorded that the habit of one peasant was to go 'to the fields, market and wrestling matches as usual'.

Outdoor games were not the only leisure activities gaining in popularity at this time. There is evidence that fifteenth-century peasants were becoming accustomed to fraternizing and consuming ale in specially designated alehouses. Compare this with the thirteenth century, when peasant alebrewing was largely a sporadic business, and communal consumption confined to special feasts or ceremonies. Yet the growing association of drinking with relaxation is evident in the preparation of Berwick (N'umb) for Henry VII's army in the 1490s, when the construction of three 'bierhouses' was ordered.[11] In some villages, the habit of naming alehouses had already been established. A Brandon (Suff) rental of the early sixteenth century refers to houses called le Ram, le Bull, le Maydhead, le Swan and le Frogge.[12] Furthermore, the more consistent use of barley malt in the brewing process, and the growing number of rural beer-brewers, indicates greater concern for both the quality and taste of the final product. Even Fortescue was moved to comment upon the English peasantry's tendency to drink ale instead of water.[13]

As they became more firmly established, so alehouses attracted moral comment. Sermons of the later middle ages warned of their dangers: 'on feast days and for

---

[9] *Ibid.*, II, pp. 57, 163, 462–3.
[10] SRO (I), S Ipswich 352, vii, p. 107; HD1538/357 temp. HVI, mm. 11, 112 and 114.
[11] *Calendar of Patent Rolls 1492–1509*, p. 87.
[12] Norfolk Record Office, MS 3992.
[13] Sir John Fortescue, *De Laudibus Legum Angliae*, ed. F. Grigor (1917), p. 61.

21   Peasants hunting rabbits

the nights following, [labourers] go off to the taverns . . . at length they get so intoxicated that they fall to ribaldries, obscenities and idle talk, and to brawls by reason of which they fight'. People of this disposition were prone to singing songs 'of fowle rebawdry and of unclennes'. Court roll evidence substantiates these claims, albeit in more sober language. At Brandon in the 1480s, the house of one full-time brewer was used for playing 'tables [backgammon], cards and other illicit games, and this at day and night'. In 1471, Joanna Skeppere maintained a 'tapster' in her house which attracted 'lecherous and suspicious men'. Alehouses in Castle Combe were supposed to close at 8 o'clock each winter evening in an attempt to regulate the drinking and gambling habits of textile workers, and those in Mildenhall at

9 o'clock.[14] Courts at Havering (Ess) began to expel pimps and prostitutes from its liberty in the 1480s, and on one Battle abbey manor Agnes Petyt paid a regular fee to keep a *domus suspecta*. In alehouses where gambling and prostitution scarcely featured, the regulars concentrated their energy on less immoral pursuits. One drunken Sussex man was accused of knocking down 'diverse signs called ale-stakes' with a bill, and at Hampton (Warws) in 1477 seven men drowned in a vat of ale after a drinking binge.

Growing references, from a variety of sources, to the unacceptable activities of rural alehouses after the 1460s indicate that the village elites – who shaped the agenda of manorial courts – were increasingly concerned with aspects of public order. In this respect the yeomanry and wealthier husbandmen had much in common with the landlords, because as employers of hired labour they shared a sensitivity to the working habits of other villagers. The empathy between landlords and the upper peasantry is implied in the labour statute of 1388, which complained that 'for the scarcity of the said servants and labourers, the husbands and landtenants may not pay their rents or live upon their lands'.[15] Such attitudes must have raised tensions in village societies, especially when the elites prosecuted reluctant workers in the manorial courts. John Grubbe, for example, was amerced by the Staverton court for taking excessive wages as a thatcher and for refusing to work for the lord's tenants.[16] To return to an earlier argument, this is less a statement of growing individualism within the village than a refusal by certain labourers to comply with the priorities of the elite.

At Havering, similar attempts by village elites to regulate behaviour have been interpreted as an attempt to discipline an idle workforce and to exercise social control over the poorer migrants and villagers. It is further argued that the imposition of such moral constraints reveals a strong element of social puritanism among the village elite, which pre-dates the emergence of puritanism in its religious form. Whilst these observations carry some weight, they must not be overstated. Participation in games attracted people from high as well as lowly social backgrounds. The parliamentary statute of 1477 commented that games were played by 'persons of good reputation . . . to their own impoverishment'. Indeed, no less a notable than the sub-prior of Durham in 1446 came from an enthusiastic local football-playing family, and the rectors of Lidgate and Ousden (Suff) were habitual players of 'backgammon for money' in the 1460s.[17] Leisure pursuits were clearly not restricted to the poor. Nor should a genuine distaste for the wilder excesses of a society exploring the potential of leisure time be mistaken for a new spirit of puritanism.

Overall, there appears to be enough evidence to suggest that wage earners were developing a stronger preference for leisure after the late fourteenth century. Moral commentaries and government statutes were, in effect, propounding a work ethic

---

[14] SRO (B), E.18/451/6.
[15] *Statutes of the Realm*, II, p. 57.
[16] SRO (I), HD1538/357, temp. HVI, m. 68.
[17] Durham Cathedral Muniments, Misc. Charter 1487; SRO (B), E3/11/1.5.

22   Peasants drinking

for the peasantry, but a work ethic constructed by the aristocracy and adopted by employers of all classes. This work ethic did not necessarily square with that of the peasantry, and their economic position was such that they were not compelled to accept it. This is not to argue that the lower ranks of society wallowed in sloth and self-indulgence. Peasant attitudes to leisure and employment would have varied over time, depending upon the season of the year and upon personal circumstances. Much wage labouring was seasonal, and parents with a young family would require more income than they would in later years. Hence there were undoubtedly times when labourers needed to work hard and consistently. But whenever possible, many part- and full-time wage earners turned to leisure and recreation as a release from the drudgery of their existence. To participate in the thrill of the hunt or the conviviality of the alehouse, however occasionally, was a symbolic achievement in a century when the peasantry gained greater flexibility and choice over what to do with their time.

Their approach to work implies that fifteenth-century labourers had a limited desire to realise their maximum potential annual income. This attitude contrasts markedly with the ambitious social mobility of the middle classes and the upper ranks of the peasantry, and to understand it requires an acceptance of the gulf in wealth which existed even within village society. The yeomanry – and perhaps the wealthier husbandmen – stood on the bottom rung of genteel society, and as such were more likely to achieve social advancement. Yet despite the improvement in real wages most peasants still earned considerably less income than the village elite. Not only did labourers lack the wealth to advance socially, but even the limited range of fifteenth-century consumer goods – such as wine, middling-quality cloths and furs, and pewter – remained relatively expensive and proved largely beyond their means. The bounds created by their limited economic position and legal status meant that the social aspirations of some peasants scarcely extended beyond the alehouse.

CONCLUSION

Limitations in the extant documentation render it difficult to reconstruct the attitudes which prevailed in fifteenth-century rural society. However, many landlords were anxious about the financial affairs of their estates, and with due cause. Economic conditions favoured, not landlords, but both the erosion of villeinage and changes in the nature of land tenures. These developments were facilitated further by the assertiveness of the peasantry, whose collective resistance to the arbitrary demands of villeinage grew. Many landlords regarded the peasantry's growing confidence with distaste bordering on contempt, but the difficulties of securing rents and tenants demanded a grudging acceptance of the changing order. On those estates where landlords continued to resist pressure for changes in serfdom, conflict intensified with peasant resentment. It can be no coincidence that tenants from the notoriously conservative duke of Norfolk's estate were so prominent in Kett's rebellion in 1549.

As manorial power waned in English villages, so communal affairs came to be dominated by elites of wealthy peasants. Their priorities were increasingly divorced from those of the village smallholders and wage earners, a numerically substantial group in some areas of the country. The aspiring social mobility which characterized most sections of fifteenth-century society was least evident among these smallholders and labourers. Simple forces of supply and demand in the labour market meant that they were less energetic in seeking work, and less assiduous in performing it. This attitude led to growing complaints about their truculence and immorality, and attempts by government statutes and village elites to regulate their behaviour. But for the lower orders, alehouse lore and occasional participation in recreational activities came to symbolize the limited advances in status and living standards that they had achieved in the fifteenth century. Material and social advancement was not the priority of all sections of society.

IO

THE POOR

Miri Rubin

The poor are always with us, but they are a difficult group to identify and discuss as a whole. Medieval people – alms givers, religious homilists as well as legislators – encountered a considerable degree of complexity when forced to define the category of poor. The definition depended on context, just as it does today. There were different definitions for religious, administrative and legal purposes. Absolute measures of poverty were recognized such as hunger and homelessness; but relative deprivation was also appreciated as a pressing need and a worthy target for charity and relief. Yet within this complexity there are some striking themes which run through descriptions and definitions of poverty, while the relative prominence of each category is historically variable and dependent on changes in demography, the price of food, the availability of work in town and countryside, the social mood. People without family and friend, people who have lost the ability to work through accident, war or disease, old people, orphans, widows, were groups repeatedly recognized in the provisions of wills, in the recommendations of homilies, in the statutes of almshouses and hospitals. A fundamental aspect of medieval understandings of poverty and its relief comes through in these definitions: that real need should be coupled with a meek spirit, or at least a grateful prayer. One of the most disturbing contemporary social images was that of the undeserving and unyielding poor person.

The examination of poverty and relief is particularly interesting in the fifteenth century: a century which saw the long-term effects of the conjunctural changes in the economy and agriculture wrought in the previous century. It is especially interesting in fifteenth-century England: a society at war both at home and abroad, in which plague was endemic, which displayed many of the social and cultural tensions which were to play themselves further out in the sixteenth century. Changes in ideas about poverty and relief in this period also offer a fruitful field for comparison with the self-conscious and purposive remaking of charity and relief in the years of the English Reformation.

The need to define the poor was not an idle preoccupation considered in the abstract, it was a pressing priority for many institutions and for individuals. Some form of giving – distribution, alms giving, exemption from levies, granting of patronage and provision of shelter – was undertaken by a wide range of institutions. First and foremost, the parish. This was a fundamental unit for contact between those able to give and the poor, not only because the parish priest was required by canon law to distribute part of the parochial income to the poor, but also because within the parish occasions customarily related to distribution of alms took place: funerals, anniversaries of the dead, masses, celebration of feastdays.[1] Furthermore, parish churches were also used as the meeting-places for voluntary bodies such as religious fraternities, many of which engaged in particular devotional and charitable activities. Be it the single church of a village, the cathedral in a large city or the urban parish church, one among many in a crowded English town, by the late middle ages the parish church saw a stream and variety of social, religious, educational, liturgical and charitable activities within and without its walls. These activities were invariably couched in the medieval language of religion and charity, but different groups possessed disparate aims. By the fifteenth century a wide range of clearly targeted activities characterized the aims of guilds and fraternities. Parish charity was for parishioners, craft fraternities aimed to help their own members. People might belong to a number of fraternities and groupings and expect help from all in time of need. Besides the religious and social organizations master craftsmen could also expect help from their craft guilds, sometimes through the mediation of the craft's social wing, the fraternity, within which duties and expectations of benefits were presented to the members. Those who paid their dues, attended masses and funerals, kept fraternity secrets and led respectable lives could reasonably expect the group's support at times of misfortune and poverty: through illness, robbery, fire, shipwreck or accident. Fraternities insisted that their help would be given only to those who had fallen into poverty through misfortune, not misdeed. The Holy Trinity guild of Cambridge provided help only when 'a brother of the said gild be oppressed by poverty . . . and be not culpable'.[2] Fraternities were important frameworks for interaction and mutual support which came to fruition after a life of productive and constant contribution to the communal fund.

In the countryside most people working on the land would have held tenancies comprising parcels of customary land for which some, by now quite low, customary dues to the lord were owed, as well as land held by lease or freeholds. In most regions access to forest, rivers and meadows, although regulated, allowed for additional sources of livelihood or grazing, gleaning, picking and gathering. A sort of 'moral economy' regulated access to such resources as well as the distribution of its fruits among the needy of a parish. These relations are poorly documented and hard to assess but relied on the necessarily close relations between the households which made up a village.

By the fifteenth century the demographic ravages of the preceding decades had left a population much depleted in number and further reduced by the allure of possibilities of service and wage labour in the towns. The low cost of entry into land meant that younger members of the land-working families might well leave their natal village and establish themselves elsewhere.[3] This state of mobility and migration, though it offered

---

[1] J. M. Bennett, 'Conviviality and charity in medieval and early modern England', *Past and Present* 134 (1992), 19–41.

[2] M. Bateson (ed.), *Cambridge Gild Records* (Cambridge, 1903), p. 116, c. 8; see also the stipulation of the Annunciation guild of Cambridge, *ibid.*, p. 66, c. 6.

[3] For a general survey, see J. R. Lander, *Conflict and Stability in Fifteenth-Century England* (3rd edn, 1977), pp. 18–45. On fifteenth-century epidemiology and demography with special reference to East Anglia,

opportunities to some, also created traps of poverty for the old who could no longer rely on the presence of a younger generation to take over their lands and look after them in their retirement. Retirement agreements contracted between an older couple or individual and another, younger, household for maintenance at old age are only one of the measures by which this problem was tackled. Widows might surrender a property and retain an interest or rights in it like the widow Juliana who entered a transaction with John Ilsent at a manorial court session at Winslow (Bucks) in June 1430 by which she surrendered a cottage and some land and he paid for it over four years and also provided her with food and allowed her to live in the cottage.[4] Besides the ever-present danger of indigence through physical incapacity which might strike through disease or accident, there was a looming danger of serious neglect and deprivation in old age; one for which individuals themselves as well as lords of manors and village elders attempted to provide. Although wills often mention bequests to old retainers this century did not see the provision of numerous specialized charitable institutions for the elderly who were subsumed into the general category of poor.

Urban guilds habitually provided help to poor and old members, but people who had passed their lives within the world of craft guilds were in any case likely to be able to provide for themselves, or to be cared for by the younger generation. The passing on of craft status from father to son thus also created a continuity in household structure and a dependence which encouraged care of the old parent on whom guild status depended. Richer townsmen might strike an arrangement with an urban religious institution for retirement as a corrodian. The corrody allowed a person to live within a religious house as a paying guest who received bed and board at a level agreed upon in the corrody contract. This was done in return for a grant made at the outset, or with the expectation of a substantial legacy at the corrodian's death. Contemporary comment attests that corrodians were usually rich people who thus procured a comfortable and safe retirement. They came to fill not only religious houses but hospital space as well.[5]

None of these possibilities for retirement and care was open to poor labourers. A classic definition of the urban poor in the middle ages was 'He who by manual labour acquires his meagre daily bread and has nothing left over after dining', capturing the

---

see R. S. Gottfried, *Epidemic Disease in Fifteenth-Century England* (Leicester, 1978). See an important discussion of wage data and work patterns in S. A. C. Penn and C. Dyer, 'Wages and earnings in late medieval England: evidence from the enforcement of labour laws', *Economic History Review* 43 (1990), 356–76.

[4] A case cited in R. M. Smith, 'Coping with uncertainty: women's tenure of customary land in England c. 1370–1430', in J. Kermode (ed.), *Enterprise and Individuals in Fifteenth-Century England* (Gloucester, 1991), pp. 59–60.

[5] See for example in the hospital of St John at Cambridge: M. Rubin, *Charity and Community in Medieval Cambridge* (Cambridge, 1987), pp. 161, 165–6, 171–3. A poet of Arras complained that the rich could enter the hospital of St-Jean-en-l'Estrée, although it was meant to take care of the sick, pregnant women and the poor: R. Berger, *Littérature et société arrageoises au XIII siècle* (Arras, 1981), p. 228 (lines 131–40); on hunger caused by speculation in the price of corn by the rich, see *ibid.*, pp. 225–7.

precariousness of a work-life which could provide for subsistence but not much for saving, or for special expenses and needs.[6] Such people benefited from the general rise in wages in the late fourteenth and fifteenth centuries, but their patterns of work were far from secure or constant. This urban labourer had figured in the traditional image of poverty. The precarious work-life of the hand-labourer, the constant search for bread, is expressed in an Anglo-French religious poem 'Del povre home qui queroit le pain aus huis' in a collection of miracle-tales of the Virgin:

Uns povres hom jadis estois	There was once a poor man,
Qui en une vile manoit;	who lived in a town.
Povres estoit e mendianz,	He was a poor man and a beggar,
As huis aloit le pain querant;	who sought bread at doorways.
Des aumones que il queroit	From the alms which he got
E de ce que afanner pooit	and from what he managed to earn
A son cors et a ses deus mains	by his body and two hands
Vivoit molt eschars e molt vains.[7]	he lived a sparse and mean living.

Such people might belong during their lifetime to a parish fraternity, like the fraternity of 'poor men' of Norwich which collected very humble subscriptions and promised relief at times of need.[8] Living in the house of a son or daughter was another possibility; and an unthreatening old person could also expect to benefit from charitable donations within the parish, funds collected on feastdays, funerals and obits which would have been distributed at the churchwardens' discretion to those in need and of good character. Eligibility for relief always depended on the image which a poor person or household presented to its community, to neighbours and potential friends and helpers. As long as relief was dispensed by people who could discern the recipient, the expectation of need for future help would have operated as a strong incentive towards conformity, good behaviour, respectable bearing. By the fifteenth century many of the earlier medieval arrangements for relief in generalized redistribution through religious institutions had given way to more directly targeted and closely scrutinized forms of charitable giving.

It is thus clear that understandings of poverty are constructed at the intersection of two processes: the process of economic, demographic and social change which refashions areas and forms of need on the one hand, and the cultural perceptions of need as they are translated into idioms of charity and evaluations held by diverse social groups on the other. The medieval language of charity was a religious idiom which informed givers and recipients of expectations and duties within the charitable exchange. Medieval theologians and canon lawyers spent much energy in discussing minute aspects of merit and duty related to charity. Who was duty bound to relieve the

---

[6] Rubin, *Charity and Community*, p. 8.
[7] G. H. Kjellman (ed.), *La Deuxième Collection Anglo-Normande des Miracles de la Sainte Vièrge* (Uppsala, 1922), p. 282.
[8] N. P. Tanner, *The Church in Late Medieval Norwich 1370–1532* (Toronto, 1984), p. 209.

poor? How much should be given? Who deserved to be helped? Some of the more radical thinkers even justified theft when this was committed by a poor person, but mainstream formulations developed a less rigorous approach, perhaps a more realistic one. People were expected to give of their *superfluous* wealth, neither to deprive their family nor to bring hardship upon themselves in the giving, and to give to those in greatest need, with preference to family, to the virtuous poor and to the categories of *pauperes Christi*: widows, orphans and those who had chosen poverty voluntarily. The emphasis on the latter category diminished considerably in the later middle ages, as a disenchantment with the orders of friars and a suspicion of movements which preached radical poverty tarnished the image of such groups. A hectic discussion on the acceptability of religious poverty in its mendicant-itinerant form began in the University of Paris in the 1260s, but by the late fourteenth century it converged with anxieties about wilful withdrawal of labour by workers to produce a powerful anti-fraternal strain, as the friars were likened to the able-bodied beggar. Not only the religious opponents of the friars but the audience of Wyclif, Chaucer, Langland and Gower believed that 'able-bodied beggars, soliciting alms under false pretences, undermine a social order founded on work'.[9] Concurrently there was a tendency in the language of legislation and of the judiciary, as well as in the vernacular literature, to see the 'common labourer', the wage earner, as an idler and wanderer, and to criticize itinerant patterns of employment (which were based on short-term contracts and could yield higher wages), as disruptive of order and wilfully harmful to the organizers of manufacture.

To try and assess how preaching, parochial instruction, traditions of mutual help and human compassion interacted with the perceptible needs of the poor to produce charitable giving and interest in relief is a considerable challenge. Not least because the inclinations towards and understanding of social obligation shift and change, and depend on the sense of well-being, cohesion and interdependence experienced in a society. The poor can be either a very close and intimate group, or a far and distant one; they can include the poor of one's family, parish or town, and exclude other groups. We witness a whole array of provision, from giving to religious orders in the metropolis such as the order of St Thomas of Acre in London, to the more common provision for the poor of a person's current or natal parish or the prisoners in the town gaol. The crucial element in recommending the intimate and familiar over the foreign lies not only in greater perceived relevance, but also in the sense of cohesion which was thus affected, and probably as importantly, in the spiritual value of prayers by recipients who knew their benefactors. Every act of giving assumed the grateful return which would contribute, through prayer, to a treasure of merit operating in the giver's

---

[9] P. R. Szittya, *The Antifraternal Tradition in Medieval Literature* (Princeton, 1986), p. 257; see further on the poetic tradition pp. 183–287, especially pp. 257–66. On Chaucer's lasting influence on this imagery, see H. S. Bennett, *Chaucer and Fifteenth-Century Verse and Prose* (Oxford, repr. 1990), pp. 22–6. On ideas of disendowment among the gentry, see M. Aston, '"Caim's castles": poverty, politics and disendowment', in R. B. Dobson (ed.), *The Church, Politics and Patronage in the Fifteenth Century* (Gloucester, 1984), pp. 45–81.

favour at that greatest moment of need, after his or her death.[10] Accumulation of such merit was an on-going enterprise; it neither required nor indicated excessive piety, rather a conventional participation in an altogether commonplace religious practice. Even if Lollards doubted and derided masses for the dead and the teachings on purgatory, these nonetheless effected widespread expectations and routines of piety and religious understanding.[11] And the fifteenth century more than any preceding century saw an explosion in the elaboration, multiplication and ubiquity of this 'accountancy of the other world'. Such understanding of merit, punishment and the after-life created the framework from which charitable giving and the understanding of poverty and the poor could never be divorced. This intimate link also created problems. Once the poor came to be seen as unequal to the task of intercession – through wilful pauperization, sloth or indiscipline – charitable attention would turn away from them, seeking other deserving recipients.

So the ubiquitous teaching of the Christian view of the poor interacted with on-going changes in social relations to influence images of the poor and thus the experience of poverty in fifteenth-century England. The product of deep conjunctural changes in the second half of the fourteenth century – dramatic demographic changes which saw a drastic fall in the availability of labour and a decline in profitability margins in land, industry and commerce – fifteenth-century society displays traits of relatively strong real wages and an abundance of working opportunities which encouraged migration, and a volatility in family structure.[12] The regional nature of variation in economic activity means that we can generalize only with the greatest caution, but one can see the fifteenth century as a period of low and stable demographic pressure, of diversification in productive activities, and of a relationship between demand for and supply of labour beneficial to labourers, particularly those of lower skill. The demand for simple manufactured goods by labourers and their families called not for the exclusive skills of a high-class metal worker, but for those of the labourers in the workshops of tailors, shoemakers, tanners and cooks. A market in domestic service had developed in the second half of the fourteenth century in which young people could gain their first job experience. The recurrent complaints of employers about the levels of wages can only be taken together with other wage indicators to establish the fact that variety, profit and conditions of work were much more beneficial for labourers than they had been a century earlier.

An idiom of complaint about the attitude of labourers towards work developed along some traditional literary *topoi*, but with a vigour unmatched in earlier periods. The

---

[10] See the provision of clothes and food for poor men at the funeral of Thomas Stonor in 1474: A. Hanham, *The Celys and their World: An English Merchant Family of the Fifteenth Century* (Cambridge, 1985), pp. 258–9. On provision for masses, see Tanner, *Church in Norwich*, pp. 91–110.

[11] See the views expressed in A. Hudson (ed.), *Selections from English Wycliffite Writings* (Cambridge, 1978), nos. 16, 18, 20a, 20b.

[12] P. J. P. Goldberg, *Women, Work and Life Cycle in a Medieval Economy* (Oxford, 1992), especially chapters 3–5.

menace of workers who bargained with their employers, who left their jobs when better conditions were on offer or who changed occupation, elicited a noisy response from those who were in a position to influence legislation. The years following the Black Death saw the issuing first of the Ordinance (1349) and then of the Statute (1351) of Labourers and the creation of a judicial system for the control of wage rates and terms of employment.[13] These were renewed in the fifteenth century, with refinements curtailing mobility and bargaining by workers, like the statute of 1402 which decreed under the pain of a 20s fine: 'no labourer [be hired to work] by the Week, nor that no Labourers, Carpenters, Masons, Tilers, Plaisterers . . . nor none other Labourers, shall take any Hire for the Holy-days, nor for the Evens of Feasts where they do not labour but till the Hour of Noon'.[14] Although the degree to which the labour legislation was applied in reality remains open to discussion and varied from region to region, at the very least its tenor reflects the mood of employers: that of frustration at a new economic order in which labour was scarce and workers were able to negotiate in conditions more favourable to them. And the meaningful division here is not between town and country, nor even between lords and peasantry; but between employer and wage earner. New measures for control of the external manifestations of status and wealth were put into force in the sumptuary legislation which attempted to limit the use of certain fabrics and colours to office holders and higher social classes.[15] The worker who demanded exorbitant wages was weighed down with culpability: it was he who kept profits of manufacture low, in his new consumption habits he aped his betters and trivialized their lifestyles, he sat in taverns and contaminated the moral fabric of the community which contained him.

The image of the productive worker, much in demand, seemed always to contain the threat of withdrawal into the world of unproductive dependence, the beggar. It is a curious and resonant transformation which combined worker and ever-threatening, menacing sturdy beggar, one which had long-lasting effects on conceptions of poverty and relief.[16] The generation which followed the labour legislators introduced a new type of legislation, one which identified the parish as the unit most suited for the control of social dangers posed by poverty by providing alms to the needy, at least those within its boundaries, from the parochial living. The statute of 1391 insisted that a

---

[13] See *Statutes of the Realm*, I (1810), p. 308, c. 7: 'Because that many [valiant] Beggars, as long as they may live of begging, do refuse to labour, giving themselves to Idleness and Vice, and sometime to Theft and other Abominations; none upon the said pain of Imprisonment shall, under the colour of Pity or Alms, give any thing to such, which may labour, or presume to favour them . . . so that thereby they may be compelled to labour for their necessary living.' For the statute of 1388: *ibid.*, II (1816), p. 56, c. 3.

[14] *Ibid.*, II, p. 137, c. 14.

[15] C. Dyer, *Standards of Living in the Later Middle Ages: Social Change in England c. 1200–1520* (Cambridge, 1989), pp. 86–7.

[16] For some images of beggars see the misericords at Winchester College Chapel and at Christ Church (Hants): G. L. Remnant and M. D. Anderson, *A Catalogue of Misericords in Great Britain* (Oxford, 1969), pp. 55, 60.

portion of every appropriated church living be allocated to poor relief: 'that the Diocesan of the Place . . . ordain, according to the Value of such Churches, a convenient sum of money to be paid and distributed yearly . . . to the poor Parishioners of the said Church'.[17] This was a desperate attempt to make an impact on parochial charity since most livings were held by vicars who collected only a small portion of the income from the parish's land and tithe income. Many parishes were appropriated to religious houses which collected their revenues and in return appointed and supported a vicar. Charitable provision suffered as funds were diverted out of the parish, and as vicarages were often established with very small incomes.[18] But it marked an important beginning in identifying the parish as the framework for distribution. Bedding to the value of £10 left by John Shipyard the Elder in his will of 1473 for the poor house-holders of St Stephen's parish, Bristol, was to be distributed by the parish vicar.[19] Such relief was aimed at the 'deserving' poor with the aim of clearing the streets of worthy beggars, thus leaving to their own fortunes and devices the group labelled 'able poor', beyond parish, occupation or stable employment.

The writers who composed for the audience of townsmen, merchants, craftsmen, lawyers and country gentlemen in this world of social adversity and economic anxiety took up the theme of poverty and begging with a vengeance. There is a great preoccupation with what the poor ate and drank, their morals, and their working habits. A rhymed poem of c. 1480 'Rauf Coilyear' describes an encounter between Charlemagne, lost in a forest, and a charcoal-burner, Rauf. The king is taken to be a traveller and is offered a meal at the collier's table:

> Of Capounis and Cunningis they had plentie,
> With wyne at thair will, and eik Vennysoun;
> Byrdis bakin in breid, the best that may be;
> Thus full freschlie thay fure into fusioun.[20]

The table of the worker groans with delicacies, some of them by his own admission products of his unlawful forays into the royal forest. His table is full and his manner is assertive. Around the person of the worker lurked suspicions of excess, hoarding, theft. There was a sense in which what working people had and enjoyed, *must* have been acquired at the expense of masters, employers, the audience of such poems.

Moralizing writers approached the problem more explicitly, and in disapproving tones. The balance of social advantage and disadvantage was clearly captured in the dichotomous pair: waster and winner, wanderer and worker. But such a dichotomy was

---

[17] *Statutes of the Realm*, II, p. 80, c. 6 (1391). The 1402 statute insists that appropriated churches 'keep Hospitality' (*hospitalite tenir*): pp. 136–7, c. 12.

[18] See an example of such failure as reported in the visitation of Thomas Bek, bishop of Lincoln, in 1343, when the abbot and convent of Torre (Devon) had failed to distribute corn in their parish of Skidbrook (Lincs): D. M. Owen, *Church and Society in Medieval Lincolnshire* (Lincoln, 1971), p. 33.

[19] Dyer, *Standards of Living*, p. 249.

[20] F. J. Amours (ed.), *Scottish Alliterative Poems in Riming Stanzas*, Scottish Text Soc. (Edinburgh, 1897), p. 89 (lines 207–10); for the dating, see p. xxxvi.

23   The deserving and undeserving poor: a cripple and a man in the stocks

no more than an illusion, an overdrawn distinction. The term 'waster' was used not only to describe the consumer, but also those who seemed to be outside a regime of stable employment and self-support. The 'wasters' could thus be the very people who depended on their own labour for everything they ate, and every stitch of clothing they wore, but who might periodically be reduced to dependence and begging.[21] In Langland's words in the poem *Piers Plowman* (*c.* 1386) there were those who 'putten hem to plough' and those who 'putten hem to pride' and the relationship between them is set up as an adversarial one.[22] Because he who begs or feigns need is the robber of the truly needy:

> For he that beggeth or bit, but he have nede,
> He is fals with the feend and defraudeth the nedy,
> And ek gileth the gyvere ageynes his wille.
> For if he wiste he were noght nedy he wolde it gyue
> Another that were moore nedy; so the nedieste sholde be holpe.[23]

Lollard writings insisted on this point, as in the satirical 'Letter of Satan to the Clergy' of 1400 where Satan avows having taught the friars 'how thei xuld increase in riches, and hate comon beggers and poore men, and that thei schuld not be poore

---

[21] A point powerfully drawn out in the insightful discussion of '*Piers Plowman*: poverty, work and community', in D. Aers, *Community, Gender and Individual Identity: English Writing 1360–1430* (1988), pp. 38–44. On patterns of employment in the later middle ages, see Penn and Dyer, 'Wages and earnings', pp. 365–6.

[22] G. Kane and E. Talbot Donaldson (eds.), *Piers Plowman: The B Version* (1975), prologue, lines 20–34, p. 228. For a general discussion of the theme, see G. Shepherd, 'Poverty in *Piers Plowman*', in T. H. Aston, P. R. Coss, C. Dyer and J. Thirsk (eds.), *Ideas and Social Relations: Essays in Honour of R. H. Hilton* (Cambridge, 1983), pp. 169–89.

[23] Kane and Donaldson (eds.), *Piers Plowman: The B Version*, passus VII, lines 67–71, p. 373. On the popularity of the friars as recipients of charity, see R. G. K. A. Mertes, 'The household as a religious community', in J. Rosenthal and C. Richmond (eds.), *People, Politics and Community in the Later Middle Ages* (Gloucester, 1987), p. 135.

in dede'.[24] Such dissimulation and deceit meant that a dilemma of charitable choice thus faced every person intent on alms giving, to seek out the worthy recipient. And it could only be solved by careful scrutiny of those who presented themselves as deserving. We can see here how trust comes to be seen as gullibility, as vulnerability to fraud, and how a well-known local virtuous poor person could become the preferred object of charity.

So the poor can be seen as a group including people permanently unable to provide for themselves, those who had fallen into indigence through some traumatic event, those who aged into it as their capacity to work declined and those who chose it for religious reasons. The latter group was supported by a dense system of recommendations to succour; their presence on the streets and roads of medieval England dramatized the alleged link between poverty and virtue. But even the itinerant religious, like poor pilgrims, did well to equip themselves with letters of recommendation. Letters not dissimilar were required from labourers on the road, as documents attesting the completion of terms of service, if not recommendations for sympathy and help.[25]

Fifteenth-century folk looked to their locality, their parish as a framework for effective help and relief. Links of solidarity seem to have operated most strongly at the local level, as coping with poverty was increasingly seen as a problem directly affecting the quality of life and the merit of a village or an urban parish. There is a discernible shift of patronage interests to the local, even among the gentry, from the monastery to the parish church. This shift is related to long-term changes in the identification of the gentry with the locality as the area of effective service and patronage. Parish churches came to bear the signs of this renewed interest, in the partitioning of parish space into family pews and the vast rebuilding projects of the fifteenth century. But even when the parish enjoyed the bounty of a local lord, most preoccupation with poor relief remained with churchwardens and able parishioners. These could organize into guilds which managed the communal funds, like the Corpus Christi guild of Kirton-in-Lindsey which was ruled in 1484 by three aldermen and whose account book records liturgical activities as well as the provision of loans against surety. Granting of loans was often seen in the middle ages as a charitable act, as it could rescue people from temporary need and allow those fallen on hard times to rebuild their businesses.[26] Bishops similarly provided letters of indulgence to recommend people who had lost fortunes or means of livelihood through misfortune and not through their idleness or sin. These people were allowed temporary begging, to get them back on their feet and permanently out of the state of dependence. Merchants, artisans and their family could

---

[24] Hudson (ed.), *English Wycliffite Writings*, no. 17 and notes.
[25] A. Gransden, 'A letter of recommendation from John Whethemstede for a poor pilgrim 1453/4', *English Historical Review* 106 (1991), 932–9. The Statute of Cambridge of 1388 required that 'servant ou laborer, soit il home ou femme' be stopped if he or she 'ne porte lettre patente contenante la cause de son aler & le temps de son retornir': *Statutes of the Realm*, II, p. 56, c. 3.
[26] Rubin, *Charity and Community*, pp. 217–21.

thus approach their neighbours and friends with the promise of spiritual benefit in return for short-term and intensive help until the disorientated member could return to productive living. An urban parish like All Hallows, London, collected only humble sums for redistribution: 2s 6d 'of men and wemen of the parysche for the charyte potte' in 1459–60, as well as 1s 11d from the Hock-Day collections of 'the wyvys of the parysshe'.[27] These are small but regular sums which allowed for some discerning distribution.

In some parishes interested benefactors created more permanent, public and ambitious arrangements for relief, in a multitude of institutions known as almshouses, which varied greatly in size, endowment and scope for provision. At the more elaborate end there was a foundation like Newton *hospitale* founded by Sir John Colvylle in 1403, a combination of clerics and poor folk in a chantry almshouse. Three poor men and a poor woman who cleaned and cooked for them were given a heavy white cloth habit and two pairs of shoes a year and supported by 6d a week. Their prayers together with the clerical effort provided a comprehensive form of religious intercession for the founder.[28] A similar, if grander, enterprise was the college/almshouse founded around 1440 by Ralph Lord Cromwell at his new castle at Tattershall. The statutes of *c.* 1460 set out a community of secular clerks and choristers together with thirteen poor men and thirteen poor women. Another Lincolnshire foundation, the Burgh chantry at Gainsborough was founded in 1498 to maintain five bedesmen at 7d per week. The combination of professional intercessors, the clergy, with the devotional group of poor remained a powerful pattern in the large-scale schemes of provision for the after-life until the eve of the Reformation.[29]

More typical were institutions attached to parish churches and providing for the parish poor. In 1451 the vill of Elsworth (Camb) founded an almshouse in the church-yard.[30] In Cambridge four new almshouses were founded between 1463 and 1484. The problem of reliable management and perpetual supervision is a perennial one in charitable foundation; in Cambridge the academic colleges were enlisted to provide the administrative backbone in three cases. They were to provide for the poor of their parish and usually provided residence and support. In Saffron Walden *c.* 1400 the almshouse took in '13 poor people' those with special needs: 'the decrepit, blind, lame'. Like the Cambridge almshouses involvement of laymen is prominent; here, twenty-four 'most worschypful pareschenys' managed the house and appointed a man and woman to work in it. He was to collect subscriptions from the more able households of the parish and she was to serve the poor men, wash them and tend to all their needs.

---

[27] C. Welch (ed.), *The Churchwardens' Accounts of the Parish of All Hallows, London Wall, in the City of London, 33 Henry VI to 27 Henry VII (AD 1455–AD 1563)* (1912), p. 7.

[28] Rubin, *Charity and Community*, pp. 142–6. See a similar effort in M. Hicks, 'St Katherine's hospital, Heytesbury: prehistory, foundation and refoundation, 1408–1472', *Wiltshire Archaeological and Natural History Magazine* 78 (1984), 62–9.

[29] Owen, *Church and Society*, pp. 99, 101. On the almshouse at Sherborne (Dorset), see Dyer, *Standards of Living*, pp. 245–6.

[30] Dyer, *Standards of Living*, p. 9.

The almshouse also distributed to the bed-ridden poor living within five leagues (a radius of around fifteen miles) of Saffron Walden.[31] Such institutions were the order of the day in fifteenth-century England. A testament could set up an almshouse by the wish of a single benefactor, like Reede's hospital at Havering (Ess) founded in 1483 for five local poor of good behaviour and recent poverty.[32] Old-fashioned hospitals run by religious communities were giving way to this more direct, discriminating and local form of giving. In the second half of the century these were often connected with attempts at the implementation of public policy: keeping the local poor, supporting the passing poor for a while and trying to get rid of the 'foreign beggars' (*extranei mendicantes*), as has recently been shown in the cases of Essex and Suffolk. Licensing and control of alehouse hours are another type of reaction to the social panic which rendered the more subtle distinctions between types of need and indigence less noticeable.[33]

Noble households not only supported the poor in permanent institutions created to commemorate the dead, but gave alms as part of their rituals and routines on festive occasions and at funerals.[34] They also gave spontaneously, when their members encountered the needy.[35] Such occasional alms appear in their household accounts, and where the identity of the beneficiary was specified, it usually fell within the categories of merit which we have already encountered.[36] The leper, sick, beggar, widow, mentioned in such household entries, reflect the notions so powerfully captured in the Pardon to the hard-suffering meek described in *Piers Plowman*:

> Ac olde and hore, that helpes ben and nedy,
> . . .
> Ac mesels [lepers] and mendenantes men yfalle in mischief
> As prisones and pilgrimes and parauntur men yrobbed
> Or bylowe thorw luther [wicked] men and lost here catel after,
> Or thorw fuyr or thorw floed yfalle into pouerte,
> That taketh thise meschiefes mekliche and myldeliche at herte,
> For loue of here lowe hertes oure lord hath hem ygraunted
> Here penuance and here purgatorye uppon this puyre erthe . . . [37]

[31] F. W. Steer, 'The statutes of the Saffron Walden almshouses', *Transactions of the Essex Archaeological Society* 25 (1958), 161–83.
[32] M. K. McIntosh, *Autonomy and Community: The Royal Manor of Havering 1200–1500* (Cambridge, 1986), pp. 239–40.
[33] M. K. McIntosh, 'Local change and community control in England, 1465–1500', *Huntington Library Quarterly* 49 (1986), 230–1.
[34] Like the Staffords, who made distributions at Christmas and Easter: Mertes, 'Household as religious community', p. 135.
[35] See for the late fourteenth century John of Gaunt's household accounts: J. T. Rosenthal, *Nobles and the Noble Life, 1295–1500* (1976), pp. 93, 152.
[36] On doorstep charity and provision in women's wills see P. H. Cullum, ' "And hir name was charite": charitable giving by and for women in late medieval Yorkshire', in P. J. P. Goldberg (ed.), *Woman is a Worthy Wight: Women in English Society c. 1200–1500* (Stroud, 1992), pp. 182–211.
[37] D. Pearsall (ed.), *Piers Plowman by William Langland: An Edition of the C-Text*, Yorkshire Medieval Texts, second series (1978), passus IX, lines 175–85, 168–9.

24   Works of mercy: feeding the hungry, giving drink to the thirsty, clothing
the naked and visiting the sick

The men and women of fifteenth-century England thus lived in a world which
recognized a substantial social obligation and moral duty towards the poor, but these
notions were webs of intricate aspirations, positions, capabilities which produced a
variety of experiences of poverty. As in all periods there were specific poverty traps
which hovered over most people: sickness, accident, widowhood and orphanhood,
the failure of crops, loss of friends and family. The position of women in youth and
later in marriage was very much dependent on that of husband or father and
fluctuated within the household as her relative importance as mother and child-
bearer changed throughout her lifetime. The indigence of workers at sickness or old
age reflected the degree to which their working life had become integrated into
associations of craft and neighbourhood; that of a customary tenant smallholder,
on arrangements made for retirement and the existence of children to care for him
and his wife. But the least changing, grinding and ever-present poverty is simply
the precariousness of the life of men and women who depended on their manual
labour for subsistence. And this is as true in country as in town; hardship is
poignantly expressed in the words of the herdsmen in the Second Shepherds' play
of the Towneley cycle, who speak of the oppressors of the poor in terms of class
antagonism:

> We ar so hamyd,
> Fortaxed and ramyd,
> We ar mayde handtamyd
> With thyse gentlery-men.[38]

Any failure in health and strength, any changes in the labour market had direct effects on the well-being of their families and dependants. When they stood in dole queues at funerals, or when their wives and children begged, they probably faced a less welcoming response in the fifteenth century than before. If they had been long settled in a parish and generally untroublesome there was a good chance of receiving help from a parish pot or an almshouse, to collect pennies and loaves at funerals and to be the subject of small gifts of food. Here the fifteenth century saw a development of more closely monitored bodies for direct distribution to known and settled poor. But the lives of many people were more complex: migration was rife; the working life cycle saw a number of changes from service sometime into apprenticeship and craft; there was seasonal movement into and out of towns; people were caught out in a hostile environment without friends; or even found themselves alone and in difficulty, or encumbered with dependants in new surroundings. They were earning better wages than their grandparents and great-grandparents had done, and were probably better nourished, but when adversity struck and found them away from family, out of work, belonging to no provident corporation, the more stringent perceptions of social obligation of the fifteenth century may well have left them, working people, without succour and, to add insult to injury, eyed with suspicion, sometimes arrested for begging, the objects of fears which haunted the better-fed, more fortunate, folk around them.

---

[38] A. C. Cawley (ed.), *The Wakefield Pageants in the Towneley Cycle* (Manchester, 1958), p. 43 (lines 15–18).

$$\boxed{II}$$

RELIGION

Colin Richmond

This is what an educated Venetian had to say about the religious behaviour of the English in the mid-1490s:

> Although they all attend mass every day, and say many Paternosters in public (the women carrying long rosaries in their hands, and any who can read taking the office of our Lady with them, and with some companion reciting it in the church verse by verse, in a low voice, after the manner of churchmen), they always hear mass on Sunday in their parish church; nor do they omit any form incumbent upon good Christians; there are, however, many who have various opinions concerning religion.[1]

Like any foreign tourist this Venetian has a variety of observations to make upon the peculiar manners and customs of Englishmen and women; some of his observations are acute, some are obvious, some are silly. He was unlike any foreign tourist, however, in where he came from. Venice around 1500 was a Renaissance city. In London he must have felt like a New Yorker in Calcutta; nonetheless, he had more of an anthropological eye than the average New Yorker abroad – which is why his report is more than merely quaint. Moreover, Venice was a civic society where religion was as intense a preoccupation as was art, indeed the former largely (but not solely) engendered the latter. In this brilliant world the humanist nobleman Gasparo Contarini in 1511 underwent 'an experience brighter than the sun'.[2] Such a deeply felt religious conversion was rare in England: Margery Kempe's may have been the only one. In other words, the religious habits of the primitive English, as vouched for by the Venetian visitor, were one thing; their religious attitudes were decidedly another.

In any writing on a vanished religion it is necessary to be anthropological: to proceed from actions to attitudes. Here we will be alliterative and examine religion under three heads, those of popularity, propriety and property. Philistinism will be the bridge between propriety and property. We begin where the Venetian began: in the parish church. He says, 'above all are their riches displayed in the church treasures; for there is not a parish church in the kingdom so mean as not to possess crucifixes, candlesticks,

---

[1] C. A. Sneyd (ed.) *A Relation of the Island of England*, Camden Soc., old series 37 (1847), p. 23. The later quotation is from p. 29.

[2] D. Fenlon, *Heresy and Obedience in Tridentine Italy: Cardinal Pole and the Counter Reformation* (Cambridge, 1972), p. 9.

censers, patens, and cups of silver'. Here is another reminder that religion in fifteenth-century England was of the kind our New Yorker (who had travelled in present-day Mexico) would instantly recognize as pre-modern. There can be no doubt that the English were devout, as by their gifts may their devotion be known. Even the most casual acquaintance with church inventories, even the most cursory perusal of wills and testaments, reveals that parishioners were familiar with their parish church and loved what they knew so well. They did not all love to the same degree; some were more capable of love than others. The inventory of Thame parish church drawn up in 1448 shows that bishops, aristocratic ladies, knights, rectors and vicars had given books, vestments, and ornaments, but plain William Bates, Henry and Agnes Clerk, Thomas and Agnes Brightwell, and Isabel Chapman were recorded as benefactors too.[3] If we take four wills of 1499, which follow one another in the register of the archdeacon of Bedford, we discover John Breteyn of Stotfold leaving measures of barley for the provision of candles to burn before images and for the repair of bells; John Lord of Millbrook leaving barley and a cow for candles and 20s towards the price of a great bell – if the parish was disposed to buy one; Richard Curteys of Hill in Warden leaving barley for candles and the bells; and William Gere of Sharnbrook leaving 1s for the maintenance of the bells and lesser sums for lights to burn before the images in the church. These men were small farmers or country craftsmen; they had wives, sons and daughters; they did not have too much to spare for the church; they gave generously of what they did have.[4]

Images and bells: these were close to the hearts (and minds) of fifteenth-century Englishmen and women. Even more notable than the expansive manner in which parishioners furnished churches was the time, energy and money they contributed to the maintenance, renovation and reconstruction of their fabric. Under the supervision (and prodding) of elected wardens naves, towers and porches were heightened, lengthened or built from scratch. In the dean of Salisbury's three visitations between 1405 and 1412 of the thirty-two churches and chapels in his charge, the fabric of only seven was being neglected throughout that period.[5] When the much diminished population of virtually every parish in England is recalled, the co-operative effort of the relatively few who remained to maintain, and often to extend, their churches has to be stressed. Some of these philanthropists may still be seen – in conventional representation. In the eastern spandrel of the doorway of the north porch of Acle church in Norfolk there are carved two figures telling their beads; they are Robert Bataly and Joan his wife. Robert died in 1494 leaving twenty marks for the building of the porch; Joan was his executor. A bell at nearby Mautby church also bears his name; to that church he left two quarters of wheat for repairs. It was not only on their deathbeds, and therefore at the prompting of their parish priest (or confessor), that men and women

---

[3] Oxfordshire County Record Office, MS DD Par. Thame C5, fols. 28–31v.

[4] P. Bell (ed.), *Bedfordshire Wills 1480–1519*, Bedfordshire Historical Records Soc. 45 (1966), pp. 79–80.

[5] T. C. B. Timmins (ed.), *The Register of John Chandler Dean of Salisbury 1404–17*, Wiltshire Record Soc. 39 (1984 for 1983), p. xxvi.

had their church in mind; as Clive Burgess has taught us, while they lived many exhibited a lively charity. One such was the reverend Thomas Cod, vicar of the church of St Margaret, Rochester, who died in 1465. Thomas's brass declares that this 'beloved and pious vicar . . . rendered great service to this church of Christ and repaired the belfry when it was in a very bad state; may eternal life be the reward of all his holy works'.

Belfries and porches. What was being built is a sure indication of social as well as religious inclinations. Change-ringing was an English craze which has persisted. Did its origins lie in a ritual of male bonding deliberately made inaccessible to outsiders (a sort of village gnosticism), or was it simple local patriotism to have a full peal? The mania for porches seems more rational. They were for a variety of secular purposes, especially if they had rooms on a second floor. At Salle in Norfolk both north and south porches have upper rooms. The south porch is of the 1440s, the north of the 1480s. The room in the north porch is imposing. It has its original stone seats; the central roof-boss of the Last Judgement was no doubt also related to the room's purpose: in it, as the manor court rolls show, important communal business was done. Not all porches are as grand as those at Salle. That at Monewdon, deep in rural Suffolk, is little more than a brick outhouse added to the church around 1500. Why was this extra space universally needed – for it was (in whatever form) all over the country? Was it because the body of the church had lost the secular and communal character it once had? By the second half of the fifteenth century altars and images had proliferated in most churches; tombs and benches may have further constricted movement. Perhaps more inhibiting than the loss of real space was the change in its character: as if the holiness of the sanctuary had invaded the nave and aisles. To do the less holy business of the community, room had to be made beyond the space now inhabited by Christ and the saints.

Porches might be regarded, therefore, as indicators of an enhanced or, at any rate, an expanding religiosity. If there had been no Reformation they too would have been taken over by the saints – as they have been in the Counter-Reformation churches of Poland, where women may discover a holy helper even when the church door is locked. Vestries or sacristies had a determinedly prosaic function from the start and have retained it; the fact that they too are being added to parish churches in the fifteenth century is of great significance. They are essentially strong rooms for storing the ornaments of the church; once a chest would have done, now, as a consequence of the generosity of parishioners, a room has become necessary. Some of these rooms retain their fortress-like barred windows, at Ludlow and Croscombe (in Somerset), for instance. We are witnessing here capital investment to protect wealth; thieves were as ready then as they are now to carry off the unattended objects of devotion: lock up your pyxes was the surprising moral of a fifteenth-century anti-Semitic horror story.[6] Such concern would not have done for the early Franciscans or for that dwindling band of moralists who regarded property (whatever its purpose) as a hindrance rather than a

---

[6] E. K Chambers, *English Literature at the Close of the Middle Ages* (Oxford, 1945), pp. 45–6.

help to devotion. Fifteenth-century churchwardens, however, almost invariably came from lower-middle-class backgrounds where an accumulative frame of mind was second nature; besides, they were also trustees, responsible to the parochial community for ornaments which were as much to the glory of God as to the honour of the parish. All this their meticulous accounts demonstrate. We must not make the mistake of believing that their close attention to the tasks of this world precluded them from taking seriously those which would gain them entry to the next.

The inscription over the vestry door at Halesworth in Suffolk proclaims that Thomas Clement and his wife Margaret were responsible for its construction and asks that prayers be offered for their souls – as do hundreds of surviving inscriptions on churches, their furnishings and their ornaments. To walk into a parish church around 1500 was to enter (as it were) an ante-chamber of purgatory. Almost everything was labelled with the names of local souls who required assistance; almost everything in use was an *aide-mémoire*; and almost every grateful recollection was of benefit to those recalled. In other words, the church and its fittings were an obit roll. It would be another mistake to believe self-conceit is to be detected here. Self-concern certainly. Yet concern for others is to be found in the very provision of a rood-screen, or font, or chalice, or clerestory, or aisle – these were for the benefit of the community for as long as they and it lasted. It is with the utmost poignancy that one notes the date 1532 inscribed on the north vestry of Melton Mowbray church; within a few years the ornaments it was built to store would be dispersed and the vestry itself change its function.

Not only ornaments disappeared from churches. So too did images. The empty niches on the exterior walls of English churches are evidence of the cultural shock of the Reformation: the elimination of the saints is as startling a transformation of attitudes as is the disappearance of the dead. The significance of this seismic shift in the mentalities of Englishmen and women cannot be overestimated. Nothing in their fifteenth-century religious behaviour or sensibility – collective or individual – prepares the historian for it, certainly not the hostility towards images of the handful of Lollards. Yet, when Michael Gamare of Wimbourne St Giles, Dorset, declared (or, rather, was accused of declaring) in 1516 that it is 'a lewde thynge and a madde condition or use occupied in this contree or paryshe that wemen will cumm and sette their candles afore the Image of Saynte Gyles',[7] we hear the authentic note of male disdain for what many of the so-called reformers of the sixteenth century called the childish behaviour of women. Such a charge is more revealing about those who made it than about those who reverenced images. Besides it was a false charge: many men of mature years and sound minds made their prayers to saints. Thomas Tyard and Robert Langton will have to stand as representatives of their fellows.

---

[7] I owe this reference to the kindness of Andrew Brown; it is from the episcopal register of Edmund Audley, bishop of Salisbury, fol. 158v.

Thomas was a Cambridge man, a bachelor of theology and a fellow of Corpus Christi College. Other well-educated men were his friends; one of them, John Seyntwary, also a theologian and fellow of Corpus, was his executor; John helped to found a bible clerkship at the College. Thomas may have moved in learned, even humanist, circles, but he was not ambitious: he held only one living in his life, that of Bawburgh in Norfolk. There he died in 1506. At Bawburgh was the holy well and shrine of a new saint, St Walstan, the patron of farmers and rural labourers. Thomas left many things to the church at Bawburgh – a silver pyx for carrying the consecrated host to the sick, what he called a 'pardon crosse', also of silver and decorated with 'margarites', for instance. To St Walstan he bequeathed a robe studded with silver coins. Indeed, Thomas may have been the author of the late fifteenth-century English verse life of St Walstan.[8] Emphasis is necessary here: Thomas was *not* an old woman from the depths of the country beyond the Ribble – where at Fernyhalgh near Preston at this time a new devotion to a holy well of the Virgin appears to have been gathering a momentum which has been maintained until now. Thomas was not a man to go in for childish and superstitious practices.

Robert Langton was from the region beyond the Ribble; he was born at Appleby. Robert in all respects went further than Thomas Tyard. He studied at Bologna as well as Oxford; he became a doctor of civil law in 1501; he was treasurer of York minster by 1509; before his death in 1524 he went on pilgrimage to Palestine, Rome and Compostella and published a book about his travels. The second part of the book itemizes the 'relykes and wondres in dyvers places' he had seen. In Italy, alongside ancient mythic marvels like the bell broken by the devil at Subiaco, and modern ones, such as the body of Simon 'that was martyred with the Jewes' at Trent, Thomas recorded at Assisi St Francis's blessing written for and given to his companion Leo, his breviary, and the St Damiano crucifix which had spoken to him.[9] We also owe to Robert the inventory of ex-votos at the tomb of Archbishop Richard Scrope in York minster, made while Robert was treasurer there: 'Item vij leges and futes argenti. Item iiij tethe and iiij herttes argenti. Item viij eyn and ij handes argenti. Item viij ymages and heides. Sanct George on horsbak of silver. A horse of silver'; and so on.[10] Was all this the 'simple curiosity', which (it has been said) 'was certainly the predominant motive of many pilgrims' of the fifteenth century? Is curiosity ever simple? That of a civil lawyer, who had studied at Oxford and Bologna, was likely to have been of a most complex variety. It would be to fall into another trap to suggest that Robert had the

---

8 Thomas Tyard's will is in Norfolk Record Office, NCC Register Ryxe, fols. 338–9. He is noticed in A. B. Emden, *A Biographical Register of the University of Cambridge to 1500* (hereafter *BRUC*) (Cambridge, 1963), p. 600. For the English verse life of St Walstan, see M. R. James, 'Lives of St Walstan', *Norfolk Archaeology* 19 (1917), 238–67. For Fernyhalgh, see Debra Eden, 'Truth, legend and continuing faith: the history of Our Lady's Well, Fernyhalgh', unpublished Keele Univ. BA dissertation, 1988.

9 E. M. Blackie (ed.), *The Pilgrimage of Robert Langton* (Harvard, 1924) pp. 26–39. Robert has a biography in A. B. Emden, *A Biographical Register of the University of Oxford to A.D. 1500* (hereafter *BRUO*) (3 vols., Oxford, 1957–9), II, pp. 1100–1.

10 J. Raine (ed.), *The Fabric Rolls of York Minster*, Surtees Soc. 35 (1859 for 1858), p. 226.

'intensely spiritual feelings of an earlier age', both because Robert would have studied theology not the law if he had, and because (anyway) earlier ages were no more spiritually intense than later ones.[11]

There are a number of important lessons to be learnt from these two examples. First, it will not do to dismiss, as the Lollards did and many historians continue to do, the role of the saints (their relics, shrines, wells and the pilgrimage of the faithful to them) as peripheral to some hard core of 'real' religion. Lollard voices, and Lollard attitudes, may not be ignored, and we must return to them, but although they disturbed the minds of some bishops they disturbed the equanimity of the orthodox so little that we are entitled to say that they disturbed it not at all. Such 'real' religion is often thought of, and sometimes defined as, more spiritual than religion which has the saints as its pivot of attitude and action. Yet, the spiritual reality of the saints is uncovered by even the most cursory examination of medieval religion. The spiritual power of once lively and ever holy men and women was evident to those who revered them because it got everyday things done; we do not in the fifteenth century observe the slaying of dragons. By the later middle ages it was for exhibiting human values to a super-human degree that men and women were regarded as saints: Zita, the much put upon but forever patient servant girl; Roche, who endured and survived the plague only to undergo humiliation at the hands of his relatives; above all, the Virgin Mary who had experienced to a praeternatural degree the sorrows of a mother, yet had not been broken by them. Such heroes and heroines were the prop and stay of one's own uncomfortable existence. Did one not draw spiritual sustenance from prayer to such models of behaviour?

Other saints kept (or made) one whole in a more obvious way; the healing power of most saints was, after all, and as we would say, physical not psychological – although, as we are painfully relearning, the two should not be so firmly distinguished, if indeed they should be distinguished at all; certainly, the material and the spiritual in late medieval religion should not be. Health was what everyone who was at all religious desired: the cure of one's body, of one's soul, of one's relations with family, friends, neighbours, of the parish and of the world. To turn directly to Christ was still felt (despite the Franciscans) to be inappropriate; only the particularly devout were bold enough for such an approach. The manner in which the devout did turn to Christ was not one, however, which commended itself to the Lollards. Reverence for the body of Christ in the consecrated host, and for relics of him, the Veronica for example, was growing apace and outstripping – as it was bound to do once the Christocentric message of the church had been received – application to local and specific saints. Their particular powers were never fully absorbed by Christ's universal authority, even if such saints were being gracefully eased from centre-stage. In this regard the Reformation was a continuation of the same show, albeit with the scenery shifted, and the gracefulness dramatically curtailed.

---

[11] The quotations are from J. Sumption, *Pilgrimage. An Image of Mediaeval Religion* (1975) p. 257.

25   The mass: the elevation of the host

Secondly, just as it is unhelpful to have a model of late medieval religion which has a less spiritual version being replaced slowly – and at the Reformation very quickly and fairly completely – by a more spiritual variety, so it is unhistorical to equate the former with popular culture and the latter with elite culture. At any rate exclusively. Erasmus did poke fun at what he regarded as stupid: 'people who've adopted the foolish but pleasurable belief that if they see some carving or painting of that towering Polyphemus, Christopher, they're sure not to die that day'. Or at what he saw as wickedness – the Virgin Mary is speaking:

> The soldier marches to a Butchery, and Slaughter, with these words in his Mouth, Blessed Virgin, put into my hands a Fat Prisoner, or a Rich Plunder. The Gamester Prays to me for a good hand at Dice . . . The Usurer Prays for Ten in the Hundred; and I am no longer the Mother of Mercy, if I deny it him.[12]

These are eternal verities. Stupidity, violence and greed did not cease in England with the demise of the saints. Thomas More, Erasmus's great friend, was a wiser man than

---

[12] *The Praise of Folly* (Harmondsworth, 1971) p. 126; *Twenty Select Colloquies* (The Abbey Classics, n.d.) p. 19.

he. For Thomas saw that if St Christopher and St Uncumber, to whom unhappy wives prayed to be free of cumbersome husbands, went, St Bridget, St Francis and all the rest would go. In other words: whereas the baby would certainly be thrown out, not all the bathwater *could* be.

Thirdly, there is a nagging doubt. Was the commitment of Thomas Tyard and Robert Langton, and men of their sort, strong enough? Clearly it was not when it came to the confrontation of the 1530s: churchmen like them caved in to the demands of the stupid, violent and greedy (especially the last). This is not to say there were not good men on the side of the bad in the 1530s; merely to say that they were the misguided idealists who would early be disillusioned. It is here, I think, that we arrive at propriety.

I have endeavoured to suggest that a 'saintocentric' Christianity is not a paradox and was not on the wane in fifteenth-century England. It was in a word popular and not (repeat not) simply with rustics. Of course, it was changing: new saints (and hence new shrines) for old; new feasts of the Virgin (the 'picturesque tenderness' of the Visitation, for example); new cults of the Virgin (the rosary, for instance); and new devotions to Christ (the Holy Name, the Five Wounds, the Sacred Heart). It was obviously vital that it could and did change; ossification meant fossilization.[13] The doubt is not about the vitality and viability of religion, and the popular practice of it. Not at all. What nags is whether the church could keep pace, or, rather and not only, whether churchmen were sufficiently enlightened to sponsor change, but whether they were innovative enough to initiate it. Alas, virtually all of the substantial developments in late medieval English religion, apart from the Wycliffite one (which may be significant), were imported: the feast of the Visitation, for example, from Bohemia, where it had been initiated by the archbishop of Prague, John of Jenstein, in the 1380s. The only English export was heresy. It is this adverse balance of religious payments which is so revealing. My impression is that by 1500 it had reached crisis proportions; the English church was living on borrowed credit; and time was running out for this mis- (or under-) managed institution.[14]

This is not to say that there was no innovation whatsoever. Osmund, the eleventh-century bishop of Salisbury, who was believed to have been the designer of the Sarum Use, which 'gradually superseded the other local uses [through the province of Canterbury] in the century before the Reformation', after a long, expensive and at the last an energetic campaign was canonized in 1456. Yet, how tame a saint: an administrator dead 350 years. St Osmund seems to sum up the fifteenth-century English

---

13 R. W. Pfaff, *New Liturgical Feasts in Later Medieval England* (Oxford, 1970), pp. 40–59; J. Catto, 'Religious change under Henry V', in G. L. Harriss (ed.), *Henry V: The Practice of Kingship* (Oxford, 1985), p. 109. For a new cover on an old shrine – made in 1455 for St Etheldreda at Ely – see Lambeth Palace Library MS 448, fol. 98v.

14 R. E. Weltsch, *Archbishop John of Jenstein (1348–1400)* (The Hague, 1968), pp. 87–90; Pfaff, *Liturgical Feasts*, pp. 42–8 (but p. 77 n. 7 ought to be noted: 'It seems that England led the way in the liturgical celebration of the Holy Name [of Jesus]').

church, just as the two other English saints of the century sum up (as I suppose does Osmund) what has been called 'the inwardness of English history': John of Beverley and John of Bridlington were advanced in status because they had helped Henry V beat the French at Agincourt. Where were the women one has to ask? There was no Colette, daughter of a master carpenter, to found refuges for fallen women and to rejuvenate a whole order of nuns; there was no Catherine of Genoa, that visionary (and witty) hospital administrator, who wrote a revolutionary treatise on Purgatory; there was no Frances of Rome, that gentle founder of an order of pious women who served the homeless poor; there was no violent ecstatic like Dorothy of Montau; no farmer's daughter rose up during the Wars of the Roses to cry enough, as Joan of Arc did in her country's civil war. And, although he listened to Margery Kempe in his garden at Lambeth until the stars came out, Archbishop Thomas Arundel did not take her enthusiasm seriously enough. Is that it: English-male complacency – evidenced (for example) in the suspicion shown in English mystical works of the later middle ages at any demonstration of emotion? Living saints are uncomfortable characters; dead ones, one is tempted to say dead and boring ones, are what English churchmen seemed to want in the fifteenth century. And where (one is bound to ask) were the Gasparo Contarinis of English upper-class society?

Not among the English nobility. Henry Bolingbroke, earl of Derby (or, one suspects, his household cofferer), always offered a paltry penny at mass, unless it was a feastday when it was invariably fourpence, and his mechanical charity epitomizes the cool, and even calculating, approach the English aristocracy took towards religion.[15] Henry Bolingbroke's son Henry V was in this respect like his father. Henry V chose to use the Council of Constance for a sectional purpose, an English purpose, *his* purpose: the defeat of France. Henry barely hesitated when making his choice, yet he made it in the full knowledge that the unique opportunity the Council offered for the reform of the church was lost by it. It is a revealing moment – for Henry V was a religious man. Does it not show (as if in a flash of illumination) that the spirit had gone out of religion in England, in upper-class England, among those who ruled in England? That spirit had gone elsewhere. Or, to put it another way, the religion of upper-class Englishmen (not necessarily English women) was no longer religion. This is where property should come in; its entrance, however, will have to be deferred for a while; propriety continues to detain us.

Henry V was one of the best minds of his age. As Thomas More was of his. Henry could not choose his career: it had been marked out for him. Thomas chose his. It was not religion. First it was the law; then it was government. Thomas was a man of parts and he played many of them. Most other more ordinarily able men, though still the cleverest and best men, stuck to one career. Both the career and the sticking are

---

[15] J. Catto, 'Religion and the English nobility in the later fourteenth century', in H. Lloyd-Jones, V. Pearl and B. Worden (eds.), *History and Imagination: Essays in Honour of H. R. Trevor-Roper* (1981) p. 47.

relevant. For, like Thomas More, the outstanding Englishmen of the fifteenth century are lawyers. They are not bishops, canons, monks or friars; nor, on the other hand, are they lawyers so devout that they became bishops, canons, monks or friars. There may have been outstanding Englishmen among fifteenth-century Carthusians, as there were among the Carthusians of the 1530s; there may have been an unknown handful among the hermits, who persisted on the margin of society in defiance of conformity, like John Grene, abbot of Leiston abbey in Suffolk, who in 1531 gave up the abbacy and became a recluse in the marshes by the sea at Minsmere, or William Thornbury, vicar of Faversham, Kent, who in 1476 resigned in order to live as an anchorite in his own churchyard.[16] It is a measure of the time that if there had been more such holy men historians are not aware of them; because society no longer flocked to such asocial folk for enlightenment – although Richard II and Henry V had asked for counsel from the hermit at Westminster and Margery Kempe visited Julian of Norwich – they may as well not have existed. Yet, it has to be stressed, society had changed not hermits – their redundancy was social not spiritual. Which is another illustration of the emptying out of the spirit from religion, as religion if it is to mean anything to people must have social meaning for them.

There was a contemporary awareness of this wholesale drainage to law – canon, civilian and common. Churchmen like Archbishops Henry Chichele and George Nevill, Bishops William Wainfleet, John Carpenter and John Alcock (among others) promoted and patronized education in general and theological education at Oxford and Cambridge in particular in a fruitless endeavour to prevail against the inevitable. Institutional inertia was not absolute. Far from it. But the fact remains that institutional energy was mainly directed elsewhere: to protecting the church's inherited position. Lawyers were what were needed for that. It is probably true to say that by the fifteenth century a preoccupation with law and property – one must go with the other – was stifling English culture; it is certainly true to say that it was eroding the capacity of the English church to produce the initiatives essential if religion was to infect social life, not simply be a reflection of it. We will take one cathedral church as an example.

Lichfield in the second half of the fifteenth century is deservedly, if not widely enough, known as a model cathedral chapter under its bishop John Hales, 1459–90, and its dean Thomas Heywood, 1457–92. Elias Ashmole commented 300 years ago: 'This good father repaired the state of the church then decayinge and therefore chose forth of the universities both learned and discreete men whome he appoynted prebendaries and governors of the church.'[17] Even before Hales became bishop there were learned men at Lichfield, like Roger Walle from Oxford, a canon from 1440 and archdeacon of Coventry from 1442 to 1488, whose books show him to have

---

[16] A. G. Dickens (ed.), *The Register or Chronicle of Butley Priory, Suffolk, 1510–1535* (Winchester, 1951), p. 59; Anon., 'Anchorites in Faversham churchyard', *Archaeologia Cantiana* 11 (1877), 24–39.
[17] Bodleian Library, Oxford, Ashmolean MS 1521, p. 109. For the canons and deans of Lichfield, see Emden, *BRUO* and *BRUC*; for the cathedral see *Victoria County History: Staffordshire*, III (1970).

26   The Feast of the Purification (Candlemas): the congregation hold lighted
candles blessed by the priest

been interested in modern history and modern poetry; while Thomas Heywood himself was a canon as early as 1433. Other canons were not only learned; they were as generously devoted to Lichfield as they were to their old colleges at Oxford and Cambridge – James Beresford and George Strangeways, for example. Thomas Milley, who may not have been to either university, though the tradition is that he had been to at least one of them, was even more innovative than they: he founded an almshouse for fifteen women which still functions as 'Dr Milley's Hospital'. It is, nevertheless, the deans of Lichfield who most impress. John Yotton from Cambridge, who was dean for twenty years after Heywood and who gave 200 books to his former college, saw to the completion of the library at Lichfield, and established an endowment for a priest either to preach the gospel (without charge) in the parishes neighbouring Lichfield, or to plead (without fee) on behalf of poor litigants in the bishop's court. The last pre-Reformation dean, James Denton, was from Eton and King's; he was associated with Bishop Geoffrey Blythe in the construction of a house in the close for the choristers, and built in the city at his own considerable cost a magnificent market cross – octagonal in shape and adorned with eight four-foot-high figures of the apostles – for (as John Leland reported) 'market folk to stand dry in'.

The list of Thomas Heywood's benefactions to the communities of cathedral and city is long and famous. It was probably notable in its own day; it was no doubt the dean himself who oversaw the drawing up of the two manuscript books which described his munificence and ensured that posterity has remained aware of it. If one of his achievements is to be singled out it is the one which is most unlike his friend Thomas Milley's, for it was undone at the Reformation; this was his chantry foundation of the Holy Name of Jesus and of St Anne. This discloses a good deal of the man. Both were fashionably recent cults, although I am not sure that it was this that attracted Thomas to them: Richard Scrope may have founded a chantry of the Holy Name at Lichfield before he was translated to York in 1398; and Thomas may, therefore, have been putting an already observed devotion on a surer footing, perhaps out of local and personal *pietas*.[18] It is Thomas's emphasis on the extra, choral services on Fridays, and the participation of the laity in these which is interesting. The chantry was founded in 1468; indulgences for those attending and offering were obtained from Canterbury in 1473 and from Rome in 1482. The great Jesus bell which summoned people to the Friday services cost Thomas £100 – surely a prodigious sum for a bell; it was cast in London and was hung in the south tower of the west front on 14 November 1477 (with a joyful dinner for all afterwards). Ten years later a fraternity of Jesus and St Anne was established for men and women of any rank. Thomas was its first enrolled member. He fully furnished the chantry: the images of Jesus and his grandmother, seven sets of vestments, two silver-gilt chalices and patens, two pewter cruets, a pax, a leather-covered mass book, an organ, stalls for the choir and so on. The thought, doubtless foolish though not frivolous, cannot be restrained – was this intended as a tourist attraction?

It would be foolish, if only because there is no indication that the main showpiece for visitors at Lichfield, St Chad, was failing in his power to attract them. It would not be foolish in the sense that Thomas Heywood may have been that sort of man. If one is prepared to think of fifteenth-century Lichfield as nineteenth-century Barchester, and as Dean Heywood as Dean Arabin (and there is, I believe, advantage in so doing), then discussions about the generation of income are as likely to have taken place in one as in the other. Thomas Heywood was not Archdeacon Grantly, but he was not, I think, Precentor Harding either. Of Thomas's generous relations with the city of Lichfield it has been justly observed that he 'was not at all original and was content to add to, or reform, existing benefactions'. It is, however, neither his this-worldliness nor his unoriginality which matters. It is Thomas's sense of propriety which does. Anne Kettle, in describing the way in which Thomas carried out in the city his jurisdiction as dean, catches what I am seeking: 'How did Heywood react when presented with this collection of ruined servant girls, shameless prostitutes, bigamous husbands and fornicating chaplains? In quite a number of cases, including one of incest, no further action is recorded . . . He was, however, concerned to follow up cases concerning marriage.' What Ms Kettle calls his 'benevolent intrusion' was not enough; it did not meet the situation.[19] This is my general contention too. A sort of 'Barchesterism' is evident in fifteenth-century English church life: there is much that is admirable, little that is discreditable. Indeed, if there had been *more* that was amiss there might have been more impropriety – that is, an enthusiasm for renewal which would let vested interests, however worthy, be damned. There were too few John Bolds in fifteenth-century England. Nonetheless, had there been more, their efforts (like his) would have

---

[18] Pfaff, *Liturgical Feasts*, p. 79, n. 3. For Dean Heywood's chantry see H. E. Savage, *Thomas Heywode, Dean* (Lichfield, 1925), and J. C. Cox, 'Benefactions of Thomas Heywood, dean (1457–1492)', *Archaeologia* 52 (1890), 617–46.

[19] A. J. Kettle, 'City and Close: Lichfield in the century before the Reformation', in C. M. Barron and C. Harper-Bill (eds.), *The Church in Pre-Reformation Society: Essays in Honour of F. R. H. du Boulay* (Woodbridge, 1985), pp. 167–8.

been thwarted by a moral and social complacency which, were it not absurdly anachronistic, could be called High Tory.

Thomas Heywood had a cadaver tomb: temporal pride above, eternal humility beneath. It is a measured attitude. Too measured is my argument: like the pennies Henry Bolingbroke's cofferer measured out for his lord to offer at mass. Moreover, the cadavers on English tombs are not as horrid as those in Spain and Switzerland – fewer worms, snakes and toads. There is in England less concentration on eternity and less contempt for the body than there is on the continent. Those extremes of behaviour, which Huizinga taught us to see as autumnal, were what were lacking in England; for, far from manifesting a world in decay, they witness to new life bursting to escape old forms of expression. English Gothic architecture captures the difference; it is perpendicular not flamboyant. Contrast, for example, King's College Chapel and Rosslyn Chapel: the latter has that essential touch of the absurd which the boring box at Cambridge entirely lacks. Where the theme of eternal values is concerned, it is more representations of death, rather than fewer, which would have indicated to the anthropologist, Venetian or otherwise, that all was well with the church and people of England. The glass of 'my Image knelyng in ytt and deth shooting at me', which Henry Williams, bachelor of law of the University of Oxford and vicar of Stanford on Avon in Northamptonshire, ordered his executors to provide in 1501 and which still survives in that church, is unique.[20] The single-minded devotion to the five wounds of Christ of Henry Pisford, grocer of Coventry and merchant of the Staple of Calais, in his will of 1525 is unusual.[21] The early fifteenth-century inscription on the north wall of the chancel of Acle church, ' . . . Death withereth children and destroyeth old men; those who wear horns or veils are not redeemed by their fortune. Therefore, harden thyself to the world and seek pardon with a pure mind . . . ', is the only one to have survived; it is likely that it was one of scores not hundreds.[22] There was only one Margery Kempe. There were no bleeding hosts and no Wilsnack, no Bernadino and no bonfires of the vanities, no Hans Böhm of Nicklashausen and no thousands of repentant poor, no *schöne* madonnas and no hysterical crowds. It is usually reckoned that these sensational manifestations of religious enthusiasm are a sign of a sickly society. The contrary is the case. They denote a powerful attachment to other values than the mercenary and must, therefore, witness to a healthy approach to life. When A. G. Dickens wrote of 'a crazed enthusiasm for pilgrimages' in the England of around 1500 he wrote pejoratively as well as mistakenly.[23] If only there had been such a craze, if only Englishmen had been crazier: the Reformation would have been more sturdily opposed and perhaps prevented. There were no Samsons in fifteenth-century England.

---

[20] R. Marks, 'Henry Williams and his "Ymage of Deth" roundel at Stanford on Avon, Northamptonshire', *The Antiquaries Journal* 54 (1974), 272–4.

[21] Public Record Office, Prob. 11/21, fol. 37.

[22] G. G. Coulton, 'A medieval inscription in Acle church', *Norfolk Archaeology* 20 (1921), 141–9.

[23] A. G. Dickens, 'The last medieval Englishman', in P. Brooks (ed.), *Christian Spirituality. Essays in Honour of Gordon Rupp* (1975), p. 179.

But there were plenty of philistines. Or, put another way, there does not appear to have been much (if any) great art. It too had to be imported. When Englishmen, Welshmen, and Scotsmen wanted high-class painted altarpieces they had to go abroad for them: Paul Withipol to Venice, Sir John Donne to Bruges, Edward Bonkill to Ghent, Sir John Weston and Christopher Kneyvet to Brussels. It does seem that in the 1480s it was English craftsmen who painted the walls of Eton College Chapel with miracles of the Virgin Mary, but their work impresses just because it was up to continental standard. Not too much must be made of art where society at large is concerned. Yet, of the English preference for, and skill at, small-scale projects in wood, alabaster and glass something may be made. There were exceptions, especially in the schemes for glazing churches, at Fairford and Tattershall, for example. Still, those who had money, like Ralph lord Cromwell at Tattershall, mainly spent it on their own comfort. It was on their houses, small and great, that wealthy Englishmen spent most – as subsequently they always have done. Professor Dickens wrote truly when he described the 'secular atmosphere' at Butley priory in Suffolk, on the visits of Charles Brandon, duke of Suffolk in the 1520s, as 'that of the rich, gracious, hearty layman in the convenient monastic roadhouse'.[24] Convenient, comfortable, complacent: these are the attitudes of the governing class in church and state in fifteenth-century England. Out of such sweetness no strength was likely to come.

In this section I have been suggesting (rather than arguing) that English religious attitudes were too balanced, too moderately held; that, in the end, there was a fatal lukewarmness. Before we arrive at why this might have been so, heresy and anti-clericalism require mentioning – if merely to be dismissed. Lollardy, when defined as a bag of assorted non-conforming beliefs (beliefs which occasionally determined behaviour), is not found to be a negligible quantity in fifteenth-century religious life. Yet, and once again, there was not enough of it, whether we define it narrowly (as hostility to images, to the physical presence of Christ in the eucharist and to salvation by the deeds or prayers of others) or broadly (as a pious stand on the need for 'poverty' in one's own life and in the life of the church). For English churchmen to rethink their religion a tougher opposition was needed than the admittedly tough Lollards, who were simply too few, too fragmented and too lower class to be met with anything other than a distaste or derision. As it was, Lollardy only did enough to harden the minds of English churchmen against enthusiasm and innovation, as their treatment of one of their number who was an enthusiastic innovator, Bishop Reginald Peacock, demonstrates. More dissent (not less) is what English religious life could have done with in the century before the Reformation.

The same may not be said of anti-clericalism, even though there was very little out and out lay hostility towards priests. At Dean Chandler's visitations in Wiltshire early in the century about a quarter of the parish clergy were complained of; 'the most

---

[24] Dickens (ed.), *Reg. Butley Priory*, p. 21.

common failing was sexual incontinence'.[25] That is not surprising. What *is* surprising is that sexual licence was not greater in a group bound to observe a celibacy which most would not have chosen for themselves. A generalization worth risking is that where a priest's sexual proclivities embraced the wives (and possibly the daughters) of his parishioners he could not be tolerated; if his woman was not one of theirs, and he was satisfactory in other ways, he might be. After all, as Peter Heath has written, 'the priest grappled with his vocation in a society of unrestrained passion and unseemly violence; not only was he surrounded by this context, he himself sprang from it'.[26] His parishioners did not expect and did not want a saint, but too anti-social a parish priest would have been too great a contradiction in terms. At the parochial level, therefore, the situation was not abnormal. It is in the relations of the upper classes with the clerical order that the potential for disaster lay. We are not discussing here the age-old contempt military elites had (and have) for the non-military clergy. A new, entirely different and not entirely explicable disdain for priests is evident among the nobility and gentry of late medieval England. The dislike of common lawyers for their clerical competitors is readily understandable. That is not, however, the heart of the matter. Church courts appear to have been disliked not because the upper class found them irksome, but because they did not punish the day to day immorality of the common people severely enough. Church courts were too populist for the magisterial elite, who desired a completely free hand to put commoners in their place.[27] To be observed here is a clash between an old ideal and a new, between the Christian ideal of the equality of souls and the capitalist one of the inequality of bodies. Moreover, it is evident that those laymen who employed priests were slipping into the habit of thinking they owned them. Here we arrive at property, the transformation of the servant into a menial, and at modernity. When Sir John Fastolf pays his chaplain less than his cook, although the former is listed among the gentlemen of the household and the latter among the yeomen, some medieval mooring seems to have come adrift – unless William Herward, the chaplain, had another source of income – which was, I think, unlikely.[28] The priest as property is a phrase that has a pre-Christian ring to it – or should it be post-Christian?

We have come to the third and final section. On the subject of ownership let us listen, in the first instance, to Judge William Yelverton: 'I have "a place to sit in the chancel and there I have my carpet and book and cushion", said Judge Yelverton in 1469 using these examples to validate the right of an individual to property in church over which the parson had no claim'.[29] It is odd to find the same man writing to John

---

[25] Timmins (ed.), *Reg. John Chandler*, p. xviii.
[26] P. Heath, *The English Parish Clergy on the Eve of the Reformation* (1969), p. 8.
[27] R. M. Wunderli, *London Church Courts on the Eve of the Reformation* (Cambridge, Mass., 1981), pp. 95–6, 102, 138–9.
[28] Magdalen College, Oxford, Fastolf Paper 8 (account of John Rafman, steward of the household, 1431–2).
[29] M. Aston, 'Segregation in Church', *Studies in Church History* 27 (1990), 245.

Paston ten or more years earlier, 'thankyng yow as hertyly as I kan . . . for that ye do so moche for Oure Ladyes hous of Walsyngham, which I trust veryly ye do the rather for the grete love that ye deme I have therto; for trewly if I be drawe to any worchep or wellfare, and discharge of myn enmyes daunger, I ascryve it unto Our Lady'.[30] Though possibly it is not: Yelverton may have had a proprietary attitude to the Virgin Mary's shrine at Walsingham. What is really rum, however, is his dating of his letter to John Paston 'on Sent Fraunces Day'. Was he thinking of the patron saint of propertylessness when he wrote that? Probably not in the least, especially as he wrote 'in hast'. One item of property Judge Yelverton had was a finger of John the Baptist. He had stolen it (so John Paston said) from the effects of Sir John Fastolf, after Fastolf's death in 1459; he also carried off 'a crosse wyth a cheyn and of the holye crosse thereynne that Sir John Fastolf dyd were dayly aboute hys nek'; it was worth £200, whereas the Baptist's finger was valued at only £40.[31] It seems (from their wills) that a great number of upper-class Englishmen and women wore some relic or other around their necks. Whether the jewelled settings of these relics were admired for their elegance, and that is the reason they were worn, or whether there was a 'talismanic' aspect to their wearing, is hard to know. That they were worn with pride, the pride of possession, may not be doubted.

Such pride is to be discovered in many other manifestations of the religious life of the nobility and gentry. Let us take as an example the chantry and hospital which Thomas lord Burgh in his will of 1496 desired to be established at Gainsborough in Lincolnshire.[32] A present-day visitor to the Old Hall at Gainsborough is startled to come upon such grandeur in the middle of so unprepossessing a town; a late fifteenth-century visitor – Richard III, say, who stayed a night in 1483 – must have been instantly aware of Thomas's new house as an expression of the pride of an *arriviste*; as the phrase goes: it had everything. Except a chapel. No more than a hundred yards away from Thomas's private suite (in a fashionable brick tower at the corner of the public hall of his house) is Gainsborough parish church; in it was what Thomas called 'my newe Chapell'. On a tomb to be 'reised and made at the northe ende of the auter of the same chapell', effigies of Thomas and his wife were to be set; that of Thomas was to show him armed and in the robes of the Order of the Garter, 'with a garter a bout my legge'. Here he was to be buried. Here was to be a perpetual chantry for himself, his wife, his father and mother, and all his ancestors. His will is as pedantic as that of any lawyer in its directions for the establishment and maintenance of the chantry. There are sixteen closely written lines alone on how, by whom, and in default of whom, and in what eventuality, the chantry chaplain shall be appointed. The chaplain may go on pilgrimage or visit his friends no more than once or twice in the year; he may be away no longer than a month; he must not be absent at Christmas, Easter and Whitsun; if

[30] N. Davis (ed.), *Paston Letters and Papers of the Fifteenth Century* (2 vols., Oxford, 1971–6), II, pp. 197–8.
[31] Magdalen Coll., Fastolf Paper 70.
[32] Public Record Office, Prob. 11/10, fol. 240v.

away, he has to depute a priest to sing mass in his place. If illness keeps him away for more than six days he has to appoint another priest to take his place. He is to sit in the chancel stalls next to the vicar. He is to live in the house which Thomas purchased from the parish clerk; it has a garden. The daily masses to be sung are specified: of the Trinity on Sunday, of the Holy Spirit on Monday, of Mary Magdalen on Tuesday, on Wednesday a requiem mass, on Thursday of All Saints, on Friday of Jesus, on Saturday of the Virgin Mary. After the offertory, and before he goes to prepare the vessels for the consecration, the chaplain has to say 'openly and in audience' the *salve de profundis* for the souls of Thomas and Margaret his wife, 'rehersyng oure names in audience', and for the souls of Thomas's father and mother, of his ancestors and heirs, and of 'other suche as comythe of me'. Daily mass is to be sung at nine o'clock or after, but not before; before mass he must ring the 'second or thirde grete belle so long space bifore he goe to masse as a man may easly go frome my Maner to the said churche'. It is evident whom these masses were to benefit.

The almshouse was another Burgh enterprise. It was to be for five poor men and in Gainsborough, though where (uncharacteristically) is not specified. Each man was to get 1d a day and to have a new gown worth 3s 4d every other year. The men were to be old Burgh servants who could no longer serve and who had 'lytell to lyve uppon'; failing such, they were to be Burgh tenants in Gainsborough, who had 'fallen unto poverte'. All were to attend daily at the Burgh masses in the church 'upon payne of lesyng of his peny . . . it to be put in the boxe with iij keys . . . except he be sike and at male case that he may not goo'. If the bedeman was literate he was to say each day matins, prime and 'oures and Evensong of oure lady'; he was also once a day to recite the psalter of the Virgin Mary on his knees in the Burgh chapel, and to accompany the priest in the saying of the *de profundis* 'in audience' during the mass itself. If he was illiterate the bedeman had to know his *pater noster*, *ave* and creed – he was not to be a bedeman if he did not know them; he also had to know 'oure lady psalter', because he was to recite it twice daily on his knees in the chapel, once before noon 'at the masse tyme' and once more in the afternoon. On those occasions too he had to be engaged in 'rememorying' the souls of Thomas and all the other Burghs. If any bedeman brawled, fought, stole or was 'vicious of his leving', and there was good evidence of such misconduct, the vicar and chantry chaplain, who had the general management of the almshouse under the supervision of the Burgh family, were to replace him with some other poor man.

The details speak for themselves. At this distance how can eternal values be distinguished from worldly ones? The overriding desire of Thomas lord Burgh to display for ever in Gainsborough his success in this life was, we may wish to say in excuse, only human. Religious fear too may have motivated him in both foundations. Where, however, is love? Is it in the penny a day for five old men broken in his service? Hardly. Five is a derisory number. Moreover, a penny a day was no recompense for all that kneeling (on arthritic knees) upon a cold Lincolnshire floor. Their labour was grossly undervalued. These were Gradgrind bedesmen: even after death their loveless employer got more than his pennyworth out of them. They were as much Thomas's property as was the chantry chaplain, who toiled away at a treadmill of masses to hasten his dead employer through a purgatory he so clearly deserved to linger in. I have (even at a great distance) made a distinction. My confidence springs from the sight of Thomas's house: such brazen self-advertisement tells one all one needs to know about him. And, by definition, his fellows.

Among whom, as we have reiterated, there was no Gasparo Contarini. Anymore than there was among that 'new' social class, the English yeomen, a Nicholas von Flue: can one imagine an English farmer – yeoman or gentleman – retiring 'from public life in protest against an unjust and oppressive decision of a local court', and becoming a hermit, who was respected and applied to by all? Well-off Englishmen were too preoccupied with property, too determined to accumulate it and so concerned with keeping it, that *their* commitment to public office had such an end principally in view. There was more of Francesco di Marco Datini about them than of Gasparo Contarini. It is symptomatic that Sir Roger Townshend, chief judge of the court of common pleas, sheep farmer and money lender should put 'Jesu Mary' at the head of the pages of his account books: it demonstrates that desire to serve two masters which Jesus declared impossible.[33] By the end of the fifteenth century – Sir Roger died in 1493 – the English landed classes were well along the path which brought them to a wholehearted worship of Mammon under the guise of a reverence for God. In the process their 'role-model' duly became a modern hero. Dick Whittington, the poor boy who becomes rich, was the opposite of those medieval heroes, Saints Alexis and Francis, rich boys who became poor.

This has become suspiciously neat. Not everything may be stuffed into a bundle labelled 'Capitalism and the Decline of Religion'. Despite the monks of Butley priory complaining in the 1530s that 'the charity of many people grows cold; no love remains in the people', Englishmen and women did not cease to be charitable and loving as the Reformation loomed. They may not be type-cast.[34] It was, after all, a provincial merchant, John Baret of Bury St Edmunds, who left probably the most communally inclined, as well as the longest, will of anyone whatsoever in the century before the Reformation:

> Item I wille the Alderman, Burgeys, gentilmen, and gentilwommen have a dyner the same day that I am enterid, with other folkes of wourshippe, preests, and good frendys, and also my tenaunts, to wiche I am moche be holde to do for hem alle, for they have be to me ryght gentil and good at alle tymes, and therfore I wyl eche of hem alle have iiijd to drynkke whanne they payn her ferme. Item such personys as my executours wylle bydde to dyner be syde I fully commytte it unto there discrecion. Item for asmoche as I levyed wele evyn I wyl they have j now [enough], and that they fayle noon at my dirige ne at mete.[35]

---

[33] British Library, Additional MSS 41139, 41305.
[34] Dickens (ed.), *Reg. Butley Priory*, p. 67.
[35] S. Tymms (ed.), *Wills and Inventories . . . of Bury St Edmunds*, Camden Soc., old series 49 (1850), pp. 18–19. For the Barets of Bury, see R. S. Gottfried, *Bury St Edmunds and the Urban Crisis: 1290–1539* (Princeton, 1982), pp. 153–9. John made his will in 1463, it was proved in 1467.

Even this may be too positive a note on which to end.

Among the town archives of Bridport are five manuscript booklets of twenty or so pages each.[36] They comprise the names of the founders of a fraternity, its rules and its accounts. The booklets are all of similar, if not the same, format. Four of the fraternities were in the parish church of St Mary; the fifth was at St Leonard's chapel. They all began in the 1420s; they all end forty, fifty or sixty years later: the last pages of the booklets are blank. What does this mean? Was the enthusiasm of a handful of men and women – there is overlapping membership – all that sustained the fraternity of the Light hanging before the Cross, or of the Torches, or of St Nicholas? When they died did the fraternities die too? Or was the enthusiasm of the next generation directed elsewhere – to the foundation of a single fraternity, for example, that of St Mary, which appears in the late 1460s? Handling these frail manuscripts with their skimpy and unrevealing accounts one is bound to wonder: what degree of religious life do they represent? Are they pathetic documents? Or is their very flimsiness a manifestation of creativity: religious desire ever seeking fresh devices? If the historian who explores the minds of the past has to admit to limited discoveries, what can the historian who examines souls confess to but bafflement.

---

[36] The booklets are in the Dorset County Record Office, Dorchester; the ones I am thinking of are Bridport CD 11, 14, 15, 16 and 22; that of the fraternity of St Mary is CD 32.

12

DEATH

Margaret Aston

In the fifteenth century dying was an art, a guide to living. 'Learn to die and thou shalt learn to live.'[1] According to the devotional assumptions of the time a good life was premised on the correct orientation towards the certainties of death, and a good death could redeem the sins of a bad life. Fears of the hereafter provided an ever-present sanction for daily morality, and provision for the souls of the dead was a central preoccupation of religion, something that affected all classes of society. Death – one's own or someone else's – was a part of daily life. Every individual longed for assurance about his or her own end, and contemporaries lived with and communed with their dead in ways that are now quite alien to us.

This profound concern of the period meets us in sources of all kinds: literary, artistic, monumental. An exploration of attitudes towards death amounts to a traverse of late medieval religion, for, as Huizinga remarked at the opening of his chapter on 'The vision of death' in *The Waning of the Middle Ages*, 'No other epoch has laid so much stress as the expiring Middle Ages on the thought of death. An everlasting call of *memento mori* resounds through life.'[2] If this seems to leave aside the cakes-and-ale side of living and believing, it remains true that to reach death without having previously confronted it, face to face, was to dice with the terrors of eternity. This was worse than foolish; it was irreligious.

Obviously there is an imbalance in what we can see and know. Wills, funeral monuments and books of hours all tell us much about the final dispositions of the highest placed and well-endowed few. But their beliefs and habits of thought, though so much more lavish and conspicuous, were not divorced from those of their servants, tenants and almsmen. Although the physical heritage of the poor is so nugatory as to be effectively invisible, we know enough from the wills of humbler people and the reconstructions of historians to be able to set the hopes of ordinary parishioners realistically alongside the world of chantries and private chapels.

Death, judgement, heaven, and hell: the four last things loomed over people in and out of church, in mural paintings, on preachers' lips, in devotional handbooks.

---

[1] F. M. M. Comper (ed.), *The Book of the Craft of Dying and Other Early English Tracts concerning Death* (1917), p. 127.

[2] J. Huizinga, *The Waning of the Middle Ages* (Harmondsworth, 1955), p. 140.

'Brethren, you shall understand that there are four last things which should principally always be kept in man's mind: the first last thing is man's bodily death; the second is the Day of Doom; the third is the pains of hell; the fourth is the joys of heaven.'³ Hell was placed before heaven. The fear of suffering was more potent than the lure of pleasure in the homiletic armoury. Meditation on death which, as Thomas More wrote (true to late medieval tradition), was of such 'profit and commodity' to the soul, entailed thinking of a host of horrors. The world was a common prison, with only one exit:

> young, old, poor and rich, merry and sad, prince, page, pope and poor soul priest, now one, now other, sometimes a great rabble at once, without order, without respect of age or of estate, all stripped stark naked and shifted out in a sheet, be put to death in divers wise in some corner of the same prison, and even there thrown in an hole, and either worms eat him under ground or crows above.⁴

Heaven and hell, the saved and the damned, were set on either side of Christ in judgement in the scene of the great Doom that dominated parishioners from the chancel arch as they worshipped in church – the saved on the Saviour's right, the condemned on his left. It was the latter about whom preachers had most, and most vivid things to say. Much was spoken in the pulpit about the pains of hell, the first of which were extremes of heat and cold. Hell fire loomed largest in contemporary imagination. It could be envisaged as the terrifying burning of a great city, all going up in flames, with tormented souls running about like showers of sparks, crying aloud for mercy. Hell's punishments were matched to the offences committed during life, and particular pains might be predicted for particular sins.

One preacher, speaking on the theme of restitution, used the story of a knight who appeared to a city burgess, riding on a black horse,

> and out of the knight's nose came smoke, and flames, and fire with brimstone. The knight was clad with sheepskins, and bore on his neck a huge weight of earth. And he said to the burgess: 'this horse that beareth me is a fiend, that tormenteth me, and beareth me to the pain of hell; for I died and made no restitution of my wrongs. I was shriven and was sorry for my sin, but I would not restore the harms that I did, and therefore I am damned.'

He wore burning sheepskins for the sheep he had wrongfully taken from a widow; bore a burden of earth for the land he had falsely obtained. The whole of creation could not express 'the pain that I suffer, and shall suffer without end'.⁵

Sir Thomas More's words about the mass burial of 'rabbles' of people, thrown into pits, are a reminder of the role played by plague in contemporary attitudes towards death. Even if late medieval imagery of death and terrestrial finality had its origins

---

³ G. Cigman (ed.), *Lollard Sermons*, Early English Text Society (hereafter EETS) 294 (1989), p. 211.
⁴ 'The Four Last Things', in *The English Works of Sir Thomas More*, ed. W. E. Campbell and A. W. Reed (facsimile of 1557 edition, 2 vols., 1931), I, pp. 77, 84, 467, 480.
⁵ A. Brandeis (ed.), *Jacob's Well* part I, EETS 115 (1900), p. 214.

before the pandemic of 1347–51, the huge scale of the human catastrophe of those years, and the repeated visitations of pestilence thereafter, etched themselves deeply into contemporary consciousness. The loss of population of between a third and a half in the mid-fourteenth century was not made up for generations, and throughout the fifteenth century plague epidemics continued to take their toll, both locally and nationally, with mortality sometimes reaching 20 or 30 per cent. The imminence of death – postponable though the thought of it must always be, as long as blood circulates and there is air to be breathed – pressed on men and women with a directness that western society in the late twentieth century knows only second-hand, from the dead and dying on the television screen as war and famine and repressive regimes make mass graves in other parts of the world.

The Black Death familiarized late fourteenth-century England with the phenomenon of mass burial. In London the unprecedented numbers of dead necessitated the opening of new burial grounds in fields outside the city, which became the sites of new religious foundations. The Cistercian house of St Mary Graces was begun by Edward III east of the Tower in a new graveyard in East Smithfield where innumerable bodies had been interred, and in Clerkenwell the London Charterhouse rose where Sir Walter Manny had provided land and a chapel for vast numbers of plague victims. Following generations took on the task of caring for the countless souls who had been so abruptly and unceremoniously cut from their corporal moorings by the disease. Even in Elizabeth's reign Londoners still knew as the Pardon churchyard the place where, according to John Stow, the bodies of more than 50,000 had been buried in 1349.

Whether or not contemporaries became fascinated by the image of death they were willy nilly surrounded by constant reminders of it. Daily life as well as religion continuously pushed reminders of the dead before their eyes. It was impossible to go through life without furnishing the mind with imagery of this kind, for the landscape itself, as well as politics and religion, thrust forward the evidence of the dead – flesh, bones and human absence. The bodies of traitors, quartered like carcasses, would be posted to places in the realm that their owners were deemed to have endangered, to be impaled as warning advertisements. After the rebellion of 1450, Jack Cade's head was set up on London Bridge, and the portions of his body displayed at Blackheath, Norwich, Salisbury and Gloucester. It surely tells us something significant of the assumptions of his subjects, as well as of the king himself, that Henry VI found this practice unchristian. According to John Blacman's memoir, the king was shocked when told that the thing he saw hanging overhead on a stake as he passed through Cripplegate was the quarter of a man who had betrayed him. He had the remains removed at once from the gateway.

Human bones, which we now prefer to keep out of sight as well as out of mind, as if their exposure to the elements and to our eyes threatened our transient hold on existence, were kept in view for spiritual health. Populous burial-places which ran out of space had to rehouse the long-buried dead to make place for the new. The bare bones removed from the ground were placed in special vaults or buildings (ossuaries or charnel-houses) in the consecrated ground, where over the decades walls of skulls and

27 Christian burial; behind, a charnel-house; below, Death attacks
a pope and an emperor

other remains accumulated. The ruins of the charnel-house are still to be seen at Bury St Edmunds. At St Paul's in London there was a chapel over the ossuary in the churchyard, served by a chaplain appointed by the mayor of London. When this charnel chapel was pulled down by the duke of Somerset in 1549, the bones removed to Finsbury Fields were said to have filled 1,000 cartloads and to have made a mound big enough to house three windmills. A human skull, artists' readiest symbol for mortality and the vanity of the flesh, was placed on the altar by John Fisher, bishop of Rochester (1469–1535), when he celebrated mass. Skulls and bones, seen on the ground or in art, kept the living in touch with their own destiny.

The land itself bore the signs of past mortality. Though accumulations of land-holdings and changes of land-use could fill many gaps, the disappearance of so many people left visible signs. The retreat from previously settled and cultivated lands brought in its wake overgrown weedy fields, derelict houses and ruined farmsteads, decaying or deserted hamlets or entire villages. In some areas open fields and plough gave way to enclosed pasture where flocks grazed. Contemporaries had evidence on the ground comparable to that which we ourselves have of departed communities from the previous century in the west of Ireland and Scotland. A black house and a cultivated patch may quickly revert to nature, without the memory of the habitation being lost. By the accession of Henry VII the message imprinted on the English landscape was clearly legible.

Plague contributed not only to the visibility and scale of late medieval mortality, but also to lay people's concern for readiness to meet the eventuality of sudden death. Mass death was (and is) shocking in itself. Mass loss of the ability to care for the dead was another kind of shock. Both sorts of horror left their mark.

'From lightning and tempest; from plague, pestilence, and famine; from battle and murder, and from sudden death, *Good Lord, deliver us.*' The prayer in the Prayer Book litany has ancient roots. Sudden death in the fifteenth century was a fate all believers prayed to be spared, for to be taken unawares by death, to die unshriven, without having confessed and received the last rites of the church, was to face the peril of everlasting perdition. The terror of dying included this incalculable risk.

> I that in heill wes and gladnes,
> Am trublit now with gret seiknes,
> And feblit with infermite;
> *Timor mortis conturbat me.*[6]

William Dunbar's famous lament for dead poets ('Lament for the Makaris'), echoed, as did others long after, the responses of the liturgy. In the sixteenth century too, the words of the church offered comfort and protection against the perils of an unprepared death.

---

[6] *The Poems of William Dunbar*, ed. W. Mackay Mackenzie (1970), pp. 20, 202. The Latin phrase is a response from the *Officium mortuorum*.

> The plague full swift goes by:
> I am sick, I must die.
> *Lord have mercy on us!*

was Thomas Nashe's prayer in the days of Queen Elizabeth, *From winter, plague and pestilence, good Lord, deliver us!*[7]

Plague, for all its devastation, was only one of the many afflictions that swept people off without warning. Times of dearth also took their toll. The drought in Spain in 1473–4 was reported to be such that grain crops were burnt up in the ground, and parents gave away children in the hope of saving them. In England, too, the tremendous heat of that summer of 1473 found victims as harvesters dropped dead in the fields. 'There was a great hot summer, both for man and beast; by the which there was great death of men and women, that in field in harvest time men fell down suddenly, and universal fevers, aches, and the bloody flux, in diverse places of England.'[8] Those who lived on the margins of existence were ill provided against such extremities. Consciousness of the imminence of such possible endings helped to foster popular beliefs in counter-remedies.

The popularity of St Christopher owed much to the belief that he could afford protection against sudden death. Wall-paintings of this saint seem to have out-numbered those of all other saints in medieval English churches, and were usually very large and placed on the wall opposite the church door where everyone would catch sight of them and gain the benefit on entering the building, or passing the open door. As one inscription put it, 'who sees this image shall not die a bad death that day'.[9] A bad death was death without the last rites. Anxiety to avoid this danger by seeking out St Christopher in this way (pleasurable but foolish as it seemed to Erasmus), might itself have been enough to encourage many at least to poke their noses inside the doors of their church, even if they did not hear mass, which was supposed to be another way of earning the same insurance.

The hour of death, when the soul took leave of the body, was a moment of extreme dread. It was a time of trial that presented the individual with greater and more grievous temptations than any encountered during life, in which the believer had to give final proof of his or her true contrition and submission to the will of God. Demons, the hounds of hell, would surround the dying with terrible assaults. There could be no doubt as to the inescapable fearfulness of death: 'the dreadful sight of fiends, which every man shall see in that hour; . . . the great battle that shall be between man and the fiend in that hour'.[10] All available assistance was needed; people should rush to aid those *in extremis* as they rushed to put out a fire. The tolling bell that announced the soul's passage out of life, warned neighbours to pause in their labours to pray for

---

[7] N. Ault (ed.), *Elizabethan Lyrics* (1949), p. 166.
[8] J. O. Halliwell (ed.), *A Chronicle . . . by John Warkworth*, Camden Soc., old series 10 (1839), p. 23.
[9] E. W. Tristram, *English Wall Painting of the Fourteenth Century* (1955), p. 115.
[10] Cigman (ed.), *Lollard Sermons*, pp. 215–16.

the person who was dying. But in the last resort, everyone had to face this contest alone, and no one from the greatest to the humblest was immune from panic fear at its prospect. Archbishop Arundel in 1414 expressed the hope that in leaving the prison of the flesh he might be delivered 'from the terrifying sight of demons', while a sermon for All Souls' Day related how a sinner had succumbed and died from 'terror and dread' of the devils surrounding her, before the priest arrived.[11]

In preparing all Christians to meet their maker the church, besides exploiting the lesson that life must be lived against the summons of death, also provided the means of self-help. Like many sermons, the late fifteenth-century play *Everyman* taught the living how to be ready for the face-to-face encounter with death. Everyman learnt how 'Death, thou comest when I had thee least in mind!'[12] and he was guided through this time of desertion and friendlessness by Knowledge. It is Knowledge who brings Everyman to priest and holy sacrament. The play reflects a characteristic of contemporary religion in concentrating on the layman's personal obligations, before coming to the assumed rite and ministry of the church. Personal devotion, including meditation on and preparation for death, could be taken a long way before one ever reached priest and sacrament. This is clear from one of the most popular of late medieval texts, the *Ars moriendi*, or *Craft of Dying*, which was virtually a do-it-yourself handbook, being a practical guide to the dreaded process of dying, that could be read and kept on hand for that last hour.

The *Ars moriendi* – Caxton's 1490 *Arte and Crafte to Knowe Well to Dye* – led its readers through the five great temptations (loss of faith, despair, impatience, vainglory and avarice) which they would encounter in dying, and also provided a series of questions by means of which *Moriens* (the departing Everyone) could in effect conduct his or her own self-examination. This preparation for the end was of course given in the expectation that the contrite individual would receive the last rites of the church, but very little is said of the ministry of the church, and the tormented sinner is given the consolation of knowing that should there not be time for confession, his full contrition of heart can save him. This was a guide to the lonely strife of the deathbed, and the block-book version of the text depicts in vivid horror the devils who surround the bed and fill the room as they try to cut *Moriens* off from the means of salvation.

Among the defences provided by the church for this ultimate spiritual contest was the sight of an image of the Passion. 'The image of the crucifix', instructed *The Craft of Dying*, 'should evermore be about sick men, or else the image of Our Lady, or of some other saint the which he loved or worshipped in his health.'[13] The crucifix (or the cross), the image of salvation that stood at the centre of every place of worship and was

---

[11] C. E. Woodruff (ed.), *Sede Vacante Wills*, Kent Archaeological Soc., records branch 3 (1914), p. 82; E. H. Weatherly (ed.), *Speculum Sacerdotale*, EETS 200 (1936), p. 227. This woman was delivered, according to the story, after her son confessed for her and did a penance of seven years' fasting.

[12] A. C. Cawley (ed.), *Everyman and Medieval Miracle Plays* (1989), p. 210.

[13] Comper (ed.), *Craft of Dying*, p. 36; cf. pp. 77–8, 93.

omnipresent on walls and beside highways and byways, was to be held before the eyes of the dying person to ward off the threatening demons. It might be the last thing seen by the expiring individual, and the sight of Christ on the cross was the final consolation of the departing, as the soul was sent on its way through the church's farewell rite of extreme unction.

Julian of Norwich describes this role of the cross during the encounter with death. Julian was granted one of the things she most dearly wanted in her search for spiritual understanding: to become ill to the point of dying, so that she would be given the last rites of the church, undergoing the physical and spiritual torment that went with this extremity, including 'the terror and assaults of the demons'. The illness came, and the expectation of death. The parish priest was called. In Julian's words; 'He set the cross before my face and said, "I have brought you the image of your Maker and Saviour. Look at it, and be strengthened".' It was an effort, but Julian did so. And the cross did strengthen her. 'Then my sight began to fail, and the room became dark about me, as if it were night, except for the image of the cross which somehow was lighted up; but how was beyond my comprehension. Apart from the cross everything else seemed horrible, as if it were occupied by fiends.'[14] The woodcuts illustrating various editions of the *Ars moriendi* enable us to enter some way into these experiences.

Julian went into darkness in which the cross was the only light. This was the fearful darkness, darkness of the forces of evil, from which all sought release. 'Quan I shal al my frendes forsake, / Cryst schyld me fro the fendes blake.'[15] The kingdom of Satan was a realm of unchanging never-ending black night, and the fear of the dark that the human psyche links with death was entrenched in Christian theology. Death could mean everlasting darkness. *Tenebrae*, darkness, features in the responses of the Office of the Dead, one of the essential constituents of the Book of Hours which was owned by so many lay people in the fifteenth century. 'Burning souls weep without end, walking through the darkness crying woe, woe, woe, how great is the darkness.' The souls remembered on All Souls' Day were those in the oven of the night, and the prayer for delivery from the paths of damnation was a prayer for release from the dark. 'Let light perpetual shine on them'[16] – the blessedness of eternal light, freed from the princes of darkness. For, as Innocent III had explained, the endless inextinguishable fires of hell burned for ever without fuel or draught, giving unimaginable heat but no light. One of the horrors of perdition was this palpable darkness that enveloped lost souls within and without. They were for eternity deprived of light.

The nocturnal office of *Tenebrae*, celebrated during the last three days of Holy Week, ritualized this association of darkness with despair, salvation with splendour of light.

---

[14] Julian of Norwich, *Revelations of Divine Love*, modern English version by C. Wolters (Harmondsworth, 1973), pp. 63–5.

[15] R. L. Greene (ed.), *The Early English Carol* (Oxford, 1977), p. 219 (no. 368).

[16] F. Procter and C. Wordsworth (eds.), *Breviarium ad usum insignis ecclesiae Sarum* (3 vols., Cambridge, 1879–86), II, cols. 279–80.

Tiers of candles were lit before the altar on a frame called a hearse (the same word – derived from the Latin for a harrow – which was used for the stand for tapers at grand funerals). During the hours when the church commemorated the desolation of Christ's suffering on the cross, these lights were extinguished one by one, leaving a single light hidden behind the altar to be raised as from the dead on Easter morning. This was in effect the funeral service of the widowed church for the bridegroom who sacrificed his life. Good Friday was the day of mourning, without bells, rich vestments, music, a day for donning 'but black, black: in black in token of our sins, for which Christ died'.[17] On Easter Day Christ answered the supplication, 'Give back, O Christ, thy light, thy servants pray', and the lights throughout the church building were rekindled in joyful celebration of the Resurrection.[18]

Though the terrors of hell remained constant in Christian thoughts of the after-life, the doctrine of purgatory introduced an entirely new dimension between the days of Innocent III and Thomas More. The establishment of belief in an intermediate region in which souls were purged, through suffering, of their remaining burden of sin, entirely altered the relationship between the living and the dead. Once it came to be accepted that the prayers of those on earth could benefit souls in purgatory, a great burden of responsibility came to rest on the living to do their best for those who had gone before them. The idea that intercession could alleviate the suffering of souls and secure remission from torment may have been present from the early church, but the pains of hell, unlike those of purgatory, could not be escaped. Travailing souls in purgatory tugged continuously at the conscience of their friends and descendants, whose capacity for prayer became a capacity to participate in divine justice. The chain of intercession linked everyone with the dead.

Foundations for soul masses grew to great numbers, thanks to the conviction that every mass celebrated for the dead relieved the suffering of those in purgatory.

> Som folk afferme in theyr opynyon,
> Seyen that they have rad hit in story,
> A Masse ys egall to Crystes passion,
> To helpe sowlys out of purgatory.[19]

These lines appear in a poem explaining the *Virtues of the Mass* that was written by John Lydgate for Alice (née Chaucer), the countess – later duchess – of Suffolk. She died in 1475, twenty-five years after her husband's murder, and was buried in the church of Ewelme in Oxfordshire where they had both long since provided for prayers as part of the well-endowed almshouse they built there. Alice de la Pole fared better than many. Her recumbent alabaster effigy on its tomb-chest ('long aristocratic features, like

[17] John Longland, *A Sermonde . . . at grenewiche* (1538), sig. k4r, cited J. W. Blench, 'John Longland and Roger Edgeworth, two forgotten preachers of the early sixteenth century', *Review of English Studies*, new series 5 (1954), 127.
[18] H. Thurston, *Lent and Holy Week* (1904), p. 417.
[19] H. N. MacCraken (ed.), *The Minor Poems of John Lydgate*, part 1, EETS extra series 107 (1911), p. 114.

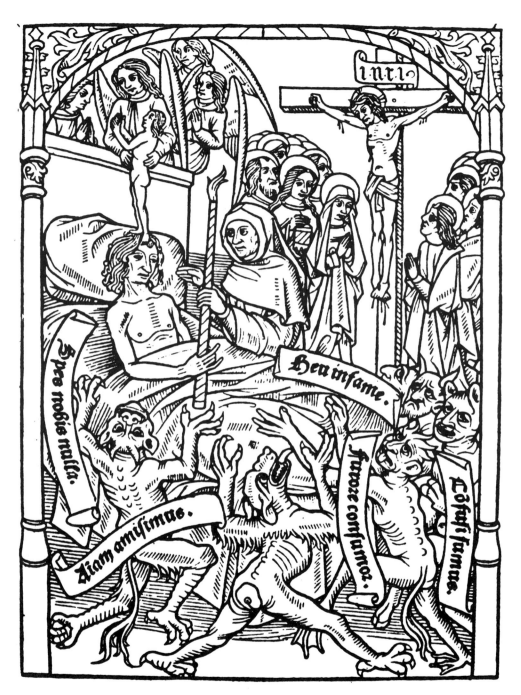

28   A good death: devils surround the bed, but the soul is received by angels

29   Prayers for the dead: three praying monks at the feet of the effigy of
William of Wykeham

a horse's')[20] remains remarkably intact, still surrounded by her chosen saints and
angels, over its emaciated *doppelgänger* of death.

The anxiety for post-mortem insurance can appear obsessive, to degenerate into an
arithmetical race that demeans spiritual objectives. Salvation – or purgatorial rescue –
began to seem calculable by number. The astronomically rich accumulated astronomic
totals of masses and indulgences. Cardinal Beaufort wanted 10,000 masses said as soon
after his death as possible. Abroad, Cardinal Albrecht of Brandenberg managed to tot
up more than 39 million years of indulgence. There were also individuals who looked
to the security of documentary proof, like a French couple who asked to be buried with
the indulgences they had obtained, as if these were a kind of passport to the world
to come. Among the methods open to ordinary mortals for earning indulgences was to
pray before certain images, which they might be able to own in the shape of woodcuts.

---

[20] J. Sherwood and N. Pevsner, *Oxfordshire*, The Buildings of England (Harmondsworth, 1974), p. 597.

The Image of Pity, Christ as the Man of Sorrows, was one such; the Pietà, with the Virgin mourning over the dead Christ, another.

Although most testators seem to have waited until death was imminent before completing the formalities of will making, many had taken thought long before for their funeral monuments and soul-masses. Those at the top end of the social scale often completed their tombs and religious foundations well before death, sometimes – like the Suffolks – embarking on such works when still in their thirties. William of Wykeham saw his chantry chapel, on the south side of his reconstructed nave at Winchester, finished before his death. In his will (dated 24 July 1403 – but he died over a year later on 27 September 1404), Wykeham referred to the 'newly constructed chapel' in which he was to be buried.[21] In the month before his death the bishop made an agreement with the prior and convent of St Swithun's for the services in this chantry. Three monks from the house were to celebrate three masses (specified in detail) every day for the souls of Wykeham, his parents and benefactors, receiving a penny a day each. If the three men performing these duties needed any further encouragement they might have found it in the effigies of the three praying monks, represented with lifelike characterization at the bishop's feet.

Given the proverbial friendlessness of the dead and the fallibility of executors, not to have made such provision was to take a serious risk. Founders and testators had to balance their obligations to their forebears against their concern for themselves, and there was always the worry that descendants might neglect their responsibilities and appropriate funds for their own interests. 'Have in mind, in mind, in mind, secuters [executors] be oft unkind.'[22] Covetousness for the goods of the departed in the fifteenth century endangered the souls of the dead as well as the relationships of the living. Forethought was essential, for spiritual as well as material reasons.

> Thenke mon thi liffe
> Mai not eu endure
> That thow dost thi self
> Of that thow art sure
> But that thow kepist
> Unto thi secture cure
> And eu hit availe the
> Hit is but aventure.[23]

The lines on an encaustic tile at Malvern Priory advertised the slipperiness of executors as a warning to beware.

The elaborate plans detailed in wills sometimes came to nought. The college of five

---

[21] R. Lowth, *The Life of William of Wykeham* (3rd edn, Oxford, 1777), appendix 17, p. xxxiii.

[22] Greene (ed.), *English Carol*, p. 226 (no. 382); cf. E. K. Whiting (ed.), *The Poems of John Audelay*, EETS 184 (1931), pp. 13, 84, 92, 227.

[23] G. H. Cook, *Mediaeval Chantries and Chantry Chapels* (1947), p. 62. 'Consider man, thy life may not endure for ever. What thou dost thyself, of that thou art sure. But that [which] thou entrusteth to thy executors' care, if it ever avails thee it is pure chance.'

priests, five clerks and three poor men that Richard lord Scrope of Bolton wanted founded 'in such place as my executors shall think best' never materialized. So the silver cup called the 'Constable bowl' which Scrope's cousin, Marmaduke Lumley, was to have had made into a chalice for the completed college never reached its destination.[24] Scrope died aged twenty-six in 1420, and was in Rouen serving Henry V in Normandy when he made his will; perhaps his proposals were unrealistically expensive. But even an existing religious house might turn down a request for prayers, on the grounds of cost. Christ Church, Canterbury, wrote to tell the earl of Warwick in 1368 that the manor on offer in Kent was not adequate to support the masses wanted for his uncle, Sir John Beauchamp. Masses for souls were a spiritual service, but they had to be paid for.

Erecting a tomb might be a more straightforward affair than the long-term endowment of prayers. Ralph lord Cromwell, builder of the castle and church at Tattershall in Lincolnshire, did not omit to provide a monument for himself and his wife ahead of time. This forethought 'for him and for my lady, like as ye se', was praised in verse, probably by one of the chaplains of his chantry college, when Lord and Lady Cromwell were interred side by side in the 1450s, 'resting under the stone'.[25]

One of the rare monuments for which the contract survives is that of Ralph Green, esquire, who died towards the end of 1417 and is buried at Lowick in Northamptonshire. He was well served by his wife Katharine and (presumably) the executors, who in February 1419 made an indentured agreement with the carvers at Chellaston (Derbyshire) for the completion and erection of this alabaster tomb by Easter 1420. This may have been the earliest opportunity, for it was just at this time that Katharine obtained control of her husband's estates. The figures of husband and wife, exact as to class, but not as individuals, were specified:

> the one a counterfeit of an esquire armed at all points, containing in length seven feet, with a helm under his head and a bear at his feet; and the other . . . of a lady lying in her open surcoat, with two angels holding a pillow under her head, with two little dogs at her feet; the one of the said images holding the other by the hand . . .

Angels with tabernacles bearing shields were to be on the sides, and the whole, gilded, painted and properly 'arrayed with colours', cost £40, payable by instalments.[26]

Even executors charged with the care of parental souls might be remiss. John Paston I (who died in London in May 1466) was ill-served by his son, the second John Paston. Expenses were not spared on the funeral, judging by the amount spent bringing the body back from the capital for burial at Bromholm in Norfolk. The payments included 6s 8d to a woman who formed part of the escort, together with the priest and twelve poor men carrying torches. The priests who celebrated at Norwich,

---

[24] N. H. Nicolas (ed.), *Testamenta Vetusta* (1826), pp. 201–2; J. T. Rosenthal, *The Purchase of Paradise* (1972), pp. 95, 115.
[25] Carleton Brown (ed.), *Religious Lyrics of the XVth Century* (Oxford, 1939), pp. 245, 340.
[26] F. H. Crossley, *English Church Monuments AD 1150–1550* (1921), p. 30.

where the procession halted, were duly rewarded, and the prior of Bromholm received various presents (including a cope), for putting up those who were busy arranging the interment.

But Sir John Paston II proved dilatory to the point of heartlessness over seeing to his father's tomb at Bromholm. Five years after the burial he was writing to his brother to ask for measurements in the church, and his mother was rebuking the latter for the lack of action. 'It is a shame, and a thing that is much spoken of in this country, that your father's gravestone is not made. For God's love, let it be remembered and purveyed for in haste.'[27] In 1476 – getting on for ten years after his father's death – John Paston III was writing to tell his mother about the ill-reports circulating at Bromholm. There was with me yesterday, he told her

> a man from the Prior of Bromholm to let me have knowledge of the ill speech which is in the country now of new that the tomb is not made. And also he saith that the cloth that lieth over the grave is all torn and rotten, and not worth 2d, and he saith he hath patched it once or twice.[28]

The prior thought that at the very least a new cloth should be sent before Easter. Finally, in May 1478, when his father's twelfth obit was approaching, John Paston II wrote to his mother, excusing himself for not being at home by midsummer when he had intended, with her help, 'to have begun upon my father's tomb'.[29] He now had a definite proposal. The cloth of gold that had been bought for his father's bier (and which was apparently loaned in 1476 for the duke of Norfolk's funeral) should be sold to pay for the tomb, and the chances of getting a 'great price' seemed good since the king was making purchases for his father's reburial at Fotheringay.

Rich aristocrats, whose religious observance had in large part moved out of church to centre on the devotions of domestic chapels, where they worshipped with their own clerks and cushions and illuminated Books of Hours, were able in effect to take such private comforts with them to the grave. Their corporal remains came back into the public buildings of the church with all the accoutrements of grand personal service. Many of the chantry foundations which were the fashion of this age amounted to private chapels for the dead: mortuaries where the great took up their last residence on earth surrounded by the spiritual luxuries which they had been accustomed to worship with when alive. Part of the community's consecrated space had been appropriated by the individual beneficiary who installed there his or her altar, sculpture, furnishings and chaplains. The celebrants may have benefited others besides the founder, but the personal objectives loomed largest.

Much less survives to recall the arrangements by which ordinary parishioners pursued the same ends. The fraternities or guilds which existed in parishes all over the

---

[27] N. Davis (ed.), *Paston Letters and Papers of the Fifteenth Century* (2 vols., Oxford, 1971–6), I, p. 359 (no. 212); cf. p. 442 (no. 264).

[28] *Ibid.*, I, p. 602 (no. 371).

[29] *Ibid.*, I, p. 510 (no. 311); cf. pp. 380 (no. 228), 489–90 (no. 295), 596–7 (no. 367).

country disappeared with the roods, saints' statues and church lights they helped to support, leaving few traces of their existence, and only a small proportion of their records behind them. They were an important part of parish life. These associations of men and women, artisans and working people, served a variety of charitable and religious purposes, among which care for the dead was important.

Parish fraternities have been called 'essentially communal chantries',[30] and those who belonged to such a group had the assurance of a decent burial and of being prayed for after death. Members' contributions paid for a chaplain who said prayers for both living and dead brothers and sisters, and celebrated obits. The rules of the fraternity of the Holy Trinity and Saints Fabian and Sebastian in the parish of St Botolph without Aldersgate in London reflect the importance of these services. They provided first, for the burial out of common funds of any member who was unable to pay for this himself; and secondly laid down arrangements for the bringing home of anyone who died within a five-mile radius. Another rule regulated the All Souls' service at which requiem mass was celebrated for 'all our brothers and sisters, quick and dead',[31] a ceremony to be attended by all members, who were fined a pound of wax for non-attendance, and who had to offer a halfpenny each. The duties of this fraternity priest included celebrating a requiem mass every Monday for all dead members.

In between these two extremes were the countless individual chantries which were not structures of any kind, but funds bequeathed to provide soul-masses for named persons and periods. Those who could not afford the full endowment of a chantry priest, but who could do better than a fraternity obit, might leave sums for the celebration of an annual or a trental (thirty requiem masses). Trentals, according to Chaucer's summoner, delivered the souls of friends, both old and young, from burning and flesh-hooks. The named beneficiaries were often the testator and his wife and their parents (ancestors, rather than siblings or predeceased offspring), and 'all the faithful departed'.

The social hierarchy of this world bore directly on the place of one's lying-in-wait for the ultimate divisions of the next. Proximity to earthly powers earned proximity to spiritual ones. The privileged who in life had worn or closely served the wearers of worldly crowns were buried where they could approach both the wearers of heavenly crowns, and the king of kings when he appeared on the day of judgement. To be interred before the altar, in the choir or chancel, meant not only to lie in the holiest part of the consecrated building, close to the daily re-enactment of Christ's presence in the mass; it also ensured a leading position when the Saviour came again from the east to judge the quick and the dead. Those buried in the nave were not so near, but still were better off than the rank and file who lay anonymously in churchyard or cemetery

---

[30] C. M. Barron, 'The parish fraternities of medieval London', in C. M. Barron and C. Harper-Bill (eds.), *The Church in Pre-Reformation Society: Essays in Honour of F. R. H. du Boulay* (Woodbridge, 1985), p. 23.

[31] P. Basing (ed.), *Parish Fraternity Register: Fraternity of the Holy Trinity of SS Fabian and Sebastian in the Parish of St Botolph without Aldersgate*, London Record Soc. 18 (1982), p. 3.

outside the walls of church or chapel. Thus Sir Walter Manny, founder of the London Charterhouse, who died in 1372, secured for his heirs the right of choice 'when taking leave of their bodies', to choose their place of burial in chancel or nave of the church, or other places belonging to the Charterhouse, 'to each according to his standing'.[32]

Finally there were the lost souls who, cut off from any hope of resurrection, were banned from burial beside other Christians, and whose bodies were either scattered to the elements or buried in unhallowed ground. Obdurate excommunicates and heretics, who forfeited communion with the church when alive, had to be prevented from contaminating it after death: likewise suicides. 'Wanhope', despair, one of the great temptations afflicting souls in their death agony, also assaulted the living, and could wipe people out of celestial as well as terrestrial existence. It caused women to overlie and suffocate their children (perhaps the commonest form of infanticide, intentional or otherwise, and a matter of concern to preachers and church legislators). It also led people of both sexes to commit the 'cursed deed' of suicide, by hanging or drowning themselves.[33]

Those who succumbed to the ultimate sin of taking their own lives were outcasts, but already in the fifteenth century desperation was distinguished from insanity. The bishop of Exeter decided in 1421 that when Maud, widow of John Hoper, hanged herself, she had previously been possessed by madness and lacked normal judgement, so there was no need (as some feared there might be) to exhume her from the church-yard at Bideford on the grounds that her burial there would pollute the place. In a more celebrated case the churchyard at Lutterworth in Leicestershire was endangered in this way for thirteen years, thanks to the failure of two bishops of Lincoln to comply with conciliar directions. Wycliffe was made a heretic thirty-one years after his death by the Council of Constance in 1415, but he was not exhumed until 1428, when his remains were burned and the ashes thrown into the nearest stream 'to the damnation and destruction of his memory'.[34] Nobody could benefit a blotted-out soul, sent thus to oblivion.

The place of burial was clearly a matter of importance – though only the fortunate had much choice in the matter. The nearness of Christ, Virgin or favourite saint, presented in image to the dying, was also sought as protection of the body after the soul had left it. Some testators asked for interment before a church's rood. A Kent rector, William Baker of Warehorne who died in 1417, wanted to be buried in the collegiate church of All Saints, Maidstone, 'next the cross in the middle of the said church'.[35] A similar request was made a few years later by John Lyndwood of Lyndwood (Linwood in Lincolnshire), one of whose sons and executors was the well-known author of the *Provinciale*, a compendium of English ecclesiastical law still in use in the sixteenth

---

[32] W. St John Hope, *The History of the London Charterhouse* (1925), pp. 10, 32.

[33] T. Erbe (ed.), *Mirk's Festial*, part I, EETS extra series 96 (1905), p. 150.

[34] W. Lyndwood, *Provinciale* (Oxford, 1679), p. 284, col. 2, note c.

[35] E. F. Jacob (ed.), *The Register of Henry Chichele*, Canterbury and York Soc., 42, 45–7 (1938–47), II, p. 105.

century. William Lyndwood was to see his father buried in Linwood church 'before the crucifix between the two doors of the church', where John's mother (the canonist's grandmother) was buried.[36]

Many others who had served the Virgin Mary in life wanted her care after death. One such was another Kent incumbent who died in 1493. Thomas Wilmott was the vicar of Ashford, and was to be buried in the chapel of St Nicholas in his church. He asked for the image of the Virgin which stood in his study to be set up at his expense in this chapel. His body was to lie awaiting the resurrection near the figure on which his eyes had rested when he looked up from his books. Like other clergy he was in a position to specify his exact burial place in his church, and there were many before him who sought proximity to the Virgin. John Harpham, a Yorkshire vicar who made his will at the time when plague had recently struck the south of England, specified that he should be interred in the lady chapel in his church of Owthorne, before the statue of the Virgin, for the better painting of which he bequeathed 6s 8d.[37]

The mercies of favourite saints were to hover round the grave. A northern squire, John Pigot, left his soul specially to the care of St Wilfrid, and asked his friends and executors, if he died within a day's journey of any church dedicated to this saint, to take him there for burial. Archbishop Arundel displayed appropriate loyalty to Canterbury in committing his soul (after God and the Virgin) to Saints Gregory, Augustine, Dunstan, Blaise and Alphege. Not many people aspired to these heights. One famous man of learning had a soft spot for a much more popular saint. Sir Thomas Littleton, whose fame rests on his authorship of the long-used legal treatise that became known as *Littleton's Tenures*, died aged seventy-nine at his birthplace, Frankley in Worcestershire, in August 1481, and was buried in Worcester cathedral in the tomb he had built during his lifetime. Littleton's will reflects a special devotion to St Christopher. The chief justice recommended his soul to the Trinity, the Virgin Mary, Christ and 'to St Christopher, the which our said Lord did trust to bear on his shoulders'.[38] His tomb was placed under an image of the saint, and the Worcester monks were to pray for his soul at the altar dedicated to Saints Christopher and George.

Plutocratic testators could get closest of all to the saints by being able to muster, not merely their images, but their bodies – or parts of them. This means offered a very special comfort, the thought that at the last trump there was a good chance of rising from the grave in the company of God's elect beside the chosen holy guardian. Henry V and Cardinal Beaufort both enjoyed this consolation. They placed their chantry chapels at Westminster and Winchester next to the respective shrines of St Edward the Confessor and St Swithun, whose relics they were able virtually to appropriate. King and cardinal rested in very special company – and the prayers of pilgrims were assured of coming their way.

---

[36] *Ibid.*, II, p. 183.
[37] The church at Owthorne, on the coast east of Hull, fell into the sea in 1816, part of the village followed in 1844, and the place seems now to have been washed off the map.
[38] Nicolas (ed.), *Test. Vetusta*, p. 362.

Henry VI planned to join the resting-place of both his parents in the hallowed entourage of the Confessor, and entered into detailed discussions with the authorities at Westminster before he was thirty. Thanks to the king's devotions at the shrine these turned into long visits, but the final decision was made. The place was on the north side of St Edward's shrine, necessitating removal of the relics to the high altar. 'Forsooth here will we lie.' The king measured the ground with his feet, and a mason was called to mark the exact dimensions with a pickaxe, leaving scratches that are still visible in the paving.[39]

Humble parishioners whose choice of burial place could get no further than the hope of joining kinsmen or friends in some corner of the churchyard might still be able to establish a posthumous material connection with a saint. Even these – the vast majority – who joined the ranks of the nameless dead in unmarked graves outside the church had ways of keeping in touch with the holy persons whose sculpted and painted features had been part of their daily worship.

The better-off could leave bequests of garments to be worn by statues of the saints. In the Devon parish of Morebath, Christian Tymwell, who died in the 1520s, gave a gown to the parish's new image of the Virgin. Women who bequeathed rings to church fabrics (like Alice Gele, wife of a Salisbury ironmonger, who was buried at St Thomas's churchyard in 1407) might assume that the gold or silver they had worn would be used to embellish a holy image. It was possible to request that your wedding ring should adorn the Virgin herself, as was done by another well-off Salisbury woman who died that year, while a Yorkshire widow, Margaret Stapleton, in 1466 left her best gold ring to hang round the neck of an image of Christ at Newburgh.

Those whose possessions never included gold could reach out towards the saints at death by means of lights. Light stood for Christ's salvation just as darkness stood for Satan's doom. As every will and funeral depiction tells us, lights of various kinds – tapers and torches, candles large and small – were an important part of contemporary devotion. There was virtually a popular liturgy of lights, which was thrown overboard by sixteenth-century reformers, for whom lighting a candle in daylight smacked as much of paganism as any kindling of new Easter fire. There was already seen to be a problem in the early church, when paganism was a much nearer threat. Jerome answered a charge of Vigilantius about the way in which relics of martyrs were being reverenced: large numbers of candles were lit while the sun was shining. 'Throughout all the churches of the East', said Jerome in justification, 'when the Gospel is to be read, lights are kindled while the sun is actually shining, not indeed to dispel the darkness, but to give a sign of joy.'[40]

Such votive lights were celebratory, not merely because light is itself uplifting, but for the very reason that they were *not* useful or needed. They were simply an extravagant

---

[39] A. P. Stanley, *Historical Memorials of Westminster Abbey* (1868), pp. 508–9, 512–13.
[40] D. R. Dendy, *The Use of Lights in Christian Worship*, Alcuin Club Collections 41 (1959), p. 79; cf. pp. 2, 108.

outpouring of honour. The altar, or the gospel, or the saint – or the body of the deceased – was honoured by the candle competing with the sun in the same way as the precious spikenard, poured from the alabaster over Christ's feet, spread a luxurious fragrance that seemed to one of the disciples an unpardonable waste. The gift of a light was open to all, and though these stands of candles lit before a saint or beside a coffin doubtless did (like the ones to be seen in Catholic churches today) illumine the gloom, that was not their purpose. They were beacons of believers' worship, of their hopes of salvation and their supplications.

Parishioners regularly gave thought to the needs of church lights when they made their wills. As a result some churches came to own bees and their own supplies of wax. A Jesus light might be supported by a bequest of sheep. Other testators, poorer or less generous, left pennies for the purpose. Late fifteenth-century wills in Hertfordshire followed convention in bequeathing 2d or 4d for the parish rood light, or a saint's light, and a similar sum to the shrine of the mother church of St Albans. The pilgrimage shrines of the saints to which healing powers were attributed were given wax offerings of a talismanic kind, as well as candles. The spiritual sources that supplicants hoped to tap by these means similarly attracted the lights of those whose pilgrimage had become spiritual. Testators who kept the saints in mind as they made their wills, hoped that their candles, burning before shrine or image, would keep them in the mind of the saint, and thereby transmit some benefit to their souls, and help transport them away from everlasting darkness towards celestial light.

Dying was itself a kind of pilgrimage, a journey in suspended time from familiar haunts towards an objective of unknown spiritual dimensions. The moment when the soul left the body was the first of a series of thresholds that had to be crossed before the individual was relocated in the community of the dead. The ritual of passing out of the world was a staged process, pegged by accepted markers, through which society – neighbours, friends and kin – surrendered its hold on the bodies of the dead, transferring them to the territory to which they now belonged, and their souls to the trust of professional soul-carers. The period of transition varied according to the status of the individual.

In theory God was no respecter of places, but everyone has an instinct for the safety of known ground. Poor and rich alike hoped to be buried in consecrated ground with which they were familiar, and possibly, since distant travel was a luxury, it was the poor more than most who were granted that wish. Everyone hoped, too, for the appropriate escort to accompany their bodies to the grave. At the top end of the social scale testators might provide for their corpse to travel considerable distances to join their nearest and dearest, or to reach their prepared tomb. Bishops with large dioceses and widely separated residences, and propertied lords with extensive estates, who led peripatetic lives moving from house to house and visiting London for sessions of parliament, convocation or business, were likely to die away from their favourite place of residence. They made plans for this.

Members of parish fraternities had to hope for the best. Their homecoming might be provided for, but only within a certain radius. The brothers and sisters of the

Holy Trinity fraternity at St Botolph's without Aldersgate were ensured of being collected and accompanied home for burial providing they did not die more than five miles away.

> If it befall that any of the brotherhood fall sick five mile each ways about London and dieth there, . . . then it is ordained that they shall wend and fetch home the body to London, and that all the brethren be ready at their warning and go against the body outside the city town's end for to bring the body in to the place with worship . . . [41]

In the early fifteenth century William lord Roos of Hamelake (Helmsley) and Belvoir provided about eighteen months before his death that if he died in the London area, he should be buried in Christ Church, Canterbury; if his end came when he was in the diocese of Lincoln, he should be taken to Belvoir priory; if he was in the diocese of York, his chosen resting-place was the abbey of Rievaulx. In each case he sought swift unpretentious removal and the repose of a religious order – Benedictine, or Cistercian. In the event he was near enough to his Lincolnshire home to be buried in the choir of Belvoir priory.

Few could contemplate commemorative funeral journeys of the monumental kind which Edward I provided when Queen Eleanor's body was brought home to London from Harby, near Lincoln, in December 1290 (taking a fortnight, at a respectful average of ten miles a day). Henry V, dying in France at the height of his glory, was brought home with full funeral pageantry, escorted by queen, nobility and household knights. Mourners dressed in white and black accompanied the chariot carrying the coffin, on which lay a lifesize leather effigy of the king, dressed in a purple mantle, crowned and sceptred, making the deceased monarch visible to all so that (as a contemporary chronicler put it) his subjects' grief and prayers might be increased. With an appropriate pause for lying in state at Rouen, it was more than two months after leaving Vincennes before the procession reached Dover, and then there was another week of lavish ceremonial before the king's bones were buried at Westminster.

Great subjects too, who did not have to count pennies, contemplated ostentatious processions for their final homecoming. Cardinal Beaufort in 1447 stipulated that if he died far away from 'my church of Winchester', his executors should pay out accordingly, arranging funeral masses in every church where his body rested overnight, with offerings of cloth of gold and 8d to every officiating priest, as well as distributing £40 in alms to the poor.[42] Half a century later, Cecily duchess of York, mother of Edward IV, who died in 1495, left the remainder of her plate to pay for the transport of her body from Berkhamstead castle in Hertfordshire to the collegiate church at Fotheringay in Northamptonshire. She was determined to make this posthumous journey of some sixty to seventy miles, so that she could be buried in the tomb of her

---

[41] Basing (ed.), *Parish Fraternity Reg.*, p. 2; cf. pp. 80–1.
[42] J. Nichols (ed.), *Collection of . . . Wills . . . of the Kings and Queens of England* (1780), pp. 321, 323; G. L. Harriss, *Cardinal Beaufort* (Oxford, 1988), pp. 376–83.

'most entirely best beloved lord and husband', Richard duke of York, who had been killed thirty-five years earlier at the battle of Wakefield.[43]

Such funeral processions both extended the transitional period in which the dead were escorted from this world into the next, and also widened the range of participants in the ceremonial. An individual's obsequies might be prolonged to a week or more, and doubtless the testators who provided for them counted spiritual as well as worldly benefits. The funeral cortège, with its attendant black-robed mourners bearing torches, probably went at about half the pace of normal travellers; the twelve poor men who escorted John Paston's body from London to Norwich in 1466 took six days, but they returned home in three. Large numbers of householders and clerks would accompany the draped coffins of the great, spreading news of their demise and collecting mourners and prayers at the towns and villages on the route.

The widowed Lady Bergavenny, who described herself in 1435 as a 'meek daughter of holy church', gave careful thought to the worship that ought to be done at her death 'to a woman of mine estate'. Not, she was hasty to add, out of pomp or vain glory, but as a memorial and remembrance of her soul to her kin, friends, servants, and others. Lady Bergavenny was anxious to be buried in a new tomb beside her husband (William Beauchamp, lord Bergavenny, d. 1411) in the Dominican church at Hereford. She envisaged quite a parade to join him. Wherever she happened to die, her body was to be kept waiting until proper black clothing had been provided for her household, and the hearse and other equipment got ready. The churches in which her body rested on the way were to receive their due rewards (gifts of cloths of gold and sizeable payments to the clergy), while the friars at Hereford, who were to say 5,000 masses as soon as possible, were given a whole suit of black vestments.[44]

The final send-off, when the body reached home and its ultimate destination in chantry, tomb or cemetery, included the funeral feast. This marked the termination of the separation rites, and as the deceased was at last delivered into the abode of the next world, those left behind closed ranks and were soldered together by a convivial social gathering. Servants, householders, perhaps tenants and townsmen, relatives and neighbours, would meet to eat, drink and celebrate the occasion, sometimes at great expense as specified in the final testament of the deceased. John Baret, a rich merchant of Bury St Edmunds (on whom more shortly) arranged for various people to be dined on the day of his interment; the alderman, burgesses, gentlemen and gentlewomen of Bury, priests, friends and tenants, not forgetting those who played the organs and sang at his requiem mass. We do not know the cost to his executors of this town feast. But in 1475 Thomas Stonor's funeral costs came to the large sum of £74 2s 5d, which included two days' fare for various people who attended the dirge and interment. The provisions included – besides ale – bread and cheese, umbles, boiled beef and roast

[43] J. G. Nichols and J. Bruce (eds.), *Wills from Doctors' Commons*, Camden Soc., old series 83 (1863), pp. 1, 3.
[44] Jacob (ed.), *Reg. Chichele*, II, p. 535.

pork for the poor men (who ate off wooden plates), and lamb, veal, roast mutton, chickens, capon, roast pigeons, baked rabbit, pheasants and venison for the gentry (who had pewter vessels, with spoons and salts of silver for the 'most worshipful').[45]

Not everyone wanted to go in such style. There were those who felt that the ostentation of death reflected the vanity of worldly display and attachment to the privileges and finery of social rank. Their final thoughts were more evangelical, and turned towards helping the poor rather than to banquets, funeral robes and banks of tapers. A group of Exeter clergy (well-placed men, all buried in the cathedral), who died early in the fifteenth century, shared this prejudice against funeral pomp, though they all made careful provision for prayers for their souls.

John Lydford, successful church lawyer and archdeacon of Totnes (d. 1407), was anxious that his funeral should avoid all superfluous expense and excess, and he explicitly banned the usual banqueting by the canons and cathedral clergy. His funeral feast, contrary to custom, was to be only for a good number of the very poor (to be chosen by his executors), and he provided in his will for the penniless, bedridden and needy, those – as he put it – 'lying in bed in their cottages and hovels'.[46] A few years later Hugh Hickling, precentor of the cathedral (who died in 1416), likewise wanted his funeral to be without the superfluities 'which tend more to the pomp of the world than the salvation of the soul', and that meant in his case no hearse of lights and no general feasting.[47] His beneficiaries too were the poor, the lame and infirm who were unable to work. Thomas Barton, a canon of the cathedral who died the same year, allowed for a procession of the poor, wearing black and carrying lights, and his funeral feast was for 200 poor, whose diet was to be roast meat and spiced drink, in appropriate moderation lest they gorge themselves. On the preceding day beggars and indigent were to benefit from his largesse – a penny apiece – and all the decrepit, blind and helpless who could not fend for themselves, in Exeter, Crediton and Ilfracombe, had 4d each.

'Naked came I out of my mother's womb, and naked shall I return thither . . . now shall I sleep in the dust' (Job 1.21, 7.21): the final levelling that is the office of death was taken to heart by some who – perhaps with enhanced scriptural consciousness – related the enforced nakedness of the tomb to the involuntary nakedness of the living poor. Even kings might lie in state naked before making the ceremonial exit that was their due, witness Edward IV, whose body, placed on a board and covered only by a loin cloth, was viewed by peers and leading Londoners for twelve hours after his death. Others deliberately chose the equivalent of a pauper's burial. Philip Repingdon, sometime bishop of Lincoln and in his youth a Wycliffite, wanted in 1424 to be buried outside the church of St Margaret, Lincoln, 'under the clear and open firmament of the sky, not in church or monastery, because I think I am unworthy of

---

[45] C. L. Kingsford, *The Stonor Letters and Papers, 1290–1483*, Camden Soc., 3rd series 29–30 (1919), I, pp. 143–4, 162.
[46] F. C. Hingeston-Randolph (ed.), *The Register of Edmund Stafford* (1886), p. 390.
[47] *Ibid.*, p. 410.

such burial', and his 'fetid' body, soon to be food for worms, should be 'put naked into a sack'.[48] Several laymen who had brushed with Lollardy made similar requests. Edward Cheyne, esquire, wanted his 'stinking carrion', covered with no cloth of gold or silk but mere russet, to be buried in the churchyard of Beckford (Glos); Sir Thomas Broke of Holditch chose interment in a shroud but no coffin in the churchyard at Thorncombe (Dev) by the south door of the church, where everyone entering church 'may step on me'. And Sir Thomas Latimer, disdaining choice of parish, specified the farthest corner of the most convenient churchyard, where, with a mere two tapers and no expense of any kind 'anon as I be dead thud me in the earth'.[49]

In an age that made poetry out of earth, corruption and flesh-eating worms, the focus on mortality took many forms. The unequal battle of the times against disease helped the church to drive home its lessons, and the habit of talking about corporal dissolution produced its own vocabulary and fashions, in art and behaviour as well as in literature. The terminology of Job – and Innocent III – moved out of the Bible and liturgy into lay people's religion and last wishes. The archbishop of Canterbury who did most to combat Lollardy prefaced his will with remarks about the putrefaction of the flesh and the cadaver of his body, and it was a sign of the times that the word 'cadaver' entered the English language (having in England, as in France, gained such testamentary usage in Latin in the fifteenth century) at the end of the period.

The example of John Baret, the rich clothier of Bury who died in 1467, will serve to draw these various strands together. Though famous in his native town, Baret never reached the national stage, but the elaborate arrangements he made for his death reflect the concerns of leading contemporaries. We have not only his excessively long and detailed will and testament (virtually a small book's worth of dispositions), but also his tomb and enough of his chantry to read the mind of this wealthy merchant, who combined delight in worldly success with a deeply engrained sense of mortality.

Baret was a man of letters, who owned books and whose connections with the abbey of Bury St Edmunds brought him into touch with the monk-poet John Lydgate. He possessed Lydgate's *Siege of Thebes* (a poem written about 1420), and also bequeathed a book called *Disce mori* (learn to die). The signs are that John Baret thought long and hard about dying and this latter text, and Lydgate himself, might both have influenced his dispositions. A vernacular treatise of this name that survives in manuscript contains a passage on the sin of covetousness that Baret could have taken to heart.

> Against this sin of covetousness the best remedy is to a man to think busily on his death
> . . . Consider the sepulchres rich and poor, and what they that lie in them were sometime
> and what now profited to them their riches and the vanity of the world that they hunted so
> busily. Now is nought seen of them but ashes . . . Imagine the richest and mightiest of the

---

[48] Jacob (ed.), *Reg. Chichele*, II, p. 286.
[49] *Ibid.*, II, p. 45; F. J. Furnivall (ed.), *The Fifty Earliest English Wills*, EETS 78 (1882), pp. 26–7; *The Ancestor* 10 (1904), 19.

world and now is he passed; all his friends, riches, worships, and all other vanity or pomp of the world have left him naked, and nothing beareth with him but sin or merit of his works.[50]

John Baret may have been impressed by what he knew of the Dance of Death, as well as the tips of his friends (academic and architectural) about the latest fashions in funeral monuments. The celebrated painting of the *Danse Macabre* or Dance of Death or of the Dead, that was completed on the cloister walls of the cemetery church of the Holy Innocents in Paris in 1424–5, was visited by Lydgate when he was in France a few years later. At the suggestion of French clerks he made an English version of the verses that accompanied the paintings, and in 1430 came a request for his *Danse Macabre* to be inscribed alongside the version of the painting at St Paul's churchyard in London. The Dance of Death, taking further the old theme of the encounter of the Three Living with the Three Dead, showed skeletal figures leading individuals from all ranks of society in a morbid dance towards the grave. Death, the great equalizer, spared no degree. Everyone could see his or her fate reflected in the painting. The familiar literary trope of the *speculum*, the mirror of mortality, makes its appearance in the opening verses of the poem. Proud folk, who were so 'stout and bold', could in these pictures see clearly the 'sudden violence' that would make an ugly end to their passage through life.

> In this mirrour every wight may finde
> That him bihoveth to goo upon this daunce.
> Who goth to forn or who shal goo be hinde
> All dependith in goddis ordinaunce.[51]

John Baret, who chose the modish form of a *transi* tomb for his memorial, made play with the mirror conceit. The cadaver, the mirror of death, was also the instructive mirror for the living, and in the tombs of various leading English figures from the 1420s on, the individual who had completed life's last dance was shown lying in state over his or her deathly partner. One such monument was requested a few years after Baret's death by Edward IV, who asked to be buried 'low in the ground' under a stone 'wrought with the figure of Death', and over this 'an image for our figure' silver-gilt, in the richness of life.[52] The admonitory decaying corpse of such *transi* lay between the representation of the deceased *au vif*, and the bones beneath the ground awaiting the resurrection and the ultimate vanquishing of death. Baret did not choose a double-

---

[50] Bodleian Library, Oxford MS Laud Misc. 99, fol. 55v, cited R. Woolf, *The English Religious Lyric in the Middle Ages* (Oxford, 1968), p. 75 n. 2; cf. p. 219 n. 6. On Baret, see R. S. Gottfried, *Bury St Edmunds and the Urban Crisis: 1290–1539* (Princeton, 1982), pp. 154–9; Gail M. Gibson, *The Theater of Devotion: East Anglian Drama and Society in the Late Middle Ages* (Chicago, 1989), pp. 72–9, 170–3.

[51] E. P. Hammond (ed.), *English Verse between Chaucer and Surrey* (Durham, N.C., 1927), p. 131; D. Pearsall, *John Lydgate* (1970), p. 177.

[52] S. Bentley (ed.), *Excerpta Historica* (1831), p. 367. The term *transi*, from the Latin *transire* (to cross over, pass on, die), is an invention of art historians.

decker monument of this kind, though his tomb represented him in the pride of life as well as the grip of death. The image of himself in the dignity of his worldly estate was smaller and more discreet than these two-tier monuments.

Baret supervised the erection of his tomb before he died, and the lengthy specification of his last wishes, written with his own hand and sealed with his silver seal (also complete several years before his end), gave careful attention to his chantry chapel in the Lady Chapel at the eastern end of the south aisle in St Mary's, Bury St Edmunds. The chapel is no more, and the tomb has been moved, but the church still bears the blazons of Baret's characteristic combination of secular pride and devotional humility.

The tomb chest shows the deceased in death and in life. On top lies the decaying cadaver in a shroud, lapped by a scroll with a Latin inscription. The words *Ego nunc in pulvere dormio* (I sleep now in dust) are placed next to the head, and the plea for mercy that follows ends with Baret's name. On the side of the monument, quite dwarfed by this emblem of mortality, is carved the diminutive figure of the living John Baret, erect in his best attire, wearing his SS collar and grasping the central 'me' of his motto 'Grace me governe'.

Baret seems to have been enormously proud of the coat of arms he had been given in person by Henry VI, who paid a long visit to Bury St Edmunds in 1433–4. His motto was plastered all over his household possessions, from rings and pendants to candlesticks and knives. Nor did there seem anything incongruous about advertising it in church. Baret's double motto, 'God me gyde' and 'Grace me governe' are still to be read on the arched braces supporting two hammer-beam angels in that part of the roof (to which he probably contributed) that was over the rood. In the panels of the ceiling over the chantry chapel 'Grace me governe' is repeated six times over, at the centre of a decorative scheme which includes Baret's initials inside an SS collar. Even the white vestment made for the St Mary's priest who was to celebrate for the souls of the donor and his parents bore his arms and motto.

The still-intact ceiling of the chantry glitters like the night sky. Its reflecting sparkle was part of the original scheme. Baret directed that 'three mirrors of glass . . . be set in the midst of the three vaults above my grave, which be ready with my other glasses and divers rolls with scripture'.[53] There was a multiple mirror in this ingenious conceit. The cadaver itself lay beneath the glimmer of a celestial vault that reflected back on the shrinking corporal substance. Meantime, generations of passers-by were to regard the cadaverous Baret as their instructive mirror. He addressed them himself. 'Ho that wil sadly beholde me with his ie / May se hys owyn merowr and lerne for to die.'[54] 'Jon Baret', soliciting the prayers of future men and women of Bury in a vernacular verse, repeated familiar maxims of mortality – 'earth to earth': 'what I was so shall you be'.

---

[53] S. Tymms (ed.), *Wills and Inventories . . . of Bury St Edmunds*, Camden Soc., old series 49 (1850), p. 20. See also S. Tymms, *An Architectural and Historical Account of St Mary's Church, Bury St Edmunds* (Bury St Edmunds, 1845–54), pp. 70, 173–4, 184–6.

[54] Tymms (ed.), *Wills*, p. 234.

30   The cadaver tomb of John Baret of Bury St Edmunds

In this meditation, expense and forward planning for his end, John Baret was very much a man of his times. He was anxious to survive in wood and stone, in the memories and on the lips of his successors, and – helped by this – to find peace for his soul. He could afford the important security of personal prayer; of being placed before God as a named individual after his soul had left his body. His chantry priest would stand at the altar's end after the reading of the gospel, and 'rehearse John Baret's name openly', so that everyone present could respond 'God have mercy on his soul', to the recipient's great relief.[55] Cardinal Beaufort's will, with its repeated stipulation that the name 'Cardinal Henry' must be used by those celebrating for him, shows the same anxiety for this individual supplication. So did Dame Margaret Leynham who in 1482 wanted to be buried beside her husband in the London Charterhouse, and who asked

---

[55] *Ibid.*, pp. 18, 21.

that small tablets bearing both their names and the names of her parents, should be placed on the altars for seven years so that these souls would be remembered 'by names'.[56]

It was almost as if, for the donor to benefit from the prayers and masses he or she endowed, the lips of the living must give God audible reminders of the personages for whom they supplicated. The countless corporation of the dead seemed disadvantaged by their very anonymity. They were not forgotten, either by testators such as these, or by members of fraternities, or by parishioners who joined in the services for All Souls' Day. But those who enjoyed the power to purchase felt safer about facing God with name tags firmly attached to the world they left behind.

We are still surrounded by many reminders of the hopes and fears of death entertained by men and women in the fifteenth century. Dying for them meant the separation of soul from body until their eventual reunion at the last judgement and resurrection. Named or nameless, they looked to those who remained behind to pray for their sojourning souls until that last tremendous day. We remember them across a credal gulf. The Reformation put an end for good to the bede rolls of innumerable souls who died secure in the belief that they would be prayed for 'for ever'. Only the fortunate few survived that hiatus, to have their names and obits celebrated by members of an altered communion.

---

[56] Hope, *London Charterhouse*, p. 96.

Suggestions for further reading

This is not intended to be a general bibliography of the fifteenth century, or even of those aspects of it discussed above. It is a selective list of the works each contributor thought likely to be most useful to a reader wishing to pursue the subject further. The specialist works cited in footnotes have not, therefore, necessarily been repeated here. Books have not usually been included under more than one heading, although many of those listed are relevant to several chapters.

The place of publication is London unless otherwise stated.

1. THE KING AND HIS SUBJECTS

Allan, A., 'Royal propaganda and the proclamations of Edward IV', *Bulletin of the Institute of Historical Research* 59 (1986), 146–54

Brown, A. L., *The Governance of Late-Medieval England, 1272–1461* (1989)

Chrimes, S. B., *English Constitutional Ideas in the Fifteenth Century* (Cambridge, 1936)
  Henry VII (1972)

Griffiths, R. A., *The Reign of King Henry VI: The Exercise of Royal Authority, 1422–1461* (1981)
  King and Country: England and Wales in the Fifteenth Century (1991)

Harriss, G. L. (ed.), *Henry V: The Practice of Kingship* (Oxford, 1985)

Hicks, M. A., *False, Fleeting, Perjur'd Clarence* (Gloucester, 1980)
  Richard III as Duke of Gloucester: A Study in Character, York, Borthwick Paper 70 (1986)

Horrox, R., *Richard III: A Study of Service* (Cambridge, 1989)

McFarlane, K. B., *England in the Fifteenth Century: Collected Essays* (1981)

Ross, C. D., *Edward IV* (1974)
  Richard III (1981)

Storey, R. L., *The End of the House of Lancaster* (1966)

Sutton, A. F., '"A curious searcher for our weal public": Richard III, piety, chivalry and the concept of the good prince', in P. W. Hammond (ed.), *Richard III: Loyalty, Lordship and Law* (1986), pp. 58–90

Wolffe, B. P., *Henry VI* (1981)

2. LAW AND JUSTICE

Bellamy, J. G., *Crime and Public Order in England in the Later Middle Ages* (1973)

Harding, A., *The Law Courts of Medieval England* (1973)

Hicks, M. A., 'Restraint, mediation and private justice: George duke of Clarence as "good lord"', *Journal of Legal History* 4, no. 2 (1983), 56–71

Ives, E. W., *The Common Lawyers of Pre-Reformation England* (Cambridge, 1983)

Maddern, Philippa C., *Violence and Social Order: East Anglia 1422–1442* (Oxford, 1992)

Powell, E., *Kingship, Law and Society: Criminal Justice in the Reign of Henry V* (Oxford, 1989)

Stones, E. L. G., 'The Folvilles of Ashby Folville, Leicestershire, and their associates in crime', *Transactions of the Royal Historical Society* 5th series 7 (1957), 117–36

Storey, R. L., *The End of the House of Lancaster* (1966)

Sutton, A. F., 'The administration of justice whereunto we be professed', *The Ricardian* 53 (1976), 4–15

3. ARISTOCRACY

Anglo, S., *Spectacle, Pageantry and Early Tudor Policy* (Oxford, 1969)

Asch, R. G., and Birke, A. M., *Princes, Patronage and the Nobility: The Court at the Beginning of the Modern Age, c. 1450–1650* (Oxford, 1991)

Bernard, G. (ed.), *The Tudor Nobility* (Manchester, 1992)

Cannadine, D., *The Decline and Fall of the British Aristocracy* (Yale, 1990) [deals with the eighteenth to twentieth centuries but makes some important points about the nature of the nobility and the processes by which it maintains itself]

Given-Wilson, C., *The English Nobility in the Late Middle Ages* (1987)

Macfarlane, A., *Marriage and Love in England, 1330–1840* (Oxford, 1986)

McFarlane, K. B., *The Nobility of Later Medieval England* (Oxford, 1973)

Mertes, K., *The English Noble Household 1250–1600* (Oxford, 1988)

Rawcliffe, C., *The Staffords, Earls of Stafford and Dukes of Buckingham, 1394–1521* (Cambridge, 1978)

Rosenthal, *Nobles and the Noble Life, 1295–1500* (1976)
    Patriarchy and Families of Privilege in Fifteenth-Century England (University of Pennsylvania, 1991)

Ward, J. C., *English Noblewomen in the Later Middle Ages* (Harlow, 1992)

4. SERVICE

Bean, J. M. W., *From Lord to Patron: Lordship in Late Medieval England* (Manchester, 1989)

Cooper, J. P., 'Ideas of gentility in early-modern England', in *idem, Land, Men and Beliefs: Studies in Early-Modern History* (1983), pp. 43–77

Given-Wilson, C., *The Royal Household and the King's Affinity* (Yale, 1986)

Hicks, M. A., 'Bastard feudalism: society and politics in fifteenth-century England', in *idem, Richard III and his Rivals: Magnates and their Motives in the Wars of the Roses* (1991), pp. 1–40

Morgan, D. A. L., 'The individual style of the English gentleman', in M. Jones (ed.), *Gentry and Lesser Nobility in Late Medieval Europe* (Gloucester, 1986), pp. 15–35
    'The king's affinity in the polity of Yorkist England', *Transactions of the Royal Historical Society* 5th series 23 (1973), 1–25

Myers, A. R. (ed.), *The Household of Edward IV: The Black Book and the Ordinance of 1478* (Manchester, 1959)

Starkey, D. (ed.), *The English Court from the Wars of the Roses to the Civil War* (Harlow, 1987)
    'The age of the household: politics, society and the arts c. 1350–c. 1550', in S. Medcalf (ed.), *The Later Middle Ages* (1981), pp. 225–90

5. EDUCATION AND ADVANCEMENT

Alexander, M. V. C., *The Growth of English Education 1348–1648* (1990)

Bennett, M. J., 'Careerism in late medieval England', in J. Rosenthal and C. Richmond (eds.), *People, Politics and Community in the Later Middle Ages* (Gloucester, 1987), pp. 19–39

Davis, V., 'William Waynflete and the educational revolution of the fifteenth century', in Rosenthal and Richmond (eds.), *People, Politics and Community*, pp. 40–59

Du Boulay, F. R. H., *An Age of Ambition: English Society in the Late Middle Ages* (1970)

Moran, J. A. H., *The Growth of English Schooling 1340–1548* (Princeton, 1985)

Orme, N., *English Schools in the Middle Ages* (1973)

    From Childhood to Chivalry: The Education of the English Kings and Aristocracy 1066–1530 (1984)

    Education and Society in Medieval and Renaissance England (1989)

Simon, J., *Education and Society in Tudor England* (Cambridge, 1979)

6. INFORMATION AND SCIENCE

Bennett, H. S., 'Science and information in English writing of the fifteenth century', *Modern Language Review* 39 (1944), 1–8

Carey, Hilary M., *Courting Disaster: Astrology at the English Court and University in the Later Middle Ages* (1992)

Cobban, Alan B., *The Medieval English Universities: Oxford and Cambridge to c. 1500* (Aldershot, 1988)

Eisenstein, Elizabeth, *The Printing Press as an Agent of Change* (2 vols., Cambridge, 1979)

Getz, Faye Marie, *Healing and Society in Medieval England: A Middle English Translation of the Pharmeceutical Writings of Gilbertus Anglicus* (Wisconsin, 1991)

Jones, Peter Murray, 'Medical books before the arrival of printing', in Alain Besson (ed.), *Thornton's Medical Books, Libraries and Collectors* (3rd edn, Aldershot, 1990), pp. 1–29

Kieckhefer, Richard, *Magic in the Middle Ages* (Cambridge, 1989)

Rhodes, D. E., *John Argentine, Provost of King's: His Life and His Library* (Amsterdam, 1967)

Robbins, Rossell Hope, 'Medical manuscripts in middle English', *Speculum* 45 (1970), 393–415

Siraisi, Nancy G., *Medieval and Early Renaissance Medicine: An Introduction to Knowledge and Practice* (Chicago, 1990)

Tester, Jim, *A History of Western Astrology* (Woodbridge, 1987)

Voigts, Linda Ehrsam, 'Scientific and medical books', in Jeremy Griffiths and Derek Pearsall (eds.), *Book Production and Publishing in Britain 1375–1475* (Cambridge, 1989), pp. 345–402

7. WOMEN

Primary sources

(in addition to those cited in the footnotes)

Blamires, A. (ed.), *Women Defamed and Women Defended* (Oxford, 1993)

O'Faolain, J., and Martines, L. (eds.), *Not in God's Image* (1979)

Osborne, M. L. (ed.), *Woman in Western Thought* (New York, 1979)

Windeatt, B. (ed.), *The Book of Margery Kempe* (Harmondsworth, 1985)

Secondary sources

Ashley, K. M., 'Medieval courtesy literature and dramatic mirrors of female conduct', in N. Armstrong and L. Tennenhouse (eds.), *The Ideology of Conduct* (1987), pp. 25–38

Barron, C. M., 'The "golden age" of women in medieval London', *Reading Medieval Studies* 15 (1990), 35–58

Bennett, H. S., *The Pastons and their England* (Cambridge, 2nd edn, 1932)

Cullum, P. H., ' "And hir name was Charite": charitable giving by and for women in late medieval Yorkshire', in P. J. P. Goldberg (ed.), *Woman is a worthy Wight* (Stroud, 1992), pp. 182–211

Goldberg, P. J. P., 'Female labour, service and marriage in the late medieval urban north', *Northern History* 24 (1986), 18–36

'Women in fifteenth-century town life', in J. A. F. Thomson (ed.), *Towns and Townspeople in the Fifteenth Century* (Gloucester, 1988), pp. 107–28

'The public and the private: women in the pre-plague economy', in P. R. Coss and S. D. Lloyd (eds.), *Thirteenth-Century England III* (Woodbridge, 1991), pp. 75–89

Hilton, R. H., *The English Peasantry in the Later Middle Ages* (Oxford, 1975)

Howell, M. C., 'Citizenship and gender: women's political status in northern medieval cities', in M. Erler and M. Kowaleski (eds.), *Women and Power in the Middle Ages* (Athens, Ga., 1988), pp. 37–60

Jacquart, D., and Thomasset, C. A., *Sexuality and Medicine in the Middle Ages* (Oxford, 1988)

Kowaleski, M., and Bennett, J. M., 'Crafts, guilds and women in the middle ages: fifty years after Marian K. Dale', *Signs* 14 (1989), 474–88

Maclean, I., *The Renaissance Notion of Woman* (Cambridge, 1980)

Penn, S. A. C., 'Female wage-earners in late fourteenth-century England', *Agricultural History Review* 35 (1987), 1–14

Power, E., *Medieval Women*, ed. M. M. Postan (Cambridge, 1975)

Scott, M., *Late Gothic Europe, 1400–1500*, The History of Dress Series, general editor A. Ribiero (1980)

8. URBAN SOCIETY

Britnell, R. H., *Growth and Decline in Colchester 1300–1525* (Cambridge, 1986)

Green, A. S. [Mrs J. R. Green], *Town Life in the Fifteenth Century* (2 vols., 1894) [inevitably dated, but still valuable]

Hilton, R. H., 'Medieval market towns and simple commodity production', *Past and Present* 109 (1985), 3–23

Holt, R., and Rosser, G. (eds.), *The Medieval Town: A Reader in English Urban History 1200–1540* (1990)

James, M., 'Ritual, drama and the social body in the late medieval English town', *Past and Present* 98 (1983), 3–29; reprinted in M. James, *Society, Politics and Culture: Studies in Early Modern England* (Cambridge, 1986), 16–47

Kermode, J. I., 'The merchants of three northern English towns', in C. H. Clough (ed.), *Profession, Vocation and Culture in Later Medieval England* (Liverpool, 1982), pp. 7–48

Palliser, D. M., 'Civic mentality and the environment in Tudor York', *Northern History* 18 (1982), 78–115; reprinted in J. Barry (ed.), *The Tudor and Stuart Town* (1990), 206–43

Pantin, W. A., 'Medieval English town-house plans', *Medieval Archaeology* 6–7 (1962–3), 202–39

Phythian-Adams, C., *Desolation of a City: Coventry and the Urban Crisis of the Late Middle Ages* (Cambridge, 1979)

Platt, C., *The English Medieval Town* (1976)

Reynolds, S., *An Introduction to the History of English Medieval Towns* (Oxford, 1977)

Rosser, G., *Medieval Westminster 1200–1540* (Oxford, 1989)

'Communities of parish and guild in the late middle ages', in S. J. Wright (ed.), *Parish, Church and People* (1988), pp. 29–55

Swanson, H., *Medieval Artisans: An Urban Class in Late Medieval England* (Oxford, 1989)

'The illusion of economic structure: craft guilds in late medieval English towns', *Past and Present* 121 (1988), 29–48

Thomson, J. A. F. (ed.), *Towns and Townspeople in the Fifteenth Century* (Gloucester, 1988)

Thrupp, S. L., *The Merchant Class of Medieval London* (Chicago, 1948)

9. RURAL SOCIETY

Bailey, M., *A Marginal Economy? East Anglian Breckland in the Later Middle Ages* (Cambridge, 1989)

'Blowing up bubbles: some new demographic evidence for the fifteenth century?', *Journal of Medieval History* 15 (1989), 347–58

Blanchard, I. S. W., 'Labour productivity and work psychology in the English mining industry, 1400–1600', *Economic History Review* 2nd series 31 (1978), 1–24

Bolton, J. L., *The Medieval English Economy 1150–1500* (1981)

Britnell, R. H., 'The Pastons and their Norfolk', *Agricultural History Review* 36 (1988), 132–44

Carus-Wilson, E. M., 'Evidences of industrial growth on some fifteenth-century manors', *Economic History Review* 2nd series 12 (1959–60), 190–205

DeWindt, E. B., *Land and People in Holywell-cum-Needingworth* (Toronto, 1972)

Dyer, C., *Lords and Peasants in a Changing Society* (Cambridge, 1980)

Standards of Living in the Later Middle Ages (Cambridge, 1989)

Dymond, D., 'A lost social institution: the camping close', *Rural History* 1 (1990), 165–92

Hanawalt, B., *The Ties that Bound* (Oxford, 1986)

Hilton, R. H., *Class Conflict and the Crisis of Feudalism* (2nd edn, 1990)

Keen, M., *English Society in the Later Middle Ages* (Harmondsworth, 1990)

McIntosh, M. K., *Autonomy and Community: The Royal Manor of Havering, 1200–1500* (Cambridge, 1986)

'Local change and community control in England, 1465–1500', *Huntington Library Quarterly* 49 (1986), 219–42

Owst, G. R., *Preaching in Medieval England* (Cambridge, 1926)

Pollard, A. J., 'The north-eastern economy and the agrarian crisis of 1438–40', *Northern History* 25 (1989), 88–105

Poos, L. R., *A Rural Society after the Black Death: Essex 1350–1525* (Cambridge, 1991)

Raftis, J. A., *Tenure and Mobility* (Toronto, 1964)

Warboys: Two Hundred Years in the Life of an English Medieval Village (Toronto, 1974)

Razi, Z., 'Family, land and the village community in late medieval England', *Past and Present* 93 (1981), 3–36

Richmond, C., *John Hopton: A Fifteenth-Century Suffolk Gentleman* (Cambridge, 1981)

Searle, E., *Lordship and Community: Battle Abbey and its Banlieu* (Toronto, 1974)

10. THE POOR

Clay, R. M., *The Medieval Hospitals of England* (1909)

Hatcher, J., *Plague, Population and the English Economy, 1340–1530* (1977)

Hilton, R. H., *The Decline of Serfdom in Medieval England* (1969)

Lis, C., and Soly, H., *Poverty and Capitalism in Pre-Industrial Europe*, trans. J. Coonan (Hassocks, 1979)

Mollat, M., *The Poor in the Middle Ages: An Essay in Social History*, trans. A. Goldhammer (New Haven, 1986)

Rubin, M., *Charity and Community in Medieval Cambridge* (Cambridge, 1987)

11. RELIGION

The following list can be supplemented by the good bibliography in R. N. Swanson (below) and by DeLloyd J. Guth, *Late Medieval England 1377–1485. A Bibliographical Handbook* (Cambridge, 1976), part XII, 'Religious history'.

Aston, Margaret, *Lollards and Reformers: Images and Literacy in Late Medieval Religion* (1984)
    'The religion of the people', in G. Barraclough (ed.), *The Christian World* (1981), pp. 157–70

Bossy, John, *Christianity in the West 1400–1700* (Oxford, 1985)

Duffy, Eamon, *The Stripping of the Altars: Traditional Religion in England 1400–1580* (Yale, 1992)

Harper-Bill, C., *The Pre-Reformation Church in England 1400–1530* (1989)

Heath, P., *The English Parish Clergy on the Eve of the Reformation* (1969)

Hudson, Anne, *The Premature Reformation* (Oxford, 1988)

Jacob, E. F., *Archbishop Henry Chichele* (1967)

McFarlane, K. B., *Wycliffe and the Beginnings of English Nonconformity* (1952)

Owen, D. M., *Church and Society in Medieval Lincolnshire* (Lincoln, 1971)

Pfaff, R. W., *New Liturgical Feasts in Later Medieval England* (Oxford, 1970)

Scarisbrick, J. J., *The Reformation and the English People* (Oxford, 1984)

Smith, H. Maynard, *Pre-Reformation England* (1938)

Swanson, R. N., *Church and Society in Late Medieval England* (1989)

Tanner, N. P., *The Church in Late Medieval Norwich* (Toronto, 1984)

12. DEATH

Aries, P., *The Hour of our Death* (Harmondsworth, 1983)
    Western Attitudes toward Death: From the Middle Ages to the Present (1976)

Barron, C. M., 'The parish fraternities of medieval London', in C. M. Barron and C. Harper-Bill (eds.), *The Church in Pre-Reformation Society: Essays in Honour of F. R. H. du Boulay* (Woodbridge, 1985), pp. 13–37

Boase, T. S. R., *Death in the Middle Ages: Mortality, Judgment and Remembrance* (1972)

Carpenter, C., 'The religion of the gentry in fifteenth-century England', in D. Williams (ed.), *England in the Fifteenth Century* (Woodbridge, 1987), pp. 53–74

Clark, J. M., *The Dance of Death in the Middle Ages and the Renaissance* (Glasgow, 1950)

Cohen, K., *Metamorphosis of a Death Symbol: The Transi Tomb in the Late Middle Ages and the Renaissance* (Berkeley, 1973)

Cook, G. H., *Mediaeval Chantries and Chantry Chapels* (1947)

Fiero, G. K., 'Death ritual in fifteenth-century manuscript illumination', *Journal of Medieval History* 10 (1984), 271–94

Finucane, R. C., 'Sacred corpse, profane carrion: social ideals and death rituals in the later middle ages', in J. Whaley (ed.), *Mirrors of Mortality: Studies in the Social History of Death* (1981), pp. 40–60

Hanawalt, B. A., 'Violent death in fourteenth- and early fifteenth-century England', *Comparative Studies in Society and History* 18 (1976), 297–320

Hicks, M., 'Chantries, obits and almshouses: the Hungerford foundations, 1325–1478' in
    Barron and Harper-Bill (eds.), *The Church in Pre-Reformation Society*, pp. 123–42
Le Goff, J., *The Birth of Purgatory* (Aldershot, 1990)
McFarlane, K. B., *Lancastrian Kings and Lollard Knights* (Oxford, 1972)
    'At the deathbed of Cardinal Beaufort', in *idem*, *England in the Fifteenth Century* (1981),
    pp. 115–37
O'Connor, M. C., *The Art of Dying Well: The Development of the Ars Moriendi* (Columbia, 1942)
Panofsky, E., *Tomb Sculpture: Its Changing Aspects from Ancient Egypt to Bernini* (1964)
Powell, S., and Fletcher, A. J., ' "In Die Sepulture seu Trigintali": the late medieval funeral
    and memorial sermon', *Leeds Studies in English* new series 12 (1981), 195–228
Richmond, C., 'Religion and the fifteenth-century English gentleman', in R. B. Dobson (ed.),
    The Church, Politics and Patronage in the Fifteenth Century (Gloucester, 1984), pp. 193–208
Rosenthal, J. T., *The Purchase of Paradise: Gift Giving and the Aristocracy, 1307–1485* (1972)
Taylor, Jane H. M. (ed.), *Dies illa. Death in the Middle Ages*, Proceedings of 1983 Manchester
    Colloquium (Liverpool, 1984)
Tristram, P., *Figures of Life and Death in Medieval English Literature* (1976)
Wood-Legh, K. L., *Perpetual Chantries in Britain* (Cambridge, 1965)

Related works mainly devoted to a later period
Gittings, C., *Death, Burial and the Individual in Early Modern England* (Sydney, 1984)
Litten, J., *The English Way of Death: The Common Funeral since 1450* (1991)
Llewellyn, N., *The Art of Death: Visual Culture in the English Death Ritual c. 1500–c. 1800* (1991)

Index